the Grace of Sophia

the Grace of Sophia

A Korean North American Women's Christology

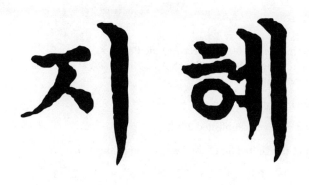

Grace Ji-Sun Kim

THE
PILGRIM
PRESS
Cleveland

For my mother,
Han Wha Ja

The Pilgrim Press, 700 Prospect Avenue East
Cleveland, Ohio 44115-1100, U.S.A.
pilgrimpress.com

Printed in the United States of America on acid-free paper

08   07   06   05   04   03   02   5   4   3   2   1

Library of Congress Cataloging-in-Publication Data
Kim, Grace Ji-Sun, 1969-
      The grace of Sophia : a Korean North American women's Christology /
Grace Ji-Sun Kim.
            p.   cm.
      Includes bibliographical references (p.) and index.
      ISBN 0-8298-1481-7
      1. Wisdom (Biblical personification) 2. Jesus Christ – Person and offices.
3. Korean American women – Religious life. 4. Women – Canada – Religious
life.   I. Title.

BS580.W58 K56 2002
232′.082 – dc21

                                                                2001058069

Contents

Contents

Preface

IN THIS BOOK I develop a Christology using Korean and Christian understandings of wisdom, which I believe will be liberative for Korean North American women who have suffered just for being who we are. I am a Korean North American woman who immigrated to Canada at the age of five. My parents left the material, social, and family comforts of Korea in search of a better place to raise their children. However, Canada was not what they had dreamt it would be. In Canada, our family experienced a constant lack of money and material goods. I could not understand why we had to live in a small, dirty, two-bedroom apartment while my friends at school lived in large homes and played in huge backyards. I was always ashamed to bring any non-Korean friends to our home because of our poor living conditions. Furthermore, I tasted immigrant reality in kindergarten, my first experience with racism. My memories are flooded with class-mates teasing me about the way I looked, the way I talked, and the way I dressed. I was a strange creature to them and so they called me names — hurtful names that penetrated deeply, becoming unhealable wounds. Words like "chink" or "go back home" left permanent scars and led me to question my own identity.

Am I a Korean, a Canadian, or both? My first visit back to Korea in 1980 made me realize that I am not a "total Korean." I just did not fit in. Koreans in Korea thought I was different from them and had become too Westernized. But then in Canada, I did not really fit in either. I was not like the other Canadians. I looked different, ate different foods, and spoke a foreign language. Therefore I was neither Korean nor Canadian and did not really have a sense of belonging. I was caught between two cultures without belonging to either. Only when I began to study the unique identity of immigrants did I come to the realization that I was "in between"[1] two cultures.

---

1. "In between" is a term that many Asian North American thinkers and writers are

Religion has always been important part in my life. In Korea, my parents grew up in the Buddhist tradition. However, soon after immigrating to Canada, our entire family converted to Christianity and became members of a Korean Presbyterian church. Our membership in a Korean church kept our Korean heritage alive. The church plays an important role in the lives of immigrants, as it becomes a haven away from the problems and difficulties of living in a foreign world. The church serves as a community where one can promote one's culture; at church I learned Korean language, history, and music. The church is an essential gathering place where Korean immigrants experience likeness, similarity, and bonding. On the other hand, the church is an institution that also perpetuates patriarchal and oppressive teachings.

My Christian upbringing made me question why I was experiencing racism from the wider society and oppression from the patriarchal Korean society. In part, these experiences of sexism, racism, and classism led me to write this book. I am in search of a Christology that can be liberative for me and other Korean North American women.

I argue in this work that in view of Korean North American women's marginalization and the inadequacies of traditional Christology, biblical Sophia, understood in conjunction with Buddhist *prajna*, offers a liberative dimension to developing a Christology for Korean North American Christian women. Jesus Sophia offers grace — unconditional love, acceptance, self-worth, dignity, and strength. Jesus Sophia as grace offers healing for the crippling effects of *han*.

This book came into being through the wondrous help of many people. First, my sincere gratitude and thanks to my editor George R. Graham, who provided many insightful suggestions and ideas to make the manuscript more readable. I am also greatly indebted to Harold Wells, Ellen Leonard, Iain Nicol, David Kwang-sun Suh, and Andrew Sung Park for their thoughtful comments, suggestions, and encouragement. My thanks go to the advisors of Pacific Asian North American Asian Women in Theology and Ministry (PANAAWTM) for their support and insistence that indeed "my project was important": Rita Nakashima Brock, Jung Ha Kim, Kwok Pui-lan,

---

using to identify themselves as people who are caught between two cultures. Hereafter, "in between" appears without quotation marks.

Nantawan Lewis, Greer Anne Wenh-In Ng, Seung-Ai Yang, Gale A. Yee, and Chung Hyun Kyung. Portions of chapter 3 appeared in *JAAT*, of chapter 4 in *Koinonia*, and of chapter 7 in *Feminist Theology*. Portions of chapter 6 appeared in *Asian American Theology: Korean American Perspective*, compiled by Sang Hyun Lee. I am grateful for permission to reprint here.

Friends and family have been important during my time of writing. I would like to thank Sharon Song, Esther Shin, and Wendy Mao for their friendship, and to my sister Karen and brother-in-law Bruce who frequently opened up their home so that Theodore, Elisabeth, and I could go over to rest, play, and eat some good Korean food. I must also thank my father-in-law and my parents for their continuous support, love, and concern. Without my mother's constant help in looking after Theodore and Elisabeth, this book would never have been finished. Above all, I must express my gratitude to my husband Perry, who has been not only a technical advisor throughout the time of my writing but an indispensable and constant wellspring of support. Last, I say thank you to my dear son, Theodore (three years old), and my daughter, Elisabeth (five months old), who have been enduring sources of joy and love during my time of writing.

~ One ~

The Search for
a Liberative Christology

IN THE PAST, theology tended to ignore the experiences of non-dominant cultures and make them invisible and inaudible. Korean North American women[1] are seeking ways to make their voices heard and their culture valued. They cannot accept the theology of the past, and they cannot accept uncritically the theological methods arising out of other experiences and contexts. These women are a distinct group of people who need to address theology out of their own unique context and experience. Korean North American Christian women need to be creative in developing a method of doing theology that considers seriously their experiences of oppression, subordination, and *han,* and also draws upon the best of their own Asian religio-cultural traditions.[2]

Han is a typical prevailing feeling of the Korean people. Hyun Young-Hak, a Korean theologian, wrote that "*han* is a sense of unresolved resentment against injustice suffered, a sense of helplessness because of the overwhelming odds against, a feeling of total abandonment, a feeling of acute pain of sorrow in one's guts and bowels making the whole body writhe and wiggle, and an obstinate urge to take 'revenge' and to right the wrong all these constitute."[3] People of Korean heritage need a relevant theology that addresses their needs

---

1. This book will focus on Korean women in the United States (including Hawaii) and on Korean women living in English-speaking Canada.

2. A "method" refers to the manner in which the practitioners of any discipline reflect upon their subject matter with a view to its comprehension and communication. Douglas John Hall, *Thinking the Faith: Christian Theology in a North American Context* (Minneapolis: Augsburg, 1989), 325.

3. As quoted by Chung Hyun Kyung, "Han-pu-ri: Doing Theology from Korean Women's Perspective," in *We Dare to Dream,* ed. Virginia Fabella and Sun-Ai Lee (Maryknoll, N.Y.: Orbis Books, 1990), 30.

1

and helps them in their process of liberation. This book attempts to
formulate a theological method that can serve Korean North American women in their quest for liberation and healing.[4] At the same time
that we focus on the need for liberation and healing, our method must
also be rigorously biblical, drawing christological insight primarily
from Scripture, because Korean North American Christian women
love and respect the Bible.

Just as African-American women could not fully identify with
white feminist theology and so have formulated "womanist theology"
and Latina women have a *mujerista* theology, Korean and other Asian
North American women also cannot identify entirely with white feminist theology. Asian North American women do not have their own
theology that they can name, but they develop instead a distinct
theology.

The intent of this book is to lead Korean North American Christian women to a more appropriate theology based on Scripture
and their own context and experience. Korean North American
women's theology is, of course, one form of contextual theology and
is methodologically akin to liberation and other feminist theologies.

This book is a pioneering work, in that Korean North American
women's theology is in a nascent stage of development and only a
few Korean North American women theologians are practicing at
present. Jung Ha Kim is a Korean American Christian sociologist
who presents research on Korean American women and the church
in her book *Bridge-Makers and Cross-Bearers*. Ai Ra Kim, a Korean
American theologian, examines the struggles of Korean immigrant
women in her book *Women's Struggle for a New Life.*[5] Further,
some Asian theologians living in the United States have done some
work on Asian women's theology. Kwok Pui-lan is a Chinese theologian who writes on contextual theology, feminist theology, and
Asian postcolonial hermeneutics of the Bible. Korean feminist theo-

4. The proposed method is a modified version of the method of Juan Luis Segundo. The
method is also constructive, and it borrows and builds on the methodological insights of
earlier liberationist, contextual, and feminist theologians, such as Kwok, Chung, etc., who
are forerunners in this area. See Juan Luis Segundo, *The Liberation of Theology*, trans.
John Drury (Maryknoll, N.Y.: Orbis Books, 1976), 8ff.

5. Jung Ha Kim, *Bridge-Makers and Cross-Bearers* (Atlanta: Scholars Press, 1997); Ai
Ra Kim, *Women's Struggle for a New Life* (Albany: State University of New York Press,
1996).

logian Chung Hyun Kyung introduces Asian women's theology in her book *Struggle to Be the Sun Again*. The most important work of Rita Nakashima Brock, a Japanese American who writes on feminist Christology and the various struggles and oppressions of women, is *Journeys by Heart*.[6]

Considering the dearth of theological literature of this genre, Korean North American women theologians need to articulate and voice the concerns of their community of women and then reflect upon these concerns theologically. Korean North American women have accumulated much *han* throughout their lives. In Korea they suffered under Confucianism, which places heavy restrictions, limitations, and major burdens upon women. When these women immigrated to North America, they remained dominated and subordinated due to other barriers and issues such as racism, classism, and ageism. Thus, their immigrant lifestyles have been burdensome as they live in two cultures that have different expectations of them. For such oppressed women, what is the good news and how can they come to understand God who is with us?

This book is written, then, for Korean North American women out of their context of suffering and oppression. I do not speak for all Korean North American women but rather from my own personal experience. This book briefly examines the Korean immigrant life and explores the needs and sufferings that arise out of their experience of coming to a foreign land. A task of Korean North American women's theology is to name, diminish, and help to heal their *han*. Since Christ is central to Christianity, Korean North American women are in search of a new Christology that can address their needs, hopes, and dreams.

Until recent times, Eurocentric patriarchalism has bound, limited, and bottled up Christology. Early Christianity used the masculine term *logos* to name that presence of God incarnate in Jesus Christ. This term drew upon Greek and Hellenistic Jewish philosophy. The divine *logos* was the means by which the transcendent God came forth in the beginning to create the world. This *logos* Christology has some

---

6. Chung Hyun Kyung, *Struggle to Be the Sun Again: Introducing Asian Women's Theology* (Maryknoll, N.Y.: Orbis Books, 1990); Rita Nakashima Brock, *Journeys by Heart: A Christology of Erotic Power* (New York: Crossroad, 1988).

negative consequences, since it perpetuated the male image of God and excluded the feminine dimension of the divine.[7] Thus, finding a more appropriate term or image to speak of the divine presence is important for the task at hand. American feminist theologians have already identified this problem and suggested alternatives to classical *logos* Christology. This book endeavors to find a relevant Christology that specifically addresses Korean North American women.

FORMS OF KOREAN NORTH AMERICAN CHRISTOLOGY

Certain Korean North American theologians have attempted to construct a Christology that addresses and meets the needs of Korean North American people.[8] Some Korean North American male theologians, such as Sang Hyun Lee and Jung Young Lee, propose a "marginal Christ" because they believe that immigrants as marginal people can identify with this image. These two scholars present many biblical images that support the image of Jesus as a marginal person. First of all, Jesus was born a marginalized child; the circumstances surrounding his birth illustrate his marginalized existence. He is said to have been born of an unwed mother far from his hometown and sheltered in a manger. Later in his life, Jesus became a friend of marginalized people: outcasts, tax collectors, Gentiles, women, the poor and the oppressed, the lame and the blind. The dominant groups of his day did not accept him, but marginal people accepted him as a marginal person. Then, on the cross, he died as a convicted criminal rejected by his friends and disciples. Jesus became an outsider and was certainly a man in between two different worlds, without fully belonging to either. According to Jung Young Lee, Jesus was in many

---

7. Many scholars argue that in John's Prologue the word *logos,* a masculine term, was used instead of *sophia,* which is feminine. Eduard Schweizer proposed that it was in fact necessary for Christian thought to substitute the masculine designation for the feminine *sophia* because of the gender of Jesus. For more discussion, refer to Elizabeth A. Johnson, *She Who Is* (New York: Crossroad, 1993), 96–100.

8. See for example the works of Jung Young Lee, *Marginality: The Key to Multicultural Theology* (Minneapolis: Fortress Press, 1995), and Sang Hyun Lee, "Called to Be Pilgrims: Toward an Asian-American Theology From the Korean Immigrant Perspective," in *Korean American Ministry: A Resource Book,* ed. Sang Hyun Lee (New York: Consulting Committee on Korean American Ministry, Presbyterian Church [U.S.A.], 1987), 96.

ways both Jewish and Hellenistic as he belonged to both groups. He was the marginal person par excellence.[9]

Moving beyond Jesus of Nazareth to Christian doctrine about Jesus, Jung Young Lee continues his argument by stating that the incarnation can also be compared to "divine immigration," in which God emigrated from a heavenly place to this world. As an immigrant in the world, Christ, like the Asian American, experienced rejection, harassment, and humiliation. Thus Jesus led a life of marginality as he roamed from one place to another. Jesus' entry into Jerusalem was a humble entry of marginality, as the entry was the symbolic penetration of marginality into the "center."[10] Therefore, Jesus is the marginal Christ. If God was in Jesus Christ, the people of God must also be marginal people. We are called to be "marginal people" in a positive sense, not only because Jesus of Nazareth was marginal, but because marginality is an intrinsic part of creation, which could not continue without its "marginal" members and components.[11] Marginality is thus part of life and makes its essential contribution.

Christ became the margin of marginality, Lee continues, by giving up everything he had. To be a servant means to have no personal worth, no innate value. Servants do not belong to the dominant group. To take on the nature of servitude after having had the nature of God means to become the precise margin of marginality.[12] Similar to Jesus, immigrants have a unique existence apart from non-immigrants. Immigrants are neither here nor there and are at times in between two cultures. They do not totally belong to their former country nor to their adopted country. Immigrants find themselves in a wilderness, living as aliens and strangers. Due to their marginalized identity, many Korean North American theologians believe that immigrants can relate to a marginal Christ.

A biblical notion of pilgrimage may also help us to discern the theological meaning of an immigrant's marginal existence. A pilgrim is someone willing to leave the security of home and to sojourn in a strange land if necessary.[13] A pilgrim is someone who lives with

9. Lee, *Marginality: The Key to Multicultural Theology,* 71–72.
10. Ibid., 83, 91.
11. Ibid., 3.
12. Ibid., 78, 81, 82.
13. Sang Hyun Lee, "Called to Be Pilgrims: Toward an Asian-American Theology from the Korean Immigrant Perspective," 95.

an ultimate loyalty to, and confidence in, the reign of God alone, which is how Korean North American immigrants may be viewed. From this knowledge, Sang Hyun Lee reinterprets Asian American existence ("wilderness of marginality") with the help of the understanding of Christian existence as pilgrimage. Our marginality in the first sense (bicultural existence) will be seen as possessing the creative potentiality of functioning in a spiritual wilderness that all pilgrims who leave the security of home in pursuit of God's promise must be willing to enter. Second, our marginality will have to be seen as a situation that calls for an ethic of rehumanization, that is, a praxis for justice and reconciliation as an essential dimension of the sacred pilgrimage to which we have been called.[14] Like Abraham, we too are in the wilderness, and our wilderness is called *marginality*. The religious meaning of our marginality (in the sense of bicultural existence) is thus a call to appropriate or use our marginal existence as the path of pilgrimage.[15]

This image of Christ as marginal is valuable; Korean immigrants can identify with a marginal Christ. Recognizing these insights of the two male Korean American theologians discussed thus far is important. They point out that a "minority" can at times be helpful. For example, the church as a minority can become a prophetic voice in this unjust world. However, some problems arise with this image. First, for Korean immigrant women, the image tends to perpetuate the status quo, leaving women who are doubly marginalized in the margins and telling them that remaining there is acceptable or the norm. The image of the church as minority reinforces the idea that suffering under oppression and domination is all right. However, this experience needs to be recognized as a result of sin and women must be liberated from it. Jesus, in his relation to marginal people, did not want to maintain them in their miserable state but to liberate them. Second, this image of the marginal Christ and the immigrant experience tends to glorify the immigrant experience, showing it as something wonderful and desirable, whereas in many cases, the opposite is true. Korean North American women and men need Christ

---

14. Ibid., 96.
15. Ibid., 98.

to liberate them from the bondage of marginality and set them free from their *han*.

Some Asian theologians like Chung Hyun Kyung have suggested another model for Christology. Chung suggests a shaman Christ who will release women from their *han*. Traditionally shamans are usually women, who perform rituals to help release people's *han*. This is a valuable contribution. This model may work for Korean women, but it will not necessarily be helpful for Korean North American women, as they are no longer totally Korean. They are not exposed to Shamanism as Korean women are in Korea. Nor can most women (even in Korea) aspire to be shamans. The image of a shaman, however, is powerful. We Korean North American women need to understand this image and retrieve it from our religio-cultural heritage, but also go beyond it.

What, then, will be an appropriate image of Christ for Korean North American women? Kierkegaard writes about the need for Christ to be "scandalous," as he is presented in the New Testament (e.g., 1 Cor. 1:21–23).[16] He writes about the wretched figure who speaks of God. Kierkegaard juxtaposes the poor Jesus with the common image of the divine. Scandal is an offense to reason. To reason that Jesus is God is offensive, for the notion of deity is associated with glory and honor. In order for Christ to be scandalous to immigrants, Christ has to be understood beyond the marginalized Christ. He needs to be scandalous to a culture that is patriarchal. The required Christology will have to shock Korean North American Christian women out of their inadequate christological understanding and perhaps necessarily be offensive to "conservative" women. Perhaps Christ needs to be rethought in female terms, metaphors, and language.

SOPHIA CHRISTOLOGY

This book proposes that conceiving of Jesus as an embodiment of Sophia can be meaningful to Korean North American women. Sophia Christology as we shall see, challenges us to move to a new level, encouraging the marginalized to be more sensitive to the twice

---

16. Søren Kierkegaard, *Training in Christianity, and the Edifying Discourse Which "Accompanied" It*, trans. Walter Lowrie (Princeton, N.J.: Princeton University Press, 1941), 105.

marginalized, who are women.[17] This figure of Sophia, which is already present in the Bible, becomes a meaningful way of portraying Christ. Since Korean North American Christian women already revere the Bible, any acceptable Christology will have to be demonstrably biblical. More fundamentally, Christian theology has to be biblical because the Bible is the indispensable source of the gospel, and the incomparable witness to the life, death, and resurrection of Jesus.

Korean North American women are torn between two cultures, Korean and North American; they try to embrace both cultures and live by them both. A key to such a tension between two cultures is to maintain a bicultural existence by selecting appropriate elements of both cultural worlds to make the best adaptation according to the demands of social circumstances.[18] However, these women often find themselves pushed to the margins as they try to maintain a bicultural existence that will satisfy both cultures. At times, the decision to use one culture over the other is not a question of which is better than the other, but rather, selecting what is good from both. An understanding of Jesus that can release them from their pain, sorrow, and *han* will have to be retrieved from both worlds. I propose that wisdom is a concept or image that can be derived from both worlds, for Korean North American women have inherited Wisdom from their Asian roots, especially through Buddhism. This Wisdom is called *prajna,* which is in some ways similar to the Wisdom called Sophia found in Christianity. Most Korean North American women are unaware of the richness of their Asian religious heritage. Yet, I suggest that, by retrieving something of their Korean culture and something from their North American Christian culture, they will be able to develop a Christology that can promote and empower their struggle for liberation.

Sophia Christology is proposed, then, as one approach that can contribute to the theological liberation of Korean North American women and release their *han* and heal them. Sophia Christ, who is

---

17. The term *marginality* in itself is a negative concept but it can also have positive aspects. For example, painful experiences in life are not good in themselves or desirable, but if appropriated in a certain way, they may deepen people and drive them to a richer quality of life than would otherwise be possible. Similarly, Sophia is akin to marginality as she builds upon the concept of marginality by conceiving the divine in feminine terms.

18. Esther Ngan-Ling Chow, "The Feminist Movement: Where Are All the Asian American Women?" in *Making Waves: An Anthology of Writings by and about Asian American Women,* ed. Asian Women United of California (Boston: Beacon Press, 1989), 368.

manifested in many ways, can be depicted within the categories of Asian religion and culture. Naming is important, and so is recognition. Through naming we recognize. But we need to exercise this the other way too — to recognize the deep things of our religious and cultural life and name them. Wisdom is a profound concept that crosses all boundaries.

North American feminist theologians, of course, have already developed Sophia Christology. This book builds upon the works of Elizabeth A. Johnson and Elisabeth Schüssler Fiorenza, who have done extensive work on Sophia. Both Johnson's and Schüssler Fiorenza's work are important and challenging, but their notions of Sophia need to be contextualized and made relevant for Korean North American women, who have distinct experiences and context. The Christology proposed in this book is a contextual Christology, because our questions are contextual, and our answers must also become contextual.[19]

As a whole, this book will develop according to the "praxis model" as described by Stephen B. Bevans,[20] a model that focuses on the identity of Christians within a culture as that culture is understood in terms of social change.[21] The key presupposition of a praxis model is that the highest kind of *knowing* is intelligent and responsible *doing*,[22] or faith seeking action. By first acting and then reflecting on that action in faith, practitioners of this model believe that one can develop a theology that is truly relevant to a particular context.[23] This model also presupposes God's revelation and understands revelation as the presence of God in history in the events of everyday life, in society and economic structures, and in situations of oppression.[24] This model is circular in that it begins with committed action, is followed by reflection, and then returns again to action. Reflection involves an analysis of action and situation and a rereading of the Bible and tra-

19. Albert Nolan, "Contextual Theology: One Faith, Many Theologies," Chancellor's Address VIII delivered at Regis College, Toronto, November 12, 1990, 5.
20. This praxis model will be discussed in detail in chapter 2.
21. Models are constructions to help us articulate what methodological task we are performing. Stephen B. Bevans, S.V.D., *Models of Contextual Theology* (Maryknoll, N.Y.: Orbis Books, 1992), 63.
22. Ibid., 66.
23. Ibid., 67.
24. Ibid., 68.

dition. The third stage is committed and intelligent action (praxis). This circle becomes a spiral as it continues within this same process.

Following this model, this book begins with a practical commitment to make a difference in Korean North American women's lives. Then the book moves into reflection, analyzing and trying to interpret the social, political, religious, and historical context of Korean North American women. The section that follows reflects upon the Bible and the tradition to understand how the gospel can be reinterpreted and understood in these women's context, using the concepts of multifaith hermeneutics. This book also briefly considers the realities of "inculturation" and "syncretism," the ways in which Christian faith becomes inserted into a new cultural situation and is influenced by them, as well as the ways in which Christianity links with other religio-cultural traditions. We therefore explore Asian Buddhist concepts of Wisdom, which may be linked to biblical Wisdom for a truly Korean North American women's contextual theology. My hope is that the Christology developed here will contribute to the empowerment of Korean North American women and make a difference in their own lives and in the lives of others. After reflecting on their understanding of who Christ is for them, I hope that readers of this book will move to committed and intelligent action.

This book begins with a brief discussion of method. The proposed method is distinct in that it will combine feminist "praxis" method with a concern for inculturation and syncretism, adopting the insights of multifaith hermeneutics. Thus the method ties in with Korean North American women's Asian cultural background. Chapter 2 attempts to illustrate that this theological method will be a step toward the holistic liberation of Korean North American women. Like other feminist and liberation theologies this method is contextual and takes into consideration the specific context and experience of a particular group.

Chapters 3 and 4 offer a contextual analysis of the situation of Korean North American women. This analysis reflects my own experience and that of other Korean North American women whom I know. I do not pretend to speak for all Korean North American women and do not claim to do scientific sociological research, but these chapters strive to provide awareness of their oppression and subordination. Through this awareness these chapters seek to gain a voice and channel for these women to release their much accumulated *han*. The social and historical context of their oppression is summarized and analyzed.

Chapter 5 explores Asian insights into Wisdom, especially Buddhist *prajna*. This chapter describes *prajna*'s character and then makes comparisons between *prajna* and Sophia. The chapter also very briefly indicates the presence of Wisdom as portrayed in Confucianism and a feminine Buddhist deity called Kuan-yin.

Chapter 6 builds upon the work of two feminist theologians (namely, Elizabeth A. Johnson and Elisabeth Schüssler Fiorenza) to understand biblical Sophia and her significance for Korean North American women's Christology. The last chapter explores ways in which Korean North American women can move toward resolving *han* through the grace of Jesus Sophia.

~ Two ~

Doing Theology in a New Way

THEOLOGY WAS "Euro-theology" for a long time. This theology tended to pay no attention to the experiences of non-European cultures. Traditional Western theology, with its emphasis on individual salvation and morality, was often disruptive of non-Western cultures, focusing only on the individual with little recognition of community or social context. Euro-theology has also been replete with assumptions of male superiority and so produced distortions regarding the being of God and of Jesus Christ. "Such culturally insensitive and oppressive attitudes have been unmasked in the last several decades as having little to do with the real meaning of Christianity, so there have been movements and pressures to make theology and church practice more consonant with what is positive and good in various cultures and more critical of what is really destructive in them."[1] The result has been the emergence in the last thirty years of other theologies such as Asian, Latin American, feminist, etc.

Although major streams of academic theology, both in the West and elsewhere, can no longer be described as Euro-theology, most Korean North American Christian women still assume and live out of a Euro-theology that they or their forebears received from Western missionaries. Today, many thoughtful Korean North American women are questioning how long this Euro-theology is going to be accepted as the only true way of understanding and knowing God. They are joining the movement to develop a theology that is more relevant and meaningful for themselves.

For such women, Euro-theology is inadequate and insufficient. The concerns of oppressed immigrant women do not coincide even with the issues of privileged white women living in North America. In ad-

---

1. Stephen B. Bevans, S.V.D., *Models of Contextual Theology* (Maryknoll, N.Y.: Orbis Books, 1992), 6.

dition, the issues of women differ greatly from those of men who have dominated the development of theology until recent times, and even of our own Korean immigrant men. Furthermore, as times change, people's concerns also change. Obviously many of the crucial issues and concerns of Augustine in the fifth century or Calvin in the sixteenth appear irrelevant to people living in the twenty-first century. Since the concerns of various people differ, one's theology should not be restricted or determined by the dominant group, but rather all people should be free to explore and develop their own theologies within chosen communities. Theological discussion should be liberating, and a space needs to be provided especially for the downtrodden to be heard.

Korean North American women's theology has to be created out of the historical and social context of Korean immigrants' struggle for full humanity. It needs to be a living theology[2] that does not remain constant but is formed and transformed by the living experience and context of Korean North American women. Theology needs to recognize and honor the experiences of the marginalized and the neglected. Many liberation theologians argue that this recognition and attitude toward the marginalized is derived from Jesus as seen in the Scriptures. Korean North American women live in the margins of society and are doubly marginalized within their own culture by the hands of powerful and abusive men. Their immigrant lifestyles have proved to be burdensome as they live in two cultures that have different expectations of them. For such oppressed women, what is the good news and how can they come to understand God who is with us? What method of theology will help to liberate them from all the bonds of domination and oppression that come their way daily?

Korean North American women need to develop a new methodology that will help them to be free of the bonds of domination and oppression. Theological method is an enormous and complex sub-discipline of theology, and I cannot claim to deal with it here in a thorough way. This chapter is only preparatory to our main subject matter of Christology. A theological method in which context/experience and Scripture play an important role is presented here.[3]

---

2. Chung Hyun Kyung, *Struggle to Be the Sun Again: Introducing Asian Women's Theology* (Maryknoll, N.Y.: Orbis Books, 1990), 100.

3. This method — a constructive method — is a modified form of that proposed by

These two components rely upon and affect one another, for this method is not static but can be viewed as a dynamic spiral. Scripture is fundamentally important because what we are doing is *Christian* theology. One's context/experience affects one's interpretation of Scripture, and likewise Scripture affects how one understands context and experiences. Therefore, this method becomes a movement, as each component affects and converses with the other to make changes in our theology and ultimately to change reality through praxis (action). The goal of doing theology, then, is not merely intellectual but practical. Because Korean women have a history and heritage in Asian religions as well as Christianity, Korean North American women's theology will need to utilize multifaith hermeneutics.[4]

CONTEXT/EXPERIENCE

The word "context" comes from the Latin word *texto,* which means to weave or join together. Context is the richly woven cultural, social, political, economic, and religious situation within which we live. Feminist theology relies on context, since theology must address and be addressed by the realities of the context.[5] Theology never occurs in a vacuum but always within a specific setting. Thus one needs to carefully examine the different historical, social, and political contexts within which we are developing our theology.

Theology that intentionally relates itself to a particular time and place has been given the name "contextual theology." All contextual theologies rightly connect theology with social existence, and of course our social existence changes over time. Although God, who is the subject of theology, is eternal, theology itself is limited by history and time. Theological language, therefore, is not universal language but a particular language for a specific social setting.[6] Hence every group of people must develop their own particular theological lan-

---

Juan Luis Segundo and also relies on the previous works of many liberation and feminist theologians who are forerunners in this area. See Juan Luis Segundo, *The Liberation of Theology,* trans. John Drury (Maryknoll, N.Y.: Orbis Books, 1976), 8ff.

4. Kwok Pui-lan discusses multifaith hermeneutics in her book *Discovering the Bible in a Non-Biblical World* (Maryknoll, N.Y.: Orbis Books, 1995).

5. Harold Wells, "Review Article; *She Who Is: The Mystery of God in Feminist Theological Discourse,*" *Touchstone* 13 (1995): 38.

6. James H. Cone, *God of the Oppressed* (New York: Seabury, 1975), 39.

guage according to their own distinct context. To do theology, we not only have to examine the context of biblical texts and the early church period, but also contemporary situations.

> We cannot afford to do theology unrelated to human existence. We cannot be "objective," but must recognize with Imamu Baraka that "there is no objective anything" — least of all theology.[7]

Since World War II, contextual theology has often been identified with the third world. Contextual theology emerged as these nations struggled to overthrow European colonial power and to reestablish the integrity of their own cultures, history, and national institutions. This form of theology has its social roots in the experience of third-world Christians as they recognized that the theology which they received was not an ahistorical, asocial or acultural theology, but was also "contextual" in an unconscious way. In considering the relationship of context to theology, these third-world Christians realized it was not that one's theological conclusions were necessarily different from place to place, but rather that the context determined the kinds of questions to be raised.[8] As contexts change, the questions also change, so that the questions and answers of the previous generation are not suitable for the next generation.

Douglas Hall outlines three reasons that theology is contextual. First, theology is contextual because it is a human enterprise. Human beings live in contexts and reflect differing times and places, in all of their thought and action. In order to speak about God, one needs to be aware of one's own contextual self. Second, theology attempts to speak of a living God and of God's relation to a dynamic creation. Third, theology exists for the sake of the Church's confession. Christians need to communicate their faith in the world and make it comprehensible for their own times and places.[9] Contextual theology has a particular interest in the search for human hope as it develops within the worldly context itself.[10] Moreover, intentionally contex-

---

7. Ibid., 16.
8. Christopher J. L. Lind, "An Invitation to Canadian Theology," *Toronto Journal of Theology* 1 (1985): 17.
9. Hall, *Thinking the Faith: Christian Theology in a North American Context,* 100, 107.
10. Ibid., 179.

tual theologies generally seek to be liberating for those who suffer hardships, oppression, and domination.

The particular context of one specific group of people obviously cannot provide the questions or answers for all peoples. People's experiences, structures, and cultures are rich and diverse in their own unique ways. Hence Korean North American women need to have a contextualized theology that addresses their own unique context, that is, specifically their immigrant status, a phenomenon that really has not been thoroughly studied from a theological perspective. Their lived experience, however, needs to be placed into immediate conversation with Scripture and tradition, if their reflection upon it is to be Christian and theological.

True contextuality means the nurture of a dialogue with one's culture, a genuine give-and-take, in which the culture is permitted to speak for itself. There the Christian community opens itself to the risk of hearing the things that it had not anticipated and to which it cannot readily respond. Thus the community of disciples sees its sociohistorical habitat not only as a field to be investigated, but as a partner in the investigation, and therefore as a contributor to the theological task itself.[11] Nothing can be accomplished without the dialogue of contemporary partners, for nothing can be achieved in isolation. Hall states that, "a theology which knows that it is not timeless will always need to know what time it is. Unless it knows this, the Christian community will not know what form of the Word is appropriate."[12]

Contextuality (as distinct from contemporaneity) means the discovery of the place-dimension of the human condition. Contextuality builds upon the apologetic tradition with its consciousness of changing time, but adds to this tradition the recognition that within any given time exist very different spatial realities that must be taken seriously by a faith that is genuinely incarnational.[13] Hence, Korean North American women's context will bring forth different expectations and understandings of theology that are distinct from those of the majority in North America. Since the reality is different "spa-

---

11. Ibid., 79.
12. Ibid., 81.
13. Douglas Hall, "On Contextuality in Christian Theology," *Toronto Journal of Theology* 1 (1985): 10.

tially," studying it and appreciating it for its differences are important tasks. These women cannot just adopt or borrow theology from the majority of North Americans but must struggle to create and give birth to their own theology that will be unique and liberating for them within their own specific context.

Contextual theology has certain dangers. For example, the danger exists that theology will merely reflect the context, or become accommodated to it, and so serve some alien agenda. Contextuality in Christian theology should not subordinate theological truth and the ultimacy of the gospel to alien ideological commitments.[14] To avoid this danger, contextual theology must remain bound and centered in Christ. In doing so, contextual theology seeks to reveal the truth and find meaning in it for here and now. In many ways, "context" and "experience" are intertwined and thus go hand-in-hand in developing a method for Korean North American women's theology.

An unique feature of feminist theology lies in its use of women's experiences. For a long time, women have been silenced. Women's experience has been neglected, as we heard only the stories of men. However, women must break away from the patriarchalism of "history" and affirm "her-story," which has been so widely ignored in traditional Judeo-Christian theology. History thus must be reread and rewritten in feminist perspective, thereby bringing forward and emphasizing the experience of women.[15] Women now need to draw upon their own experience to understand God in their lives. Women have been excluded in the historical development of theology, and their experience is now exploding as a critical force, exposing classical theology as based in male experience. Women's experience must be affirmed and remembered as a complex of events, feelings, and struggles that are shared by women in various circumstances of life. Women, especially black, third-world, and immigrant women, experience much suffering and oppression, and theology must emerge out of the particular experiences of these "oppressed people of God,"[16] if it is to address their situation and make sense to them.

---

14. Harold Wells, "Ideology and Contextuality in Liberation Theology," *Liberation Theology and Sociopolitical Transformation in Latin America,* ed. Jorge Farcia Antezana (Burnaby, B.C.: Institute for the Humanities, 1992), 62.

15. Jacquelyn Grant, *White Women's Christ and Black Women's Jesus: Feminist Christology and Womanist Response* (Atlanta: Scholars Press, 1989), 13.

16. Ibid., 3, 9, 10.

In appealing to experience, feminist and liberation theologians are also not falling into the false dichotomy between *changeless* truth and purely relative and *changing* truth. Concern for context is not just a popular appeal to the idea that everything is *relative* and nothing really matters. Rather, it is an attempt to deepen and correct our vision of God's promise by understanding that everything is *related*.[17]

Resorting to experience shows us how all the facets of our life are interconnected and that our faith and theology must also be profoundly affected by our experience.

Our particular method of using women's experience hears the stories of the oppressed and marginalized Korean North American women. These women need to examine and reflect on their own experience. The stories of male, chauvinistic history and philosophy have much dominated and occupied their homeland. These women suffered greatly in their strict, demanding roles as wives, mothers, daughters, and daughters-in-law. Their bodies often reflect the torturous lifestyles that they are enduring. Their hands reveal the difficult work that they perform and their feet show the hard path that they tread. Theology that is not in touch with their life experience cannot be a living theology.[18] These women need to value and acknowledge their struggles against all forms of injustice and domination.

Recounting and retelling Korean North American women's stories can lead to a deeper comprehension of their unique social context, including a better understanding of their political, historical, economic, and religio-cultural situation. These women carried many dreams and great hopes when they left their homeland to live in a free democratic country in North America. When they arrived, however, other battles were to be fought, and thus they did not gain the much anticipated liberation. Instead, they found themselves caught between two cultures that demanded and expected different roles from them. They also found that their new country had its own problems, as it required them to fulfill two major roles: housework, which includes cooking, cleaning, and rearing of children, and also working outside of the home

---

17. Letty Russell, *Household of Freedom: Authority in Feminist Theology* (Philadelphia: Fortress Press, 1987), 30, 31.

18. Jung Young Lee, *Marginality: The Key to Multicultural Theology* (Minneapolis: Fortress Press, 1995), 1.

to make a living. North America also became a place where they experienced much racism, as well as the sexism not unlike that of their homeland. They were looked down upon and treated with discrimination and hatred, just because of their race, and sexism added insult to injury. Understanding the experiences of these women who have their roots and destinies in between two worlds is an important step.

Korean North American women's theology can be seen as one specific type within the wider genre of feminist theology. The critical principle of feminist theology in general is the promotion of the full humanity of women. Women need to name themselves as subjects of authentic and full humanity. The naming of males as norms of authentic humanity causes women to be scapegoated for sin in both original and redeemed humanity.[19] Therefore the experiences of marginalized, ethnic women need to be validated and upheld as a source for doing theology. Korean North American women truly need to articulate their experience and claim their space as participants in the act of liberation. They need to act as agents of change and work toward a new future where women can claim their true humanity and be liberated from the numerous bonds of oppression. The appeal to experience is an invitation to look at how faith is shaped by life and how it can grow, change, and deepen as the contexts of life and learning shift.

SCRIPTURE AS A BASIC SOURCE

The use of Scripture in formulating theology has been a long tradition within the church. In the Reformed/Presbyterian tradition especially (of which this author is a part), Luther's method of *sola Scriptura* has been basic. Luther, and Calvin following him, fighting their own contextual battles in sixteenth-century Europe, denied that popes or councils have authority higher than or equal to Scripture. In the context of religious/ecclesiastical oppression of their time and place, Scripture was profoundly liberative. For them, *sola Scriptura* did not mean, however, that a Christian could simply read the Bible and automatically come up with Christian truth. Luther and Calvin did not believe that the Scriptures could be interpreted in isolation from tradition and learning. Moreover, with hindsight we can see today that

---

19. Rosemary Radford Ruether, *Sexism and God-Talk* (Boston: Beacon Press, 1983), 19.

the theology of the reformers was acutely contextual for their own time and place. Thus *sola Scriptura* did not mean, and cannot mean today, that theology was to be done from Scripture only — rather that Scripture stands alone as the incomparable source of truth in the Church. Without the Scripture we have no gospel.

A basic thrust of liberation appears throughout the Bible, as evident in Exodus through to Christ and Pentecost. Luther himself was well aware of the fallibility of the Bible.[20] Yet, even though it is fallible, Scripture continues to hold authority for the Church because it still bears Christ to humanity.[21] Scripture is "canonical," acknowledged as authoritative by the ecumenical church, because it is seen as the primary and most proximate witness to decisive revelatory events, especially the life, death, and resurrection of Jesus Christ.

Today, much debate and concern occurs among theologians about the interpretation of the Bible. Many turn to context to help them understand the meaning of particular passages for here and now. Context is also used in a historical sense, the surrounding circumstances or events that originally led to the formation of particular texts in the Bible. Biblical texts make sense only if they are read with insight into the social, political, and religious contexts of their own time.[22] The Bible originated in a patriarchal society. The story of salvation is told from a male point of view, and males overwhelmingly dominate biblical stories. The creative reflection and participation of women is neglected and marginalized, and the function of women is most often restricted to the important one of bringing forth sons for the men who are the bearers of the promise.[23]

Due to this patriarchal bias, one needs to read the biblical words with a critical eye and be aware of their origin and intent. Schüssler Fiorenza suggests,

> the revelatory canon for theological evaluation of biblical andro-
> centric traditions and their subsequent interpretation cannot be

---

20. Harold Wells, "The Making of the United Church Mind — No. II," *Touchstone* 8 (1990): 18–20.

21. Ibid., 19.

22. Letty M. Russell, "Exploring the Context of Our Faith," *Changing Contexts of Our Faith,* ed. Letty M. Russell (Philadelphia: Fortress Press, 1985), 22.

23. Elizabeth A. Johnson, *She Who Is: The Mystery of God in Feminist Theological Discourse* (New York: Crossroad, 1993), 76.

derived from the Bible itself but can only be formulated in and
through women's struggle for liberation from all patriarchal oppression. It cannot be universal but must be specific since it
is extrapolated from a particular experience of oppression and
liberation.... The personally and politically reflected experience
of oppression and liberation must become the criterion of appro-
priateness for biblical interpretation and evaluation of biblical
authority claims.[24]

Thus, feminist theologians need to search the Bible for what is
redemptive for women and use it for their liberating purpose.

Hence, one needs to formulate a criterion for accepting or rejecting biblical passages. One will focus upon and emphasize the Bible's
own liberating message. For example, in this book I shall discuss the
retrieval of biblical Wisdom as a source for Korean North American
women's Christology. But one must no longer accept the patriarchal
stories as God-ordained stories. Rather, women must examine them
with apprehension and trepidation. The Bible needs to be studied
very carefully and examined for its proper role in helping and liberating women from the bondage they experience within society, church,
and home. A method of deciding what is useful or not for women
is to move toward a critical evaluation of the Bible to uncover and
reject those

> elements within all biblical tradition and texts that perpetu-
> ate, in the name of God, violence, alienation, and patriarchal
> subordination, and eradicate women from historical theological
> consciousness. At the same time, such a feminist critical herme-
> neutics must recover all those elements within biblical texts and
> tradition that articulate the liberating experiences and visions of
> the people of God.[25]

In the end, the ultimate norm by which the Scriptures are judged is
whether they are oppressive or liberative.[26]

---

24. Elisabeth Schüssler Fiorenza, *In Memory of Her: A Feminist Theological Reconstruction of Christian Origins* (New York: Crossroad, 1990), 32.
    25. Ibid., 32.
    26. Pamela Dickey Young, *Feminist Theology/Christian Theology: In Search of Method*
(Minneapolis: Fortress Press, 1990), 31.

Scripture has an unavoidable impact on the lives of Christians, and Korean North American feminist theologians need to decipher the role of Scripture in formulating their theology. Throughout much of recent Korean history, missionaries have used the Bible as another form of domination and for the export of Western beliefs and philosophy. The Bible today is still used to perpetuate Western domination and cultural imperialism in Korea as many Korean clergy emphasize the absolute truth of the Bible over Korean culture, history, and religion. The wealth of truth of the Korean religious cultural traditions came to be regarded as inferior to the truth of Christianity.[27] This absolute truth of the Bible was indoctrinated into the minds of vulnerable Korean people, who live in a very different world from the West and who have encountered God in their own unique ways, long before the Western people ever came into their land.

Korean North American women who live in between two worlds usually accept the Protestant missionary view of the Bible as the only authority for understanding God, and thus see it as the ultimate revealer of truth. They also revere the Bible, in part at least because they have found it instructive, comforting, and liberating. They have been inspired by the message of the loving, compassionate God and the stories of Jesus. For them the Bible is the written word of God and they believe in its literal truth. Some of these women almost worship the Bible as an absolute authority that requires their unconditional acceptance of and obedience to its commandments. However, this understanding prevents women from seeing the conflict between biblical and modern knowledge.[28] They fail to understand the patriarchal origins and bias of the Bible. For the Bible to be truly liberating to them, they need to acknowledge its androcentric and cultural biases. Korean North American women need to look beyond a narrow understanding of the Bible and read and interpret it with an awareness of its problems and fallibility. As a Korean North American woman, I believe that my sisters and I need to expand our horizons and explore the possibilities of reading the Bible together with our own Asian heritage and beliefs; Scripture needs to be dissociated from Western thought and power and freed from many of its traditional Western

---

27. Chung, *Struggle to Be the Sun Again*, 107.
28. Ai Ra Kim, *Women's Struggle for a New Life* (Albany: State University of New York Press, 1996), 144, 145.

interpretations and understandings if it is to liberate Korean North American women. The Bible and context/experience should interact with one another and provide crucial components for a Korean North American women's theology. Douglas Hall states the matter well:

> In that mode of reflection which we call Christian theology, there is a meeting between two realities: on the one hand the Christian tradition, namely, the accumulation of past articulations of Christians concerning their belief, with special emphasis upon the biblical testimony and on the other hand, the explicit circumstances, obvious or hidden, external and internal, physical and spiritual, of the historical moment in which the Christian community finds itself. Theology means the meeting of these two realities. It is the struggle of imagination-intellect which occurs in that meeting, the ongoing encounter between the claims of the tradition and the lived experience of the present.[29]

Such a meeting forms the basis for the Christology developed in this book.

MULTIFAITH CONSIDERATIONS

To link biblical faith to our own Asian and Korean heritage, we must engage the dynamics of multifaith relations. A full treatment of interfaith dialogue is beyond the scope of this work, but we must briefly consider some current concepts that are often used to clarify the relationships of religions and cultures to each other: multifaith hermeneutics, inculturation, and syncretism.

Multifaith Hermeneutics

A helpful methodological concept for Korean North American women's theology is multifaith hermeneutics. While Kwok Pui-lan uses the term to describe theological method within the Asian Christian context, the term also applies to the context of Korean immigrant women living in North America. Kwok explains that earlier Asian theologians attempted to bridge the gap between the Christian worldview and the Asian mind-set through the process of indigenization.

---

29. Hall, "On Contextuality in Christian Theology," 3, 4.

Christian faith was presented in Asian idioms, symbols, and concepts to make it less foreign. Motifs and Christian doctrines were compared to those in various traditions of Asia.[30] Many Asian theologians are finding this approach inadequate and turning to multifaith hermeneutics. Multifaith hermeneutics can be described as the task of relating Christian biblical interpretation positively to other religious texts and traditions. Korean North American women's theology must be related to their own religious past. Multifaith hermeneutics assumes the willingness to look at one's own traditions from other perspectives, the maturity to discern both similarities and differences in various traditions, and the humility to learn from other partners in the conversation. Multifaith hermeneutics requires us to affirm that other religious traditions have as much right to exist as Christianity.[31] The interaction between Asian Scriptures and Christian Scriptures is not meant to prove that they are compatible or incompatible, but aims at a "wider intertextuality" and a fruitful and continuous cross-cultural dialogue.[32]

Korean North American women need to claim the power to read the Bible with their own eyes in light of their experiences. Kwok Pui-lan suggests that a "dialogical imagination" must become operative in biblical interpretation. This approach invites more dialogue partners by shifting the emphasis from one Scripture (the Bible) to many Scriptures, from responding to one religious narrative to many possible narratives. Dialogical imagination shifts from a single-axis framework of analysis to a multiaxial interpretation, taking into serious consideration the issues of race, class, gender, culture, and history. Dialogical imagination uses Asian cultural and religious traditions and sacred texts as dialogical partners in biblical reflection and "the social biography of the people" as hermeneutical keys for biblical interpretation.[33] Such a method can be adapted for immigrants, because they can obtain something of value from both worlds and synthesize them, for the sake of an authentic interpretation for those who live in between two worlds. Dialogical imagination needs to look at both the biblical reality and the East Asian reality and utilize them to chal-

---

30. Kwok, *Discovering the Bible in the Non-Biblical World*, 57.
31. Ibid., 58.
32. Ibid., 63.
33. Ibid., 36.

lenge the established order. Korean North America women may thus be free to read the Bible critically and to be liberated from their age-old captivity to patriarchy, colonialism, and Western imperialism.[34] Furthermore, this approach will enable them to view the Bible from within the perspective of their own historical and bicultural heritage.

Koreans have a long history of spiritual stories that speak of God and God's encounter with humanity. Missionaries rejected these rich religious and spiritual stories as "unchristian," and the Bible was given to them as the only true revelation of God.[35] Koreans need, however, to retrieve their own indigenous religious and spiritual stories for the sake of developing their own theology. Furthermore, Korean North American women are immersed into the cultural stories of North America, which they also need to take into consideration. Somehow, these women need to claim truth from both worlds and not neglect the experiences of their Korean foremothers who experienced much mistreatment from missionaries and the Japanese and Korean men. These women must search elsewhere for truth and also be open to Confucianism, Buddhism, and Shamanism, which are already part of their tradition, finding ways to synthesize the best of these traditions with their understandings of the Bible.

The idea of synthesizing and borrowing from one's own history and culture and from others is nothing new. The Bible itself presents evidence of this type of outlook. For example, biblical wisdom literature reveals an openness of the Jews to what can be learned from Egyptian or Mesopotamian wisdom.[36] These people looked beyond their own religious circle to understand and articulate Wisdom. Wisdom was originally an instrument of contextualization, as the Jews borrowed the characteristics of Isis, who was a prominent Egyptian goddess, and ascribed it to *Hokmah* (Sophia).[37] The contextualizing process is comparable to the hermeneutical circle of liberation theology; that is, contemporary knowledge was placed in conversation with the authoritative source, which was in turn interpreted and critiqued by practical

---

34. Chung, *Struggle to Be the Sun Again,* 107.
35. Ibid., 107.
36. Wesley Ariarajah, *The Bible and the People of Other Faiths* (Geneva: World Council of Churches, 1985), ix.
37. This subject is discussed further in later chapters.

worldly wisdom and experience.[38] Likewise, Christians should also look beyond Scripture to find theological truth and meaning.

Moreover, many biblical passages affirm that God is God of all nations and not just the Israelites. For example, Amos puts all nations, including Israel, under God's judgment. Amos writes, "The Lord says, 'People of Israel, I think as much of the people of Sudan as I do of you. I brought the Philistines from Crete and the Syrians from Kir, just as I brought you from Egypt' " (Amos 9:7). God cares for all people, and thus we need to also respect and care for all the different people in the world. Even the book of Malachi insists that God is God of all nations and that other nations are honoring God. "Now, you priests," he says, "try asking God to be good to us. He will not answer your prayer, and it will be your fault. . . . I am not pleased with you, I will not accept the offering you bring to me" (Mal. 1:9–10). And then comes the challenge, "People from one end of the world to the other honor me. Everywhere they burn incense to me and offer acceptable sacrifices. All of them honor me" (Mal. 1:11).[39] All people thus belong to God, and God's presence and wisdom are found among all nations. In the same manner, Korean North American women, as people of God, also need to look beyond the Bible and retrieve valuable truths about God from their own rich spiritual and religious stories and traditions.

Multifaith hermeneutics affirms that truth and wisdom are found not only in the Bible but also in the cultures, histories, and religions of other people. We have already seen that the Bible itself affirms this in various places, challenging us to look at it from a much broader worldview and cultural framework. Asian theologians debate among themselves about how to assess their religious and cultural traditions. Some regard Asian Scripture and hermeneutical tradition as important resources for a cross-cultural reading of the Bible. Others point to the failure of the earlier indigenization efforts, which tended to romanticize traditional Asian culture and to overlook present-day sociopolitical struggles.[40] Using one's own religious and cultural tradition, but using it critically, is very important.

---

38. Harold Wells, "Trinitarian Feminism: Elizabeth Johnson's Wisdom Christology," *Theology Today* 52 (1995): 333.
39. Ariarajah, *The Bible and the People of Other Faiths*, 7, 11.
40. Kwok, *Discovering the Bible in a Non-Biblical World*, 66, 67.

Instead of assuming that any faith tradition is monolithic, one should be alert to the varying influence the tradition has had on people of different races, classes, and genders. One should include spiritual traditions that are intellectual and written, as well as the popular and the oral. The influence and use of Scripture in the life of the community — including liturgy, drama, song, and aesthetics — must also be taken into consideration.[41] Multifaith hermeneutics heightens one's consciousness of the hermeneutical assumptions underlying Eastern and Western traditions, which one can explore by looking at the relation of hermeneutics to language and reality on the one hand and to history on the other. Hermeneutics has to do with much more than the study of a given text; it includes the perception of truth behind the text and the relation of the text to the ethos and practice of the religious community. A multifaith approach to hermeneutics reveals the divergent assumptions of Asian theologians when they relate the biblical story to the Asian story. That the Asian story is a forerunner or a preparation for the Gospel has largely been rejected because that belief still assumes the missionary approach. Many Asian theologians do not think the biblical story is a fulfillment of or superior to the various Asian stories.[42]

Women who participate in the work of multifaith hermeneutics may see the issues more from the perspective of gender. For example, these women insist that women's stories be included among the people's stories. They lift up stories women have told that give meaning to their lives and empower them in their struggle against male oppression. Many women who are less concerned with the boundary between orthodoxy and heterodoxy have created religious meanings in their dialogical appropriation of different traditions.[43]

In order to move toward the multifaith interpretation of Wisdom that this book is exploring, two important terms, syncretism and inculturation, must be understood. These terms, similar and yet distinct, play an important role in the movement toward an understanding of Sophia as a Christology for Korean North American women. Because we wish to draw upon Asian religio-cultural sources, as well as biblical and other Christian ones, we are inevitably involved in

---

41. Ibid., 67.
42. Ibid., 67, 68.
43. Ibid., 69, 70.

some degree of syncretism. And because we wish to articulate faith in Christ in a way that speaks to the culture of Korean North American women, we are inevitably engaged in inculturation. Sophia Christology for Korean North American women requires one to search the various Asian religious traditions to discover sources that help us to comprehend Sophia. Syncretism and inculturation are methodological tools for a multifaith understanding of Wisdom.

Inculturation

"Inculturation" speaks of contextualization, i.e., the communication of faith in a manner relevant to a particular culture. Other common terms (besides contextualization) have been "adaptation," "indigenization," and "incarnation." For various reasons, the term "inculturation" has gradually gained favor. Peter Schineller offers a widely accepted definition of inculturation:

> incarnation of Christian life and of the Christian message in a particular cultural context, in such a way that this experience not only finds expression through elements proper to the culture in question, but becomes a principle that animates, directs and unifies the culture, transforming and remaking it so as to bring about "a new creation."[44]

Inculturation is an ongoing way of engaging in Christian life and mission. This engagement takes place within families, schools, seminaries, and churches. Indeed, wherever Christians are, they are inevitably involved in the process of inculturating their faith.[45] Inculturation is the necessity of the historical intersection of cultures and the determination to blend them with an integrity that respects both faith and cultures.[46] Inculturation thus has to do with the interaction of what may be referred to as "faith" on the one hand and culture on the other — the ongoing dialogue between faith and culture. Where Christianity is concerned, inculturation is the creative and dynamic

44. Peter Schineller, *A Handbook on Inculturation* (Mahwah, N.J.: Paulist Press, 1990), 6.

45. Ibid., 12.

46. Theoneste Nkeramihigo, "Inculturation and the Specificity of Christian Faith," in *What Is So New about Inculturation?* ed. Ary Roest Crollius and Theoneste Nkeramihigo (Rome: Pontifical Gregorian University, 1984), 22.

relationship between the Christian message and a culture. This relationship is inevitable because the Christian faith cannot exist except in some cultural form.[47] The concept is important for Korean North American women's theology, which needs to find ways to inculturate its received faith into the women's own particular context.

In order to further grasp this concept of inculturation, defining "culture" is necessary. Many definitions of culture are available. Tylor suggests that culture is "that complex whole which includes knowledge, belief, art, morals, law, custom and any other capabilities and habits acquired by man as a member of society."[48] Culture is what a person learns, or acquires, as a member of a society. Clifford Geertz defines culture similarly as a "historically transmitted pattern of meaning embodied in symbols, a system of inherited conceptions, expressed in symbolic forms by means of which human beings communicate, perpetuate and develop their knowledge about and attitudes toward life."[49] Religion as a human phenomenon or human activity must thus affect and be affected by culture.[50]

As these definitions indicate, culture is a way of living, behaving, thinking, and reacting that includes the group's value systems and the institutions of family, law, and education. As the sum total of learned behavioral patterns, culture is constantly changing. Therefore, where Christianity is concerned, contextualization is always a continuing task.[51] The Gospel enters a culture and examines it. It affirms what it perceives as good and true and seeks to elevate that goodness and truth to an even more exalted level. At the same time the Gospel challenges and corrects what is seen as evil and sinful so as to purify the culture. While the Gospel can indeed become inculturated in every human situation, it also transcends every culture.[52] Inculturation at

---

47. Aylward Shorter, *Toward a Theology of Inculturation* (Maryknoll, N.Y.: Orbis Books, 1988), 4, 11, 12.

48. Sir Edward Tylor as quoted by Aylward Shorter, *Toward a Theology of Inculturation*, 4.

49. Clifford Geertz, *The Interpretation of Cultures* (New York: Basic Books, 1973), 89.

50. Shorter, *Toward a Theology of Inculturation*, 5.

51. Bruce J. Nicholls, "Towards a Theology of Gospel and Culture," in *Gospel and Culture*, ed. John Stott and Robert T. Coote (Pasadena, Calif.: William Carey Library, 1979), 70.

52. Robert Schreiter, "Inculturation of Faith or Identification with Culture?" in *Christianity and Cultures*, ed. Norbert Greinacher and Norbert Mette (Maryknoll, N.Y.: Orbis Books, 1994), 15.

its best is the renewal of culture, within the framework of Christianity and the "transforming dialogue" of culture with the Gospel.[53]

The process of inculturation is one of integration, in the sense of an integration of the Christian faith and life into a given culture and also an integration of a new expression of the Christian experience in the Church. The inculturation of the Church is the integration of the Christian experience of a local church into the culture of its people.[54] The Church's mission needs to involve correlating the Christian message with present situations. "In this way gospel values become inculturated or localized. Inculturation is not achieved, however, merely by importing grace from outside, as if it were not already available in the situation, but by stirring up the grace of God that has already been decisively offered through Jesus Christ."[55] Inculturation is the transformation of cultures in light of the Gospel, the evangelization of every aspect of the people, and the naturalizing of the Church in every culture. In working toward these goals, authentic inculturation will respect the character of each culture.[56] These goals will ultimately help people understand Christianity within their own culture. However, Christianity itself and its theological expression will also be transformed, taking on fresh, new, and dynamic forms appropriate to the culture in which it lives.

Karl Rahner, writing from a Roman Catholic perspective, suggests that three major epochs in Church history have revealed the Church's movement toward inculturation. The first is when the Gospel was spread through Jesus' preaching to the Jewish people. This process was continued after his death by his followers who lived among and shared their belief with the Jewish community. The result was a Jewish Christianity, in which Christians retained many of the Jewish traditions such as their prayers, the law of circumcision, and some dietary

53. Shorter, *Toward a Theology of Inculturation*, 263.
54. Ary Roest Crollius, "What Is So New about Inculturation?" in *What Is So New about Inculturation*, ed. Ary Roest Crollius and Theoneste Nkeramihigo (Rome: Pontifical Gregorian University, 1984), 14, 15.
55. Schineller, *A Handbook on Inculturation*, 73.
56. Peter Schineller, "Inculturation: A Difficult and Delicate Task," *International Bulletin of Missionary Research* 20 (1996): 109.
It is evident that inculturation was always present within the Church and even played an important role in shaping the Christianity that we know today. As the Church grows and spreads to different parts of the world, inculturation will continue to play a key role in allowing people to live out their faith authentically.

laws. The second epoch began with Paul's conversion and his mission to the Gentiles as he took the Gospel to them. Since the Gentiles' culture and religion was very different from Jewish culture and religion, Paul began to adapt and modify the Gospel to enable them to understand it. The result was a Gentile form of Christianity, one that did not demand circumcision and engaged in dialogue with Greek and Roman philosophy. According to Rahner, this Christianity has existed for almost two thousand years, until the Second Vatican Council. Western European Christianity, which stemmed from Greco-Roman traditions, has become the predominant and basic form of Christianity. The third epoch is the world church. The Catholic Church, while still remaining Roman, is becoming more diverse in the expression and celebration of its one faith, one baptism, and one Lord. The church was to be a "church in the modern world" with its rich diversity of cultures and traditions.[57]

The term "interculturation" is another term for inculturation. David J. Bosch states that "inculturation" implies the Gospel as the subject and a culture as the object as though one is the giver and the other the receiver. Bosch realizes that Western Christianity has domesticated the gospel in its own culture. This resulted in the gospel becoming foreign to every other culture and assumed that the Western Gospel was a fully indigenized, universalized, and completed product. Bosch thus argues that the term "inculturation" is inappropriate due to its negative connotation.[58]

Three main reasons or bases exist for inculturation. First, inculturation has a biblical basis, rooted in the incarnation of God in Jesus Christ: "The word became flesh and dwelt among us" (John 1:14). According to the New Testament, Jesus preached the good news and called his followers to continue his work after his death and resurrection. Therefore, God in Jesus Christ became incarnated in one particular time and place. Jesus' entire life and ministry can be the central paradigm in which people discover and inculturate the gospel into particular contexts. This process of inculturation continues in the speeches of Peter found in the book of Acts and in the letters

57. Karl Rahner, *Concern for the Church: Theological Investigations XX*, trans. Edward Quinn (New York: Crossroad, 1981), 85–87.
58. David J. Bosch, *Transforming Mission: Paradigm Shifts in Theology of Mission* (Maryknoll, N.Y.: Orbis Books, 1991), 447–55.

and speeches of Paul. Paul teaches and relates the gospel to Greek philosophy and the various religions of that time (Acts 17).[59] Furthermore, the four Gospels, with their differing narratives and theologies, indicate the necessity of inculturation, for the story of Jesus is multifaceted and the communities to whom the gospel was preached were also different and diverse. Each of the Gospels provides both a different instance of inculturation, and furthermore, differing messages to be inculturated.[60]

Second, theological bases exist for inculturation. Theology can be described as a critical reflection on one's faith as it is influenced by one's culture. The relationship is mutual, in that faith seeks to influence and transform a culture; culture in turn transforms theology. Theological understandings therefore both have an impact on culture and are affected by culture.[61]

Third, strong contextual and experiential reasons for inculturation are present today, because we are living in an age of mission and of intense intercultural activity, with tremendous challenge to and activity on the part of the church. In many places, the church is spreading. The church urgently needs to respond to the different cultures that it encounters, lest it be meaningless to them. We are also in an age of global awareness, which includes the awareness of cultural diversity[62] — a diversity both within nations and among nations. In our newly globalized world context, inculturation is inevitable and needs to occur intentionally and responsibly.

Several obstacles may deter the progress of the deep rooting of Christian faith in the rich variety of human cultures. One obstacle is the complexity of cultures, for so many cultures exist even within one country. Into which culture does one inculturate the Gospel? We must respect and appreciate the varied contexts that exist today within one nation or society. Another obstacle is the demand upon time and energy. The faith brought by missionaries reflected mainly American, British, or Canadian expressions of the Christian faith. Inculturation should be happening naturally and without haste, but many people are urgently engaged in catching up, correcting the lack

---

59. Schineller, *A Handbook on Inculturation*, 6–8.
60. Ibid., 8.
61. Ibid., 45.
62. Ibid., 6.

of inculturation in the past. Yet another complexity is the nature of inculturation as it encompasses all areas of life. This task is indeed colossal and should be approached slowly and comprehensively. All of these conditions require a positive and hopeful outlook.

Change brought about by authentic inculturation must not be seen as a loss or diminishment, but growth in the true catholic nature of Christianity. We are not losing anything but are gaining richness and authenticity for our faith. Solid, clear theological underpinnings, without loss of identity or the essentials of faith, are necessary if Christian faith is to explore new possibilities with confidence. Established and emerging churches need to maintain close relationships if emerging churches are to avoid going off on tangents and if established churches are to avoid stagnation. Christianity is a living religion that changes and grows as it moves from one culture to another. The church should not remain the same but must also change and adapt itself to ever-changing societies and cultures. Further, all Christian believers must be encouraged to take part in the process of inculturation. If believers want to grow and change, they must actively engage themselves in the process. Inculturation occurs in a secular, pluralistic, and often unjust world, involving the cross and demanding a conversion from the old to the new. Inculturation reaches down and touches the very mystery of our personal relationship with God.[63] To this creative engagement, every individual, every church, every culture is called.

Theology cannot be content to remain with the successful formulation of one specific time and place, as though it were valid for all times and places, but must be constantly a re-creation of each time and place. Inculturation is a necessary and crucial way for the Church to engage in dialogue throughout the world.[64]

Syncretism

A related and complementary concept (together with multifaith hermeneutics and inculturation) is syncretism. The concept is a vast one about which a huge literature exists. Here we can only touch briefly

---

63. Schineller, "Inculturation: A Difficult and Delicate Task," 110, 112.
64. Marcello De Carvalho Azevedo, *Inculturation and the Challenges of Modernity* (Rome: Centre "Cultures and Religions" — Pontifical Gregorian University, 1982), 52.

on the phenomenon. "Syncretism" has generally been used pejora-
tively within the Church, but in recent years the term has become
more acceptable within theological circles as theologians recognize it
as an inevitable and universal reality. Many ways to define syncretism
exist. Visser't Hooft defined it negatively as the denial of the uniqueness of any religion and the mixing of various religions, in an attempt
to bring various religious traditions into one great synthesis.[65] This
practice would be unacceptable to most adherents of nearly all the religions, for each religion has its own uniqueness of belief and practice,
even though many aspects may overlap with other religions.

Contrary to traditional understandings, pure Christianity does not
exist, never has existed, and never can exist. According to nearly all
religions, the divine is made present through human mediations.[66]
Syncretism is thus a normal condition for the incarnation, expression, and objectification of a religious faith.[67] Not only is syncretism
inevitable within Christianity, but it may be seen positively as a historical and concrete way in which God comes to people and saves them.[68]
Within Christianity, syncretism needs to be based on a very clear christological position. Jesus Christ crucified and risen needs to remain its
center and criterion. While many things can be borrowed and mixed,
limits exist as to what can be blended if any religious tradition is to
avoid losing its own identity and its unique message.[69] Syncretism,
I would contend, must thus be Christ-centered where Christians are
concerned.

Anthropologists point out that syncretism has always been "part

---

65. D. C. Mulder, "None Other Gods" — "No Other Name," *The Ecumenical Review*
38 (1986): 209.

66. Leonardo Boff, *Church: Charism and Power* (London: SCM Press, 1985), 91. According to E. Hoornaert, without paganism, Christianity loses its vitality and becomes dry
and sterile. Paganism is necessary to Christianity as the soil is to the garden. Paganism
brings life to Christianity as it offers it the opportunity to testify to its faith. Eduardo
Hoornaert, *The Memory of the Christian People*, trans. Robert R. Barr (Tunbridge Wells,
England: Burns & Oates, 1989), 261.

67. Ibid., 93.

68. Ibid., 99. W. Pannenberg has shown that syncretism has always been present within
Christianity and has suggested that it might be seen as a positive characteristic, because it is
the way in which the universal Christian message incarnates within other cultures. For more
discussion, see Andre Droogers, "Syncretism: The Problem of Definition, the Definition of
the Problem," in *Dialogue and Syncretism: An Interdisciplinary Approach*, ed. Jerald Gort,
Hendrik Vroom, Rein Fernhout, and Anton Wessels (Grand Rapids: William B. Eerdmans,
1989), 13.

69. M. M. Thomas, "The Absoluteness of Jesus Christ and Christ-Centered Syncretism,"
Ecumenical Review 37 (1985): 395.

of the negotiation of identities and hegemonies in situations such as conquest, trade, migration, religious dissemination and marriage."[70] The oldest use of the term "syncretism" is found in Plutarch and refers to the inhabitants of Crete, who, in facing a common enemy, overcame their differences of opinion and temporarily joined forces. In the seventh century, the notion took on a negative characteristic and came to refer to the illegitimate reconciliation of opposing theological views.[71] Much later Erasmus spoke of syncretism as a positive union of seemingly disparate points of view. In mission history in recent centuries, however, "syncretism" was generally a pejorative term referring to surreptitious activity of native converts who clung to their older religious ideas or practices, incurring the hostility of missionaries.[72]

Throughout Judeo-Christian history, syncretism can be divided into at least four periods. The first period is the history of Israel in the last century before the Exile. Foreign cults were introduced to the Israelites and the God of Israel was conceived as one of many gods in which there were only relative differences. In Deuteronomy, Jeremiah, and Ezekiel, a sharp prophetic reaction to this syncretistic crisis occurred. That reaction was not simply an exhibition of fanatical intolerance, but an expression of the deep conviction that to mix Yahweh with other gods is in fact to deny the specific claim that the God of Israel makes. The second wave started with Alexander's conquests and found its climax in the period of the Roman empire. Gods from Egypt, Syria, and Persia found their way into Rome, Germany, and Britain, and all kinds of attempts were made at synthesizing the various beliefs. Some philosophers saw the numerous gods as different forms of the one god, and an emperor like Julian tried to make a syncretistic religion the basis of his empire. Then the third period occurred in Europe in the eighteenth century. During this time, people of the Enlightenment were looking for a common fac-

---

70. Charles Stewart and Rosalind Shaw, *Syncretism/Anti-Syncretism: The Politics of Religious Synthesis* (London and New York: Routledge, 1994), 19–20. Harold Wells discusses this in "Korean Syncretism and Theologies of Interreligious Encounter: The Contribution of Kyoung Jae Kim," *Asia Journal of Theology* 12 (1998): 57.

71. Andre Droogers, "Syncretism: The Problem of Definition, the Definition of the Problem," in Gort et al., *Dialogue and Syncretism: An Interdisciplinary Approach*, 9.

72. Carl F. Starkloff, "Inculturation and Cultural Systems (Part 2)," *Theological Studies* 55 (1994): 281.

tor in all religions and reacting against claims of uniqueness by the Church. People like Rousseau thus made "natural religion" a serious competitor of revealed religion. The fourth period is occurring now and consists of the growing influence of comparative religion and the renaissance of Asian religions.[73]

Leonardo Boff suggests, from a contemporary Roman Catholic perspective, four fundamental criteria for true syncretism. One is Scripture, which itself presents a purification within Judaism and primitive Christianity. Second is Christian praxis supported by the traditions of the universal church, and the third is the decisions of episcopal synods. The fourth is the tradition of the prophets and of Jesus in the defense of human freedom and spontaneity in the cultural universe.[74]

A key theorist of syncretism is R. J. Schreiter. According to him, in light of the historical facts about syncretism, three basic aims of a new definition are present. The first is theological as we seek to find new expressions of the Christian faith that will allow new voices to be heard. The second is cultural. One needs to find a universal discourse in which aspects and particularities of a culture will be respected and at the same time linked to other communities around the world. The third is missiological. Missiology's concern about crossing boundaries is now a central concern in theology. Therefore theology is becoming missiology.[75]

Leonardo Boff offers a critical discussion of six kinds of religious syncretism. The first is "syncretism by addition," in which persons simply add other practices and beliefs to their own religion. This addition, which takes place without genuine interrelation, is certainly a pejorative sense of syncretism. Second is syncretism as accommodation, when the dominated people's religion is as a strategy for survival adapted to the religion of those who dominate. This adaptation produces conflict within the religious experience of the dominated peoples. Third is syncretism as a mixture, in which the individual or group "pours together" various elements in order to satisfy needs, but lacks any coherent religious vision of the world. This type of

73. D. C. Mulder, "None Other Gods" — "No Other Name," 212, 213.

74. Boff, *Church, Charism and Power,* 104.

75. Robert J. Schreiter, "Defining Syncretism: An Interim Report," *International Bulletin of Missionary Research* 17 (1993): 53.

syncretism leads to confusion. Fourth is syncretism as agreement, according to which no unique revelation exists but many equivalent paths to the divine are available. In this process, an attempt is made to harmonize in order to create a universal religion for all people, but this approach ignores the specificity and uniqueness of each religion. The fifth is syncretism as translation. In this approach, says Boff, one religion uses the expressions of another to communicate its own central message, but no real mutual learning from the other has occurred. The sixth is syncretism as adaptation, when a religion is exposed to other religious expressions and assimilates them according to its own identity. This movement involves adaptation and reinterpretation so that one's true religious identity is still preserved while genuinely learning from the other. This process is continuous as the religion continues to incarnate itself in different cultures.[76] What is attempted in this work is syncretism in this last sense, in which the insights of two or more religions are genuinely integrated without violence or loss of identity on either side.

Korea is a multireligious country where different world religions have existed side by side in various periods of its history.[77] Many evidences of syncretism are present in Korea among several religions. The Korean theologian Kyoung Jae Kim tells us that when *Pungryudo* (the henotheistic religion of the ancient Han people believing in the heavenly God, the God of light and life, called *Hananim*) and Shamanism met, an integration occurred. The *Hannism* of *Pungryudo* was the henotheistic faith of the ancient Han people. Because of societal change from hunting to agriculture, people related to spiritual beings in their daily lives, seeking healthy children, healing, and success in agriculture. To meet this void, *Pungryudo* was integrated with Shamanism. Such a fusion between religions does not preclude the possibility that each religion will hold its own character.[78]

Most Christians in Korea have been highly resistant to syncretism

---

76. Boff, *Church, Charism and Power,* 90, 91.

77. Suh Nam-dong uses the term "confluence" to describe the syncretistic activity in Korea. Confluence is the coming together of two religions, much like two rivers flowing into each other to form one river. Suh Nam-dong, "Historical References for a Theology of Minjung," in *Minjung Theology,* ed. the Commission on Theological Concerns of the Christian Conference of Asia (Maryknoll, N.Y.: Orbis Books, 1983), 177.

78. Kyoung Jae Kim, *Christianity and the Encounter of Asian Religions: Method of Correlation, Fusion of Horizons and Paradigm Shifts in the Korean Grafting Process* (Zoetermeer: Uitgeverij Boekencentrum, 1994), 105, 107.

even though their religious practices indicate an implicit or unconscious syncretism. The horizons of Shamanism, of Buddhism, and of
Confucianism have not only changed and developed within themselves, but have also integrated with each other over many centuries
to create a syncretic religio-cultural society. This adaptation does not
mean that their specificities have disappeared, but that they have mu-
tually influenced one another, and all play a key role among Korean
people.[79] This phenomenon of adaptation and borrowing continued when Christianity made its way into Korea. Finding elements
of the older religious traditions more or less unconsciously present in
Korean Christianity is not difficult. For example, components of Confucian filial piety remain, as do recognizable behavioral roles for men
and women. Elements of Shamanism's emphasis on physical, emo-
tional, and spiritual healing and Buddhist styles of meditative prayer
are also apparent.[80] Despite all these elements and evidences of syncretism, Korean Christians tend to deny its reality in their lives and
their forms of Christianity.

Despite this denial, syncretism has played a key role in the growth
of Christianity in Korea. The appearance of Roman Catholicism
occurred without the help of Western priests, but through certain
Korean neo-Confucianists who were convinced through their own
study that Roman Catholicism was true. As Catholicism spread, it
began to threaten the Korean ruling elite, because of its rejection
of ancestor worship. Severe persecutions followed, and thousands
of Catholics were martyred in the early nineteenth century. Despite
this, Catholicism survived and was officially tolerated from 1886.
Then in the late nineteenth century, Protestant missionaries entered
Korea and focused on the working class. Christianity evidently fed
the spiritual hunger of many Korean people and helped them to resist the oppression that they suffered from the local elites. Christianity
became a life-giving force that promoted women's rights and the abo-
lition of class barriers.[81] Kyoung Jae Kim believes that the spirituality

---

79. Ibid., 106.

80. Wells, "Korean Syncretism and Theologies of Interreligious Encounter: The Contribution of Kyoung Jae Kim," 60.

81. Kyoung Jae Kim discusses this matter in *Christianity and the Encounter of Asian
Religions: Method of Correlation, Fusion of Horizons and Paradigm Shifts in the Korean
Grafting Process* as cited by Wells, "Korean Syncretism and Theologies of Interreligious
Encounter: The Contribution of Kyoung Jae Kim," 64.

and religious understandings of Mahayana Buddhism, Shamanism, and Confucianism all helped the Korean people to receive the gospel. Many Christian concepts (Spirit, redemption, heaven, etc.) were easily understood and accepted because of the people's religio-cultural heritage.[82]

Feminist theologian Chung Hyun Kyung discusses syncretism as a necessary element for becoming truly Asian Christians. She argues that Asian women need to move away from the doctrinal purity of Christian theology, which they uphold very strongly, and take the risk of affirming the life-giving element of syncretism. What matters to these women's survival is not doctrinal orthodoxy but liberation for themselves and their communities. Furthermore, the life force can empower them to claim their humanity. Asian women need to selectively choose life-giving elements of their culture and religions and weave new patterns of religious meaning that will liberate them from oppression and hardship.[83]

In sum, multifaith hermeneutics, inculturation, and syncretism are ways to the survival and meaningfulness of Christianity in relation to various human cultures. We have seen that inculturation is the introduction of Christianity into a particular cultural context, in such a way that the insight and wisdom of cultures shapes new forms of Christianity. Inculturation, especially where Asian cultures are concerned, is likely to involve religious syncretism. There are good and bad forms of syncretism. I have argued that syncretism is inevitable, and may be positive when a religion assimilates other religious expressions into itself, while both religious identities are maintained. I have stressed that there is no pure Christianity, since from its earliest stages syncretism and inculturation occurred spontaneously. It would be a tragedy, then, for Asian Christians and particularly Korean North American Christian women simply to accept Western Christianity as "authentic" and "pure." We need to adapt and borrow from our own cultural and religious background so that our Christian faith may be more meaningful, yet remain Christ-centered.

82. Kim, *Christianity and the Encounter of Asian Religions*, 118, 119.
83. Chung, *Struggle to Be the Sun Again*, 113.

PRAXIS

Korean North American women's theological method cannot be merely a description and analysis of their own context/experience, or a rereading of Scripture, or an abstract consideration of multifaith relations. It must lead to some change or social action for a better, more just society.[84] Korean North American women's theological method must fight against the oppressions that they experience through their own culture, history, and religions, and also place them in solidarity with others who suffer. Therefore their theological method cannot be static or abstract, but must be constantly moving and making a practical difference in their lives and in society. Stephen B. Bevans well articulates this notion of doing theology for social change in his discussion of "praxis" as outlined in his book *Models of Contextual Theology.* The praxis model is a way of doing theology that is formed by knowledge at its most intense level — the level of reflective action. In discerning meaning and contributing to the course of social change, praxis takes its inspiration from "present realities and future possibilities."[85] This model focuses on the identity of Christians within a culture as that culture is understood in terms of social change. This approach grows out of the conviction that commitment to social change leads to a deeper and more challenging knowledge of God.[86]

The key presupposition of the praxis model is that the highest kind of *knowing* is intelligent and responsible *doing,* or faith seeking action.[87] By first acting and then reflecting on that action in faith, practitioners of this model believe that one can develop a theology that is truly relevant to a particular context. Thus, theology is conceived more in terms of an activity, a process, a way of living.[88] This model also presupposes God's revelation, and understands revelation as the presence of God in history in the events of

---

84. This is much like Segundo's idea of "changing reality" in his theological methodology called the hermeneutic circle. For further discussion see Juan Luis Segundo, *The Liberation of Theology,* trans. John Drury (Maryknoll, N.Y.: Orbis Books, 1976), 8, and Rosemary Radford Ruether, *To Change the World* (New York: Crossroad, 1990).

85. Stephen B. Bevans, *Models of Contextual Theology* (Maryknoll, N.Y.: Orbis Books, 1992), 63.

86. Ibid., 64, 66.

87. Ibid., 66.

88. Ibid., 67.

everyday life, in society and economic structures, in situations of oppression. God's presence is one of beckoning and inviting, calling people of faith to locate God and cooperate with God in God's work of healing, reconciling, and liberating. Thus all people are called to "theologize."[89]

This praxis model is circular in that it begins with committed action, is followed by reflection, and then returns again to action. Reflection involves an analysis of action/situation and a rereading of the Bible and tradition. The third stage is committed and intelligent action (praxis). This circle becomes a spiral as it continues in the same process. Praxis thinking insists that real theory emerges out of action and evokes more responsible, real activity.[90] This model regards theology not as a generally applicable, finished product that is valid at all times and in all places, but as an understanding of God's presence in very particular situations. For Korean North American women, this model offers them much hope as a corrective to a theology that is too general and impractical, and that claims to be universally relevant.[91]

•

The theological method that I have proposed — drawing upon many sources — is constructive and offers much hope for Korean North American women who have suffered unjustly. This contextual/praxis model with particular sensitivity to multifaith considerations has potential to broaden Korean North American women's horizons and inspire them to take action to rectify the injustices that they have encountered in their own context/experience, while assisting them to renewed liberative understandings of Scripture.

---

89. Ibid., 68.
90. Ibid., 73.
91. Ibid., 71.

~ Three ~

The Korean Context

KOREAN NORTH AMERICAN WOMEN have come, of course, from Korea to North America — either they or their mothers or grand-mothers. We must therefore know in some depth the religio-cultural historical context of Korea if we are to understand them and their spiritual and cultural needs. Korean women's history is characterized by patriarchal religion, thought, and culture, deriving in large mea-sure from the Confucianist tradition that has played a major role in determining their lives: how women are to behave, who they are to obey, and what they are to do with themselves. Noting the Confucian influence upon Korean society is thus essential. Because of certain oppressive aspects of Confucian society, many women have accumu-lated *han*. They suffer deeply from *han* but do not have the necessary channels to resolve it. Korean culture and society, despite many pos-itive dimensions, are such that women find it very difficult to break out of their traditionally restricted roles.

An ancient legend speaks of Korea's origin. Korean tradition places the founding of the tribal state in the year 2333 B.C.E. by a spirit king of divine origin named Tan'gun. Many versions of his birth are told. One of them begins by stating that a lovely maiden rested beside a clear stream. She thought deeply upon the gods of the heavens and often pondered the spirits of the mountains and seas. Finally a god in the heavens saw her and fell in love with her. Disguised as a gentle breeze, the god descended from the heavens and caressed her with his breath. From this caress, a son was conceived and born. His name was Tan'gun, and he became the first ruler of Korea.[1]

During its long history, Korea developed a rich cultural and reli-gious civilization. Throughout Korea's history, three major religions,

---

1. Bong-Youn Choy, *Koreans in America* (Chicago: Nelson-Hall, 1979), 3.

Shamanism, Buddhism, and Confucianism, have had a profound influence on the social and cultural development of the country. They have shaped and formed Korea into its present form and have had an impact on the lives of Korean women, profoundly influencing the consciousness and political attitudes of society as a whole toward women. Under Shamanism and Buddhism, women were relatively free, as these two religions placed only limited restraints on women's social and moral behavior. However, when Confucianism was adopted as the official religion during the Yi dynasty (1392–1910), women became severely restrained. Confucianism's moral code for women was strict and oppressive. In this chapter, Shamanism and Buddhism are discussed only briefly; our attention focuses on Confucianism, as it is the religion that, more than any other, initiated and reinforced oppressive conditions for Korean women. Our purpose here is not to describe these religions in their entirety but to note their significance for the place of women in society.

SHAMANISM

Shamanism is Korea's oldest religion and the most basic and pervasive form of Korean religiosity or spirituality. Shamanism is a belief in an unseen world of gods, demons, and ancestral spirits that affect daily life. Since its earliest time the mass culture of Korea has been shamanistic in its basic characteristic and tone. Shamanism is a religion of the oppressed, poor, and socially marginalized, and many Koreans today continue to be practitioners of shamanism. Rituals are performed to cure the sick, to comfort lost ones, and to reconcile broken families. Shamanism features the expulsion of evil spirits, believed to be the malevolent presence of those who have died with *han*.[2] Shamans, the majority of whom are women, perform certain tasks. The possibility that women could become shamans has provided relative freedom and a certain dignity and status for women and has liberated some women from the bondage of household duties.

Female shamans have three basic functions: they are priestesses, healers, and diviners. Priestesses play the role of intermediary be-

---

2. Virginia Fabella, "A Common Methodology for Diverse Christology," in *With Passion and Compassion,* ed. Virginia Fabella and Mercy Amba Oduyoye (Maryknoll, N.Y.: Orbis Books, 1988), 111–12.

tween gods and human beings. Only the priestess has access to the spirit world through certain rites, and they are believed to communicate directly with the spirits. Shamans talk to the spirits and comfort people who live under severe life conditions. Shamans even feed and make happy the unhappy wandering spirits of the deceased who have no permanent place to settle. They preside in national ceremonies such as when prayers are offered for rain and blessings.[3] As healers, shamans are believed to drive out evil spirits and receive the favor of the good gods when a family experiences sickness. As diviners, shamans foretell the future of the nation as well as of individuals. Many women find these activities to be a way of freeing themselves from the monotonous routine of daily life.[4]

Shamanism is the only Korean religion where women have been at the center throughout its development. Women shamans were relatively freer under Shamanism than Confucianism. When Confucian society did not allow women to freely go out in public, female shamans were the privileged few who had the freedom to do so. They could actually participate in public life and display their abilities as professionals. Women shamans also became "big sisters" to many deprived women as they helped and encouraged them to live fully. People also listened to these women as they prophesied and drove evil spirits away.

BUDDHISM

Buddhism, a vast and complex religious tradition found in many forms in many Asian societies, originated in northern India and Nepal by Gotama the Buddha who lived about twenty-five hundred years ago. Since then, the practice has spread far beyond the boundaries of its original homeland to embrace most of Asia. Doctrinally, Buddhism has been essentially egalitarian from its beginnings. The same teachings were given by the Buddha to both his female and male dis-

---

3. David Kwang-sun Suh, "Liberating Spiritualities in the Korean Minjung Tradition: Shamanism and Minjung Liberation," in *Asian Christian Spirituality: Reclaiming Traditions,* ed. Virginia Fabella, Peter K. H. Lee, and David Kwang-sun Suh (Maryknoll, N.Y.: Orbis Books, 1992), 33.

4. Yung-Chung Kim, ed. and trans. *Women of Korea: A History from Ancient Times to 1945* (Seoul: Ewha Womans University Press, 1976), 14–16.

ciples, for the same spiritual path was open to all.[5] Therefore, within Buddhist teachings, no theological or philosophical excuse existed for inequality between male and female. As with Christianity, which teaches equality but does not always exercise it, Buddhism too has not always been egalitarian in practice. At times throughout Buddhist history, women have been treated as second-class citizens. In comparison with the Confucian society, however, women living within the prominently Buddhist society were much freer and less oppressed.

Women practitioners of Buddhism actively participated in various Buddhist events held for the people's general welfare, for national security and peace, and to honor those who died during war. Buddhism penetrated deeply into the everyday life of the people, and women believers had several ways of serving Buddha. One way was to shave their heads and become nuns. Some women took this path when they were still young, while others did so after they were widowed. Another way to follow Buddha was to offer manual labor. Many women believers contributed to the building of temples through their labor as well as by offering donations.[6] Partially through women's hard work and dedication, many beautiful Buddhist temples were built all over Korea. Women thus became active workers and contributors to the rise of Buddhism within Korea.

The influence of Buddhism allowed Korean women relative political and social freedom and status between the Silla (fourth century C.E.–918) and the Koryo dynasties (918–1392), which preceded the Yi dynasty. In the Silla period, three women rulers occupied the throne, and queen-mothers often acted as regents for young kings, exerting enormous political influence and power. During this era the female right to head the family was acknowledged. During the Koryo period, when Buddhism was predominant, women interacted with men outside the house with relative freedom and without social constraints. Koryo poetry and songs written by women vividly portray their freer and flexible images, which seem to be absent during the Confucian Yi dynasty.[7]

---

5. Nancy Schuster Barnes, "Buddhism," in *Women in World Religions,* ed. Arvind Sharma (Albany: State University of New York, 1987), 105.

6. Kim, *Women of Korea: A History from Ancient Times to 1945,* 14–16.

7. Elizabeth Choi, "The Status of the Family and Motherhood for Korean Women," in *Women of Japan and Korea: Continuity and Change,* ed. Joyce Gelb and Marian Lief Palley (Philadelphia: Temple University Press, 1994), 191.

In both Buddhism and Shamanism, women could become active participants and leaders, but they were still under the dominance of men. In times of trouble or unrest in the country, however, women became easy targets of victimization during both these religious periods. In Shamanism, for example, some female shamans became victims of angry kings who were infuriated by their ominous predictions about affairs of state. From the later part of the Buddhist Koryo dynasty on, shamans slowly began to lose their power and came under tight government control because of public disapproval of their conduct.[8]

In Buddhism, women also became victims when economic power and privilege enjoyed by the Buddhist temples involved them in secular activities. As the temples grew wealthier, many monks neglected their original duties and became corrupt. In obedience to the monks' preaching, many women adherents gave offerings and alms. By manipulating women's piety, monasteries were easily able to collect money from women believers. Rather than controlling or restricting the monks' behavior, King Hyonjong (r. 1009–31) prohibited women of all social classes from donating money to temples and shrines, and even from becoming nuns. This prohibition eventually caused a strong reaction against women's participation in the religion.[9] These incidents were scattered and few, however, and compared to Confucian society, Korean women living under Buddhist or Shamanistic societies were relatively free. For example, before the sixteenth century, men and women bathing together naked in the same pool was quite common. "Couples could also marry after meeting at a festival and falling in love. Women were free to walk in public. In accordance with *Chu-tzu Ka Re*[10] even though funerals or celebrations were led by the first born son of the family, daughters or sons-in-law conducted the ceremonies."[11] After the assimilation of Confucianism into daily life, all of these customs changed dramatically. Women began to experience deplorable oppression and hardships.

8. Kim, *Women of Korea: A History from Ancient Times to 1945*, 15.
9. Ibid., 22.
10. This is a book written to give examples and explanations of ritual ceremonies for marriage, funerals, and other ancient ceremonies which should be remembered and celebrated. Elli Kim, "Confucianism and Women in Korea," in *Faith Renewed II: A Report on the Second Asian Women's Consultation on Interfaith Dialogue* (Seoul: Asian Women's Resource Centre for Culture and Theology, 1991), 151.
11. Ibid., 146.

CONFUCIANISM

As with Shamanism and Buddhism, our purpose here is not to under-
take a complete study of Confucian practices, but to look briefly at
Confucianism in order to seek its significance for the lives of Korean
women, including Korean North American women. Confucius (551–
479 B.C.E.) offered moral or ethical answers to questions regarding
life's meaning and order in society.[12] His answers would dominate
Chinese philosophical thinking for about two millennia and also profoundly impact Korean society. "Confucius" is the Latin rendering by
seventeenth-century Jesuit missionaries of "K'ung Fu-tzu," or Master K'ung whose name was K'ung Ch'ui. K'ung did not have a very
high profile during his lifetime. The highest public office K'ung ever
occupied was at the age of fifty as a kind of police commissioner in
his home state, and that was only for about a year. In over ten years
of travel, K'ung visited many feudal states, seeking, but never finding
a ruler who would use his advice. In old age, he devoted more time
to teaching disciples, while also occupying himself with music and
poetry, occasionally conversing with rulers or ministers. K'ung became historically influential only after his death, which was at about
the age of seventy, from natural causes. K'ung did not develop any
systematic doctrinal structure in which manners, morals, law, philosophy, or theology were clearly distinguished. The teachings were
systematized only with Mencius (c. 371–289 B.C.E.) and Hsun-tzu
(c. 298–238 B.C.E.).[13]

Confucianism has perhaps a stronger cultural hold in Korea than
in any other nation in the world, and any discussion of Korean society and women would be incomplete without some understanding of
Confucian history and moral code.[14] Confucianism made its way into
Korea during the Yi dynasty, the last Korean kingdom (1392–1910)
established through a military *coup d'état* led by General Yi Song-Ge,
later known as King T'aejo. He instituted Confucianism in place of
Buddhism as the creed of the new government. Historians generally
consider that he made this change largely for political reasons, for
during the Koryo period Buddhist priests controlled a great portion

12. Julia Ching, *Chinese Religions* (Maryknoll, N.Y.: Orbis Books, 1993), 53.
13. Ibid., 54.
14. Joyce Gelb and Marian Lief Palley, eds., *Women of Japan and Korea: Continuity and Change* (Philadelphia: Temple University Press, 1994), 3.

of the land and thus the national economy. Buddhist priests were essentially the rulers in many local areas, and when Yi seized power he needed to shift power from the Buddhist priests to groups that supported him and sought to be the new ruling class, a new Confucian aristocracy.[15]

Confucianism had a special appeal to Yi dynasty rulers, then, because it supported their own hold on power and easily kept people below them in good order. Therefore, to eliminate Buddhism, rulers and scholars attacked it not only as an institution harmful to the national economy, but also as a conglomeration of superstitious doctrines harmful to society. They confiscated extensive temple land and gave it to the Confucian aristocrats. King T'aejong (r. 1400–18 C.E.) destroyed all but 250 temples, and when Sejong (r. 1418–50 C.E.) came to power, only 36 temples were allowed to function.[16] Slowly the Buddhist religion of the previous dynasty thus began to fade, and the new religion and philosophy of Confucianism was instituted throughout the country.

Since the Yi dynasty, Confucianism has deeply affected the development of Korean people's consciousness and lifestyles,[17] playing a vital role in stimulating the cultural development of the country. The Yi dynasty rulers wanted to enlighten the people through Confucian ethics in order to maintain a well-regulated state.[18] Confucianism as a state creed discouraged "progress" but preserved the existing established order and assured power and position for the literate and educated.[19] By preserving the status quo, Confucianism — an ethical and moral system designed to govern all social relations in the family, community, and nation — thus served the advantage of the rulers by stressing a rigid vertical order of human relationships based on age, sex, and inherited social status.[20] Like many other religious and moral

15. Choy, *Koreans in America*, 18.

16. Kim, *Women of Korea: A History from Ancient Times to 1945*, 80.

17. Ai Ra Kim, *Women's Struggle for a New Life* (Albany: State University of New York Press, 1996), 5.

18. Cho Kyung Won, "Overcoming Confucian Barriers: Changing Educational Opportunities for Women in Korea," in *Women of Japan and Korea: Continuity and Change*, ed. Joyce Gelb and Marian Lief Palley (Philadelphia: Temple University Press, 1994), 209.

19. Choy, *Koreans in America*, 18.

20. Inn Sook Lee, "Korean American Women and Ethnic Identity," in *Korean American Ministry: A Resource Book*, ed. Sang Hyun Lee and John V. Moore (Louisville, Ky.: General Assembly Council–U.S.A. Presbyterian Church, 1993), 194.

systems, Confucian thought exalted men and subordinated women, and thus Confucian infiltration in Korea had negative consequences on women.

Confucian Thought and Moral Code

Confucian culture today in Korea is very different from when it was prominent during the Yi dynasty. The Confucianism discussed in this section is a description of past Confucianism, yet many of its beliefs and practices undergird Korean reality today.

Confucianism practices a sacrificial cult of veneration for Heaven and for ancestors, and allows for sacrifices of incense and foods even to semi-deified historical personages, including Confucius himself. Confucianism does not have monastic orders and has no organized priesthood outside of the recognition of the emperor himself as a high priest. The emperor is the only person qualified to sacrifice to Heaven, but the heads of families can act as mediators between the ancestral spirits and the living. In fact, Confucian emphasis on family life and progeny was in principle opposed to clerical or monastic celibacy, while Confucius's teachings on social responsibility abhorred any self-imposed isolation from society, unless it was motivated by social protest.[21]

Ancestor worship, the major ritual of Confucianism, portrays the male as both dominant and supreme. This precept reunites the ancestors with living family members through the male and thereby strengthens the identity of the family's lineage. The oldest man in the family, the first son, is the ritual priest, and all men participate in the ceremony. The rituals and ceremony of ancestor worship exclude women, reinforcing their marginality. Women function as men's assistants, as they manage only the necessary preparations, such as cooking the food and setting up the ritual table. This ritual illustrates concretely the sexual inequality between men and women.

Confucianism sees human society in terms of personal relationships and ethical responsibility resulting from such relationships. The five relationships are ruler-subject, father-son, husband-wife, elder-younger brother, and friend-friend. Three of these are family

---

21. Julia Ching, *Confucianism and Christianity: A Comparative Study* (Tokyo: Kodansha International, 1977), 9.

relationships, while the other two are usually conceived in terms of the family model. For example, the ruler-subject resembles father-son, while friendship resembles brotherliness. Confucian society regards itself as a large family, and the responsibilities ensuing from these relationships are mutual and reciprocal. The system of five relations emphasizes a basic sense of hierarchy, and the only truly horizontal relationship is that between friends.[22]

In this hierarchical social order human relationships tend to become fixed and rigid, with the superior partners — fathers, husbands, rulers — exercising more right and privilege and the inferior partners performing more duties and submission. The patriarchal family system was consolidated with the assistance of Confucian ideology, and women were increasingly relegated to a subordinate role.[23]

The adoption of the Confucian moral code during the Yi dynasty led to the deteriorating status of women. The freedom and relative equality experienced by women during the Koryo period was abolished with the institution of Confucianism. Confucius had little to say about women, but what he did say was decisive and far-reaching in its effect.

> He based his whole teaching about human society upon the patriarchal family, ancestor worship, and the duty of filial piety. The function of woman within this system was simple and clear. It could be summed up in one four-letter word — "obey." Woman is a creature born to obedience.[24]

A woman was to obey her father while at home, her husband when married, and her son if widowed.[25] From Confucian cosmology came the notion that the female *yin* force, essential for harmony, ought to be passive and docile, following the lead of the more important male *yang* force.[26]

Confucianism limited female education to the formation of feminine virtues and domestic skills. Women were taught home manage-

22. Ibid., 96, 97.
23. Ching, *Chinese Religions,* 167.
24. David Mace and Vera Mace, *Marriage: East and West* (Garden City, N.Y.: Doubleday, 1959), 67.
25. Ching, *Chinese Religions,* 167.
26. Denise Lardner Carmody, *Women and World Religions* (Englewood Cliffs, N.J.: Prentice-Hall, 1979), 96.

ment, self-discipline, courtesy or propriety to their husband's family, and how to rear and educate children.[27] Women were limited to the home, and Confucian thought clearly dictated what a woman could or could not do. The religious and social freedoms once experienced by women under Shamanism and Buddhism were totally confiscated under Confucianism.

Marriage

Under the Yi system, marriage was so important that room barely existed for an unmarried woman. Even up to 1930, society offered virtually no alternative except that of becoming a Buddhist nun for unmarried women or women who disliked domestic life.[28] Therefore, every effort was made to marry off daughters, as it was crucial for a woman to marry lest she be labeled as a social outcast and misfit. One woman recounts the story of her parents' efforts to have her crippled sister married off. Her parents knew that her sister needed to get married, and her father concluded, "She must marry and have a son who will look after her in her old age. I cannot allow her to grow old like a ghost in her brother's home when we are no longer around to care for her."[29] In his effort to have his daughter married, the father offered a handsome reward to any matchmaker who could locate a kind family with a son of marrying age. But no family accepted. Then the father lowered his standards and asked for any type of man, even poor or without parents. He included a handsome dowry, but no one responded. With no luck, but desperate to marry off his crippled daughter, he asked his own servant to marry her. The father proposed to the servant, "I will give you land, a house on that land, and food to fill the house. You will never have to work as a servant in another man's home ever again if you agree to marry my second daughter."[30] The servant agreed to the marriage, and the parents were relieved

---

27. Cho Kyung Won, "Overcoming Confucian Barriers: Changing Educational Opportunities for Women in Korea," 207, 210.

28. Hesung Chun Koh, "Women's Roles and Achievements in the Yi Dynasty," in *Korean Women in Transition: At Home and Abroad,* ed. Eui-Young Yu and Earl H. Phillips (Los Angeles: Center for Korean-American and Korean Studies, California State University, 1987), 32.

29. Helie Lee, *Still Life with Rice* (New York: Scribner, 1996), 92.

30. Ibid., 94.

of their tremendous burden and anxiety that their crippled daughter would become a social outcast.

As in many other traditional societies, marriage was a union of two family lines even more than the union of two individual people. Young people did not choose their marriage partner; only parents could arrange a marriage. Any romance between a boy and a girl was regarded as disgraceful and sinful and was supposed to be unfilial to parents.[31] In some cases, matchmakers were paid by parents to find the right marriage partners for their children. In certain cases, marriage became more like a business transaction than a union between two lovers. Women became human pawns for their fathers to move around and for fathers-in-law to accept or reject. There was also the practice of the husband's family paying a price for the bride, which further lowered a woman's status, as it presented her as merchandise to be bought and sold. If a family was too poor to raise their daughter, the preference was to let her be brought up by her future husband's parents. Thus at a young age (seven or eight), the future bride was sent to the groom's family. In this situation the bride became an additional worker in the house, expected to help with all the housework and the care of younger siblings. Most often the poor girl's family would rather do this than sell her into slavery or prostitution.[32]

At marriage a bride passed out of her natal family and joined the family of her husband. The reception of the bride into her husband's home stressed that she had replaced his mother as the prime childbearing female. A ceremony three months after the wedding established the bride's place in the ancestral line of her new household. Her first obligation was to honor her husband's parents and ancestors by raising up children to continue the line.[33] Therefore, marriage for a woman meant becoming the housewife of another family, performing ancestral sacrifice, giving birth to a son, and serving her husband's parents.[34]

31. Soon Man Rhim, "The Status of Women in Traditional Korean Society," in *Korean Women in a Struggle for Humanization,* ed. Harold Hakwon Sunoo and Dong Soo Kim (Memphis: Association of Korean Christian Scholars in North America, 1978), 12.

32. Soon Man Rhim, *Women of Asia: Yesterday and Today* (New York: Friendship Press, 1983), 86.

33. Carmody, *Women and World Religions,* 97.

34. Sung-Hee Lee, "Women's Liberation Theology as the Foundation for Asian Theology," *East Asia Journal of Theology* 4 (1986): 5.

The obligation of providing a male heir became women's sacred duty, to assure the continuation of the ancestral cult. The more sons a woman produced, the more security the family had in transmitting its name through several generations. Men are the source of status and authority, and givers of social recognition to women.[35] The necessity of having sons also offered an excuse to the husband to take on a second wife, in cases where the principal wife was childless or had only daughters. The practice of concubinage often eventually reduced women to sex objects for men to manipulate and enjoy. Furthermore, this practice was a constant threat to the first wife as it brought insecurity and jealousy into the relationship.[36] The more Confucian Korean society became, the more subordinate and oppressed women became.

In Confucian society, a woman was subject to seven evils that justified the expulsion of a wife from the household: disobedience to parents-in-law, failure to bear a son, adultery, jealousy, hereditary disease, garrulousness, and larceny.[37] Although not always strictly enforced, any violation of these seven evils could become sufficient condition for the husband to divorce his wife. Even though a husband could easily divorce his wife for reasons that benefited him, a woman had no grounds whatever for divorce. She was expected to endure any hardship, injustice, or unhappiness for the sake of the family and children. Thus an ideal wife was passive, quiet, and chaste; she was expected to be an obedient daughter-in-law, devoted wife, and dedicated mother.[38]

Further, to be a true Confucian woman during the Yi dynasty, a widow must never remarry, for she continued to be obligated to the ancestors of the family into which she had married. She was to remain loyal to one man and family even though widowers were always encouraged to remarry, as they often did.[39] A woman could even be a widow from birth if her parents had arranged her marriage before she was born. As a child widow she had to dress in white mourning clothes and when she approached marriageable age at around

---

35. Nantawan Boonprasat Lewis, "An Overview of the Role of Women in Asia — A Perspective and Challenge to Higher Education," *East Asia Journal of Theology* 3 (1985): 141.

36. Ching, *Chinese Religions,* 167.

37. Kim, *Women of Korea: A History from Ancient Times to 1945,* 86.

38. Choi, "The Status of the Family and Motherhood for Korean Women," 191.

39. Carmody, *Women and World Religions,* 96.

thirteen, she was expected to go and live in her dead groom's home and serve his parents for life.[40] This example dramatizes the inequality and oppression that existed between men and women during the Confucian era.

Women's place was not in public like men, but was confined to the home. According to "Naeoebop," a set of rigid rules concerning the distinctions of the roles of husband and wife, upper-class women spent most of their lives at home, shut off from the world, thus demonstrating the clear division between men's and women's places in society. Women were prohibited from enjoying outdoor games. If women wanted to participate in any social activities, they needed permission from either their husband or from the head of their family, who was a male. Hence, one of the terms for "wife" was *anae* (inside person), which means that she was expected to remain within the confines of the family compound. Such restrictions on women's social activities in the Yi dynasty were thought to be an unavoidable and necessary precondition for establishing a new family order based on Confucian values. The rulers of the new dynasty were convinced that the disorder in the Koryo dynasty was due in part to women's frequent social activities. Once again women were blamed and victimized for whatever problems or shortfalls that occurred within society. Under such strict prohibitions, women were allowed in the streets only at night, after the men were restricted to their homes by a 9 P.M. till 2 A.M. curfew. And when outside, women could not roam freely but had to veil their faces.[41]

This social dichotomy between men and women was also carried into the home, as men and women were further segregated within the domestic scene. Houses were divided into male and female sections, and men entering into the women's section and vice versa unless the master of the house gave his permission was considered improper.[42] Women were confined to the women's quarters, which were usually the kitchen and their own sleeping quarters. Even girls, after the age of seven, could no longer associate with boys or men. They were more and more confined to the inner quarters of the house, where

---

40. Lee, "Korean American Women and Ethnic Identity," 195.
41. Kim, *Women of Korea: A History from Ancient Times to 1945,* 84, 86.
42. Cho, "Overcoming Confucian Barriers: Changing Educational Opportunities for Women in Korea," 209.

they received instruction in domestic duties from their mothers and grandmothers.[43] Not only were women deprived of free movement in public, but they were restricted even within their own home.

Lack of Identity and Rights

During the Yi dynasty, the formal structure of society did not officially recognize women's existence. They were treated as lifelong minors subject to a man's direction. A woman could neither obtain prestige and power, nor inherit her father's property.[44] Furthermore, women were deprived of the simple but important possession of names, by which they could be called, identified, or recorded. Even commoner males were granted the privilege of a name, but this simple privilege was not granted to women. Even a high government official's wife could not enjoy her own name.[45]

Without a name, women were only identified by their positions relative to men and thus lost their own sense of identity as individual persons. If women did not marry, they were at a further disadvantage as to gaining a socially acceptable identity. Without a name, women were called "so-and so's daughter" or "so-and so's mother." When they were married only the name of their original family was entered into the husband's family registry. Even in the registry of their own families, only the name of the son-in-law, her husband, was recorded. Women's names were never entered. Furthermore, women could not carry on the family line, nor perform the worship ceremonies for their own ancestors. For social and legal purposes, married women left their own homes permanently. Therefore, if their husband threw them out of the house for any reason, they were without a place to go and without a person with whom to be identified.[46] These Yi dynasty women thus became persons without a name but only a face.[47] That they had no name deepened the already ignominious status of women in Korea.

---

43. Marina Deuchler, *The Confucian Transformation of Korea: A Study of Society and Ideology* (Cambridge: Council on East Asian Studies, Harvard University, 1992), 258.

44. Haejong Cho, "Republic of Korea: Those Left Behind," in *Women in the Villages, Men in the Towns* (Paris: UNESCO, 1984), 191.

45. Rhim, "The Status of Women in Traditional Korean Society," 21.

46. Kim, *Women of Korea: A History from Ancient Times to 1945*, 85, 86.

47. Lee, "Women's Liberation Theology as the Foundation for Asian Theology," 2.

Furthermore, women were not given human rights. Confucian beliefs fix in their minds the ideal Confucian woman, who is passive, obedient, chaste, and subordinate to men. Within the home, men retained all the significant rights and privileges, and the institutional suppression of women actually extended to the family. To attain virtue in Yi society, women had to lead lives of complete self-sacrifice,[48] neglecting their own wishes and desires for the sake of the family. These women did not live for themselves but for men, children, and the family, and thus could not separate their own identity from those of their husband and children. Their social selves became their subjective selves. Thus they were nameless; their existence was totally immersed in their men, and their own selves were negated.[49]

In sum, some major Confucian dictums dehumanized women during Korea's Yi Dynasty: women should be trained to serve others; parents should arrange their daughters' marriages; a wife belonged to her husband's family after marriage and visits to her parents were almost nil; a woman was known by her husband's or son's name; a woman could not carry on a family line; daughters could not legally inherit property from their parents.[50] Hence, women were at a great disadvantage in relation to men. They were, in a sense, nonpersons.

Han

We have seen that the influence of Confucianism in Korean society resulted in severe measures of oppression against women. Korean women often suffered unjustly at the hands of cruel men, and the oppressive social system continuously negated women as persons. Koreans have articulated *han* as a mode of responding to the tragic situation of the oppressed. In terms of its etymology, *han* is a psychological term that denotes repressed feelings of suffering, through the oppression of others or through natural calamities or illness. Sometimes translated as "just indignation," *han* is deep spiritual pain that rises out of the unjust experience of the people. *Han* appears in-

---

48. Cho, "Overcoming Confucian Barriers: Changing Educational Opportunities for Women in Korea," 207, 210.

49. Kim, *Women's Struggle for a New Life*, 16, 25.

50. Lee, "Korean American Women and Ethnic Identity," 194.

evitably in the biography of Korean women and in their stories.[51] Through their suffering and turmoil, Korean women experienced and accumulated much *han* throughout their lives. *Han* is not only an experience of women; it is a typical prevailing feeling of the Korean people, for the nation as a whole has endured many defeats and disasters. Korean people embody this *han* as they experience oppression and suffering in their daily lives. *Han* is "the suppressed, amassed and condensed experience of oppression caused by mischief or misfortune, so that it forms a kind of 'lump' in one's spirit."[52] It is "an underlying feeling of Korean people. It is a dominant feeling of defeat, resignation, and nothingness. But on the other hand, it is a feeling with a tenacity of will for life which comes to weaker beings."[53] *Han* comes especially to women, who are the most disadvantaged.

Of course, this reality is experienced to some degree by oppressed and marginalized people everywhere. Koreans as a people, however, have been among the most downtrodden in the world. The feeling of *han* comes from the sinful interconnections of classism, racism, sexism, colonialism, neocolonialism, and cultural imperialism that Korean people put up with every day and have endured for many centuries.[54] In recent history, Koreans have suffered under brutal Japanese occupation from 1909 to 1945. They were under the domination of superpowers, the Soviet Union and the United States, who both wanted control over Korea during the Korean War in the 1950s. Within Korea even today, much discrimination exists among the classes of the rich and the poor who are separated by a very wide gap. Korea, through its experience of invasion and colonialism, has become a land of spirits full of *han*. *Han* is brokenheartedness but also the raw energy for the struggle for liberation. In Korean tradition, people who were killed or who have died unjustly became wandering spirits, *han*-ridden spirits that are everywhere seeking the chance to make the wrong right. The living people's responsibility is therefore

---

51. Kwang-Sun David Suh, "A Biographical Sketch of an Asian Theology Consultation," in *Minjung Theology: People as the Subjects of History*, ed. the Commission on Theological Concerns of the Christian Conference of Asia (CTC-CCA) (Maryknoll, N.Y.: Orbis Books, 1983), 24, 25.

52. Chung, "Han-pu-ri: Doing Theology from Korean Women's Perspective," 30.

53. Suh Nam-Dong, "Towards a Theology of Han," in *Minjung Theology: People as the Subjects of History*, ed. the Commission Theological Concerns of the Christian Conference of Asia (CTC-CCA) (Maryknoll, N.Y.: Orbis Books, 1983), 58

54. Chung, "Han-pu-ri: Doing Theology from Korean Women's Perspective," 30.

to listen to the voices of the *han*-ridden spirits and to participate in the spirits' work for making right whatever is wrong.[55]

In Korea, the suffering people are called *minjung,* which is an untranslatable word even in Korean. When broken down, the word *min* can be translated as "people" and *jung* as "the mass." The term *minjung* came to be used first during the Yi Dynasty when the common people were oppressed by the ruling class. Since then, *minjung* denotes all the common people who have come to be regarded as the subjects of Korean history.[56]

Specifically, *minjung* are "the oppressed, exploited, dominated, discriminated against, alienated and suppressed politically, economically, socially, culturally and intellectually, like women, ethnic groups, the poor, workers and farmers, including intellectuals themselves."[57] They are the *han*-ridden people. They live with *han,* accumulate *han,* and die with *han.*[58] *Han* is thus a key concept for Korea's distinctive *minjung* theology. "*Han* is the experience of the minjung and minjung theology is the theology of *han.* By releasing the power of *han,* the minjung find liberation."[59]

Minjung theologians try to articulate theology out of the concrete historical experience of the Korean *minjung. Minjung* theology is the theological articulation on the political experience of Christian students, laborers, professors, farmers, writers, and intellectuals. "It is a theology of the oppressed in the Korean political situation, a theological response to the oppressors, and it is the response of the oppressed to the Korean church and its mission."[60] *Minjung* comes from the experience of Korean Christians who are suffering in the political and social struggles for justice and full humanity.[61] *Minjung* theology grew out of *minjung* experience, such as torture in prisons, dehumanization in workplaces, and underground movements of resistance.[62]

55. Marianne Katoppo, "The Concept of God and the Spirit from the Feminist Perspective," in *Feminist Theology from the Third World: A Reader,* ed. Ursula King (Maryknoll, N.Y.: Orbis Books, 1994), 390.

56. Jung Young Lee, ed., *An Emerging Theology in World Perspectives* (Mystic, Conn.: Twenty-Third Publications, 1988), 4.

57. Chung, "Han-pu-ri: Doing Theology from Korean Women's Perspective," 30.

58. Suh, "Liberating Spiritualities in the Korean Minjung Tradition: Shamanism and Minjung Liberation," 33.

59. Lee, *An Emerging Theology in World Perspectives,* 9.

60. Suh, "A Biographical Sketch of an Asian Theological Consultation," 16.

61. Ibid., 17.

62. Lee, *An Emerging Theology in World Perspective,* 8.

Minjung are present wherever sociocultural alienation, economic exploitation, and political suppression exist. Women are therefore *minjung* when they are dominated by men, by their family, or by sociocultural structures.[63] Historically in Korea, women may be said to suffer the worst *han,* because of Confucianism's strict imposition of laws and customs discriminating against them.[64] Women are the *minjung* of the *minjung* and are deeply burdened with *han.*

Women have not had the public channels that men have had to express their *han,* which has led to a sense of helplessness in their lives. They have been enclosed within the home to take care of the family and household. Women have been discouraged from taking on leadership positions and play only a minimal role in society.[65] Some changes, however, have occurred in recent years, so that Confucian rules and practices are no longer strictly in place either in Korea or in North America. Today women have names, hold jobs in the workplace, and receive education together with men. The Confucian religio-cultural diminishment of women is still a powerful factor, however, and is especially strong in the consciousness of middle-aged and older Korean people. Some women are now professionals, but women are still greatly underrepresented in all the spheres of social and cultural power.

Suffering has become the beginning point for Korean women's reflection on their search for full humanity. In their brokenness and struggle, many Korean women have met and come to know God. "To know God for them, means to understand the ultimate purpose of their lives and to discover the meaning of existence in this history and cosmos.... [Their] understanding of humanity is directly related to their understanding of who God is and what God does in the midst of their suffering and their struggle for liberation."[66] Korean women are victims of oppression, but in spite of this, and perhaps even through this, they can become agents of liberation. Korean women cannot define humanity apart from their own suffering.[67] Therefore, a step

---

63. Suh, "A Biographical Sketch of an Asian Theological Consultation," 35.
64. Suh, "Towards a Theology of Han," 58.
65. Chung Hyun Kyung, *Struggle to Be the Sun Again* (Maryknoll, N.Y.: Orbis Books, 1990), 39.
66. Ibid., 39.
67. Ibid., 39.

toward Korean women's liberation is to become acutely aware of their *han* and to find ways to release it.

Han-Pu-Ri

Two modes of dealing with *han* are available to Korean women: accept it or reject it. The acceptance of *han* can be defined as resignation and is called *jung han*. Here women try to be at peace with their situation and to live out a dutiful life for the reward of a better fate in the next life. Some Christian missionaries perpetuated this *jung han* in Korean Christian women's lives as they encouraged Korean women to be passive and to accept their own victimization. Women were encouraged to suffer internally, just as Jesus suffered on the cross, because it was God's will. This mode does not change anything, as it amounts to mere submission or resignation to fate. The second way to deal with *han* is to refuse it, which is known as *won-han*. Women need to use their *han* to be empowered by it to overturn and overcome the oppressed state in which they find themselves.[68] Women need to be angry about their situation and seek meaningful social change. Of these two modes of dealing with *han, won-han* is the route that Korean women need to take if they are to rectify their situation. They can no longer remain in the passive mode and accept things as they are, but must fight back to change the injustices in society. But where will they find the strength and courage for such resistance?

A major goal of doing theology for Korean women is to release this *han* in the sense of *won-han*. The process that untangles and resolves accumulated *han* is called *han-pu-ri*. The term originally came from the Korean shamanistic tradition as the shamans played the role of the priest/ess of *han-pu-ri* in his or her community. The shamanistic *kut* (ritual) gave the opportunity for the voiceless ghosts to speak their stories of *han*. The community then must resolve the *han* of the ghost collectively, either by eliminating the source of oppression for the ghosts, or by comforting or negotiating with them. In this way *han-pu-ri* has been an opportunity for collective repentance, group therapy, and collective healing for the ghosts and their communities in Korean society.[69]

---

68. Ibid., 39.
69. Chung, "Han-pu-ri: Doing Theology from Korean Women's Perspective," 34.

Shamanism still continues to be an attractive, effective, and positive way for a large segment of Korean women to resolve their *han*. With no hierarchy, no church, and no building, Shamanism is the one truly indigenous religion of Korea — a way of controlling the animistic spirits and forces that are believed to hold sway in one's life, fate, and *han*.[70] However, for Korean Christian women, is Shamanism the answer to their pain and suffering? Unlikely, especially in North America. Does Christianity hold any good news that can help Korean women find inner healing? Christian women need to reexamine Christianity and discover whether Christ is able to resolve their *han*.

Korea's major religions have had a profound impact in the lives of women. As we have seen, Shamanism and Buddhism did not restrict or limit women's roles as much as Confucianism did, but the Confucian influence is still operative today even among Korean North American women. In many ways, Shamanism is an inadequate tool for the resolution of *han* if it does not empower women to resist. Thus we need a liberative understanding of Korean religions, which can be combined with Christianity, to strengthen women's resistance. This requires, I shall argue, a fresh approach to Christology, but first we turn to the immigration context of Korean North American women.

---

70. Hwain Chang Lee, *Confucius, Christ and Co-Partnership* (Lanham, Md.: University Press of America, 1994), 22.

~ Four ~

The Immigration Context

WHEN KOREAN WOMEN immigrated to North America, the Confucian culture did not leave them. Rather, it accompanied them to their new land, and its influence is evident in church, family, and home. From the beginning of the immigration of "picture brides" to recent immigrants, Korean North American women have suffered much *han*. To be truly liberative for these women, Christian faith and theology must address their particular circumstances. This chapter examines the effect that the immigrant churches have had on these women's roles in family and society. The limitations and restrictions that they have experienced in the home evidently have also been endured in the church. The burden of *han* that they carried in Korea has remained with them in their new land.

A BRIEF HISTORY OF IMMIGRATION

For Koreans, emigration has been a foreign concept and has not been accepted well because leaving Korea meant cutting off one's roots and blood ties. The act of leaving Korea became a kind of social or spiritual death. Because it meant breaking ties to their ancestral past, most people were not attracted to the idea of moving far away to another land. However, when the missionaries came to Korea, they encouraged emigration among the newly converted. Missionaries like the Rev. George Heber Jones offered an image of the United States as "the land in which milk and honey overflowed," and thus for these new Korean Christians, emigration offered promise and hope for a new life. From the beginning, emigration and Christianity had a close relationship, and Christianity became the main religion of emigrants from Korea. Immigration of Koreans into the United States began in 1903, and nearly half of the first 101 immigrants on the first ship to the United States (55 men, 21 women, and 25 children) were from the Rev. Jones's Yongdong church in Inchon. The history of the first Korean Methodist church in North America offers a clear indication of this missionary's impact on Korean emigration.[1]

The major motives for Koreans to emigrate to America in the early twentieth century were economic and political. Korea had recently experienced several famines, and for this reason some people were eager to move to a better land. Furthermore, the sugar plantations in the Hawaiian islands were experiencing massive, well-organized protests by overworked Chinese and Japanese male workers, and another source of cheap labor was therefore needed.[2] Many single Korean men seized the opportunity to leave their poverty-stricken country and sailed to America with high hopes of earning money.

Korean immigration to the United States occurred in three major waves. Korean political exiles had moved to the United States as early as 1885, but the first significant wave of immigration was to Hawaii (1903–5). The first wave can be described as immigrants who were concerned with the Korean political situation or interested in Christianity and the Christian churches. This era saw the importation of many brides into North America, the birth of a second generation in the immigrant community, ethnic dormancy, rapid acculturation, and rising rates of intermarriage due to the lack of young Korean women. The second wave was after the Korean War (1950–53) and involved a more heterogeneous group, consisting of wives of American servicemen, war orphans, and students. Little data exists about them because they did not form their own groups but integrated themselves quickly into the dominant culture due to their immediate connection with American families. This group is not treated at length in this chapter.

The current wave, still in progress, began as a result of immigration reform through the 1965 Immigration Act[3] in the United States. These immigrants are contending with a multitude of issues, including cultural and linguistic differences, parent-child stress, and changes in roles, especially among women. They are also dealing with concerns

1. Ai Ra Kim, *Women's Struggle for a New Life* (Albany: State University of New York Press, 1996), 28.
2. Jung Ha Kim, *Bridge-Makers and Cross-Bearers: Korean-American Women and the Church* (Atlanta: Scholars Press, 1997), 3.
3. Harry H. L. Kitano and Roger Daniels, *Asian Americans: Emerging Minorities,* 2d ed. (Englewood Cliffs, N.J.: Prentice-Hall, 1988), 113.

such as cultural conflict in norms and values, achieving a healthy identification in a predominantly white society, and varied levels of acceptance of Korean immigrants by both the majority and other minority groups already living here.[4]

Canada has a much shorter immigration history, beginning in the early 1960s. Only an estimated 250 immigrants appear before 1965. The first Korean who entered Canada was a theological student who studied at Pine Hill Divinity Hall in the class of 1915. The first settler is identified as a trained medical doctor who came to the University of Toronto in 1949 on a refresher course and remained.[5] With a revision in the Canadian Immigration Law in 1965, the number of Korean immigrants began to increase, surpassing 1,000 for the first time in 1971.

This chapter examines the Korean North American women's context by specifically examining the hardships of picture brides, the struggles of third-wave women, the role of the immigrant church, and the identity of Korean North American women.

PICTURE BRIDES: THE FIRST WAVE

Since most male workers in the first wave immigrated to North America at a young age (seventeen to twenty-five years old), many remained bachelors for a long time because of the lack of young Korean women. These men wanted to marry and thus sent pictures back to Korea with hopes of being matched with a suitable bride. In some cases, the pictures worked and marriages were arranged. Many brides, however, arrived on U.S. shores having been deceived by their prospective husbands, as the husbands were usually ten to twenty years older than the brides: the pictures that these men sent all too often showed them when they were much younger. Since the culture viewed as a disgrace an engaged woman who returned to her home, these women married the men who deceived them.[6] These women formed the first group of

---

4. Ibid., 113, 116, 118.

5. Hee-Min Park, "The Relevant Ministry to Korean Immigrants in Metro Toronto Area," Doctor of Ministry thesis, Knox College, University of Toronto, 1982), 9, 10, 55.

6. Kim, *Women's Struggle for a New Life*, 37, 40. The phenomena of Korean picture brides did not occur in Canada.

Korean women to immigrate to America (1910–24), and they later became known as picture brides.

The main motive for the picture brides to leave Korea was to escape the oppression of Confucian society. An interview with an eighty-seven-year-old picture bride states, "Ah, marriage! Then I could go to America! That land of freedom with streets paved of gold!...Since I became ten, I've been forbidden to step outside of my gates, just like all the rest of the girls of my days...becoming a picture bride, whatever that was, would be my answer and release."[7] Many of these picture brides were assertive and decisive in character and willpower. They were brave and ambitious, as they independently chose a new life that brought them to America. They seemed to have decided their own fate, since there is no evidence that their fathers (or brothers) sold them as "picture brides." In their bravery and autonomy, they were quite different from their traditional or "ideal woman" counterparts. They sought a new life and decided to risk their oppressive past and present for an unknown but hopeful future.[8]

The reality of immigrant life was quite different from what the picture brides anticipated. Their roles did become more diverse, and their status became relatively more equal to that of men. However, they still lived for others, mainly the family, and men continued to be the focus of their lives.[9] Even though these women came to America to escape the traditional Korean family, the patriarchal structure was inevitably transported. In the new land, however, they began to carry on the burden both of household tasks and outside work. Picture brides were often overworked as they struggled in the new land to make their home a better place to live. Women were responsible for such normal household chores as cooking, cleaning, sewing, and raising children. Immigration, however, also forced most women to come out of their homes in order to supplement their husbands' income. Most women worked in the sugarcane plantations alongside their men (sixty-five cents a day for men and fifty-five cents for women) for an average of ten hours a day, six days a week. Sometimes they worked with babies strapped to their backs and returned home to prepare supper.

---

7. Ibid., 30, 31.
8. Ibid., 31.
9. Ibid., 41.

For years on end, many of these women survived with no more than four hours of sleep a night.[10]

On the plantations of Hawaii and on the farms of the western United States, Korean women cooked, washed, and cleaned for their families, and, for a fee, performed these chores for bachelors or married men who had come without their wives. In doing so, these women assumed even more work, such as washing and pressing the men's laundry and growing vegetables. Women who did laundry for a fee had to lug water from the well or the outdoor faucet, scrub the clothes on washboards, hang them out on lines to dry, and iron them with irons heated on stoves. The work was demanding, but the income was better than laboring in the fields. In many families, such supplemental earnings made the difference between starvation and survival. Women who fed unattached men had to wake up at 3 or 4 A.M. to cook breakfast for as many as forty persons and to pack an equal number of lunchboxes in primitive kitchens.[11] Many of the couples operating such boarding houses managed to save money that they later used to set up small businesses in Honolulu and other urban areas, where women contributed directly to the family income by working in the fields or operating the boarding houses.[12] The lifestyle was burdensome for these young women who left all that they had to live a more comfortable life abroad, only to discover that it was just as difficult, or more so, than their previous lifestyle in Korea.

Some of the hardships that the picture brides endured have been well recorded. One story about the Rev. Sin-Kyu Paik and his wife tells of their life with children and how they moved to Riverside to pick oranges. Living in a former chicken shack, the entire family survived on Mrs. Paik's earnings from cooking for Korean bachelors. One of the children recalled:

> Although there were about ten families, there were a lot of bachelors. About thirty of them. Since we're poor, father got the idea that mother should cook for the bachelors. You know, that gives

---

10. Mary Paik Lee, *Quiet Odyssey: A Pioneer Korean Woman in America,* ed. with an introduction by Sucheng Chan (Seattle: University of Washington Press, 1990), lvii.

11. Ibid., lvi.

12. Eun Sik Yang, "Korean Women in America: 1903–1930," in *Korean Women in Transition: At Home and Abroad,* ed. Eui-Young Yu and Earl H. Phillips (Los Angeles: Center for Korean-American and Korean Studies, California State University, 1987), 169.

us food and a little money. So my poor mother had to cook for thirty to forty bachelors. Every morning she would get up at three or four o'clock and with the makeshift stove, cook for them. I always had to get up at three o'clock in the morning and help her pack the lunches.[13]

Mrs. Paik was a comparatively small woman, yet she not only survived the ordeal but also gave birth to eight more children. These picture brides' perseverance, dedication, and their will to survive gave vitality and stability to their families and the community.[14]

Many of the hardships that the picture brides endured have been repeated in the lives of Korean women who immigrated during the third wave. This group of women constitutes the present majority, and their thoughts and experiences primarily inform the theological and christological development of this book.

WOMEN'S ROLES TODAY: THE THIRD WAVE

The majority of contemporary Korean immigrant women were married when they came to North America. They came in order to improve their life conditions, but more particularly to advance their husband's careers and to provide their children with a Western education. Their measure of a good life was centered on the success of their husbands and children, and many women supported their husbands and families while their husbands studied.[15] Immigrant life has often proved to be very harsh for these family-oriented women.

While all Korean immigrants in North America are weighed down with multiple responsibilities, the women bear the heaviest burden of all. They suffer the oppression faced by all immigrants, as well as the disadvantages experienced by most women. They work outside of the home, but instead of finding careers that offer self-actualization and identity in work, Korean North American women more often work in factories or labor-related jobs,[16] in spite of the fact that some of these women are well-qualified workers with credible degrees or

13. Sonia Shinn Sunoo ed., *Korea Kaleidoscope* (Sierra Mission Area: United Presbyterian Church, U.S.A., 1982), 97.
14. Eun Sik Yang, "Korean Women in America: 1903–1930," 171.
15. Kim, *Women's Struggle for a New Life,* 62.
16. Sook Ja Paik, "Korean-American Women's Underemployment and Dual Labor Bur-

other qualifications. The problem they face is that many employers are seeking North American experience and thus do not count the numerous and valuable Asian work experiences that these women may have. A young second-generation Korean-Canadian woman recounts the struggle of her own mother, Young Ju Park Kim, in finding employment.

> In my mother's situation, coming to Canada meant a drop in her class status. In Korea and in Hong Kong, my mother had been an art teacher and was pursuing her career and passion for art. However, in Canada, she no longer worked in a profession, but found herself in a factory job. Even getting this factory job was a feat in itself. Because of systemic discrimination, such as the requirement for "Canadian experience only," my mother's many years of teaching experience (over ten years) were seen as insufficient credentials for Canadian employment.[17]

Korean North American women must contend with both societal discrimination toward women and male domination within the immigrant community. As a consequence, these immigrant women are among the lowest paid and most oppressed of workers.[18] They often work more hours than men, and in spite of their full-time employment, they are expected to perform all the family tasks. They carry the burden of performing the traditional household tasks, as well as bearing and raising children. Immigrants are still influenced by the Confucian philosophy that women are born to be sacrificial, submissive, and devoted servants to their husband and children, and the women themselves have usually internalized these expectations. Thus they have a lifetime commitment to lengthy child-bearing and child-rearing, which deprives them of their own life, identity, and voice. Instead women's lives, identities, and voices are extensions of their families' life, identity, and voice. As much as they like to deny it,

---

den," in *The Korean-American Community: Present and Future,* ed. Tae-Hwan Kwak and Seong Hyong Lee (Seoul: Kyungnam University Press, 1991), 259.

17. Zestaline Kim, "Korean-Canadian Women: Voices of First Generation," Women's Studies thesis, McMaster University, Hamilton, Ontario, 1997, 32.

18. Edna Bonacich, Mokerrom Hossain, and Jae-hong Park, "Korean Immigrant Working Women in the Early 1980s," in *Korean Women in Transition: At Home and Abroad,* ed. Eui-Young Yu and Earl H. Phillips (Los Angeles: Center for Korean-American and Korean Studies, California State University, 1987), 221, 233.

many immigrant women's roles are still defined and determined to a great extent by the Confucian society of their homeland.[19] Young Ju Park Kim recounts the painful story to her daughter of not being able to pursue her dreams, for the sake of her family.

> The pressures were so hard that tears would just come streaming down my face. I cried a lot. For fifteen years, I completely forgot about my art and drawing. When we first came, doing artwork was an impossibility. So, I had a lot of stress. Your dad would always say to me, "Honey, by constantly thinking about life, it becomes difficult. Just forget everything and live — eat, sleep, work, raise children — don't think about your artwork or anything." That sounded okay to me, so until you were in middle school, I didn't do anything. Then when you were in grade six, I began my artwork for the first time.[20]

Countless numbers of immigrant women have gone through similar sacrifices for their families; they have sacrificed their personal goals and aspirations and have instead become workers and helpers for men.

The double burden that many women immigrants face involves a great deal of stress and sacrifice. For these women, social adaptation is hard, as they came from a country where they were mainly confined to their homes and discouraged from engaging with the outside world. Though Korean North American women can function in the public sphere, many of them rarely interact socially with the larger society.[21] They remain isolated and stay within their own ethnic group. These women also suffer the extra psychological burden of their negative self-image; they tend to blame themselves for any upset experienced in the domestic environment and attribute the cause to their own failure to fulfill their "womanly" role.[22] Korean North American women,

---

19. Hwain Chang Lee, *Confucius, Christ and Co-Partnership* (Lanham, Md.: University Press of America, 1994), 6, 9.

20. Kim, *Korean-Canadian Women: Voices of First Generation*, 32.

21. Lee, *Quiet Odyssey: A Pioneer Korean Woman in America*, lix.

22. Young-In Song Kim, "Korean Women's Experience in the Crossfire of Cultural Conflict," in *The Korean American Community: Present and Future*, ed. Tae-Hwan Kwak and Seong Hyong Lee (Seoul: Kyungnam University Press, 1991), 266. Positive changes are happening to the status and expectations of women. Younger women are not necessarily experiencing marriage as oppressive and burdensome. Some are finding joy and happiness in their marriage.

as a result, live with much anguish, pain, sorrow, and *han*. Their personal desire to escape the oppressive elements of Confucian culture was not fulfilled, as those elements, in large measure, immigrated with them.

The Role of the Immigrant Church

For many of these women, the immigrant church is a major institution in their lives. The historical establishment of Korean-American churches in the United States began with four churches during the first wave of immigration: the Hawaii Methodist Church (established 1903), San Francisco Korean Methodist Church (1904), Hawaii Korean Anglican Church (1905), and the Los Angeles Presbyterian Church (1905). By 1967, there were thirty Korean-American churches, growing to three thousand by 1989.[23] Many immigrants go to church: in 1986, 79–80 percent of Korean immigrants were affiliated with Korean churches, compared to a church membership rate of 15–18 percent in Korea. Of these church participants, 40 percent became Christians after immigrating to the United States.[24]

In Canada, two Korean Presbyterian churches were organized in Toronto in 1967, and in 1969 a Korean Catholic Church was established. Then with increasing numbers of immigrants in the 1970s, the existing congregations were unable to meet the needs of newcomers, and the ministers who came here as immigrants themselves started new congregations in response to the growing population. The history of Korean immigrant churches in Canada can be divided into three phases: the first occurred in the 1960s as the beginning period; the second occurred in the 1970s as the churches grew as well as divided due to conflict; the third period occurred in the 1980s as the churches faced the challenge of developing a new style of ministry for immigrants.[25]

The churches have proven to be an extremely important community for immigrants, with four major sociological functions. First, the churches provide fellowship for Korean immigrants and serve as a social center for meeting people and making friends. The churches

---

23. Kim, *Bridge-Makers and Cross-Bearers: Korean-American Women and the Church,* 7.
24. Kim, *Women's Struggle for a New Life,* 67.
25. Park, *The Relevant Ministry to Korean Immigrants in Metro Toronto Area,* 56, 58.

represent a group tie that is lacking in the larger community, as they bring together people with common experiences, sufferings and goals. They help immigrants adjust to the host society by giving valuable social services and information. The churches also become a means of identifying with the dominant culture, as adherence to Christianity has been a means of gaining sympathy from the white community.[26] Second, the churches serve as centers of education — of Korean as well as of English language, of North American culture as well as biblical knowledge, and as centers of activism for early immigrant women. Third, churches confer social status and positions of leadership upon adult members, which is important for men because it gives them leadership roles that are difficult to obtain within the dominant society. Many men are able to exercise power and authority within the church, giving them a certain status within the community. Fourth, the churches reflect, more or less, the traditional Confucian Korean cultural and social structure and system. Churches have offered a vehicle for "Americanization and also offered sites for cultural preservation and elaboration,"[27] where people can come together and reinforce their ethnic identity. Churches strengthen the Korean identity of immigrants by maintaining Korean cultural traditions.[28]

These churches fulfill many of the social and psychological needs of the immigrants. The churches, however, also perpetuate the suffering of women by restricting their roles and participation. For women in the immigrant community, these churches have been, in many ways, a source of domination and oppression.

Women in the Church

The Korean North American church predominantly reflects the conservative, hierarchical, and male-dominated characteristics of traditional Korean culture. Most senior ministers were trained in Korea and tend to hold old-country values in which traditional sex-role differentiation is clearly marked and practiced within the church. Ministers are almost all male, as are elders and ordained deacons. Church committees are chaired either by a male elder or an ordained

---

26. Kitano and Daniels, *Asian Americans: Emerging Minorities,* 122.
27. Kim, *Bridge-Makers and Cross-Bearers: Korean-American Women and the Church,* 15.
28. Kim, *Women's Struggle for a New Life,* 67.

deacon, and other important decision-making positions of the church
are largely filled by men. Women can only become lay deacons, whose
main concerns are service and mission work. An honorary position
called *kwonsa* is, however, reserved for experienced church women.
Kwonsa do not hold any decision-making power in the church, so
the position is basically for elderly women who cannot be ordained
elders[29] because of their gender.

Women's leadership or authority has not been well accepted in the
Korean immigrant churches during most of the twentieth century, and
the roles women are usually allowed to play are largely as assistants
to men. Women's roles and status in the churches have been largely
influenced by Confucian thought and practice. In the modern Korean
Christian church, women lack positions of leadership even though
they comprise the majority of the church membership. Women are excluded from many important roles but are allowed to serve as invisible
helpers behind the scene.[30] They are mainly relegated to kitchen-
related services in the church, which means that churchwomen repeat
the daily routines of housework when they go to church on Sundays.
Therefore, in many respects, the Korean North American church systematically justifies the devaluation and subordination of women[31]
as the church continues to be ruled largely by Confucian and patriarchal Christian notions of gender hierarchy, replicating the cultural
standards established back in Korea.

Most Korean North American women in the churches accept and
adjust to this Korean-Christian social environment. In such cases, the
Christian God is seen as legitimating female inferiority and shaping
women's rationalization into a process of accepting the given social
reality. Korean immigrant women, regardless of professional or religious background, generally subscribe to a sexist anthropomorphic
understanding of God. They try to live their Christianity in accordance with the elements of Korean culture, which dictate that women
are, or should be, inferior to men by nature and social function. In

29. Eui-Young Yu, "The Activities of Women in Southern California Korean Community
Organizations" in *Korean Women in Transition: At Home and Abroad,* ed. Eui-Young
Yu and Earl H. Phillips (Los Angeles: Center for Korean-American and Korean Studies,
California State University, 1987), 289, 290.

30. Kim, *Women's Struggle for a New Life,* 52.

31. Kim, *Bridge-Makers and Cross-Bearers: Korean-American Women and the Church,*
135.

so doing, many Korean North American Christian women accept and legitimate their patriarchal society and the status quo religious realities.[32]

In many ways, Korean Christianity in the immigrant church communities has become detrimental to those women who want to develop their own potential as persons and want to improve their roles and status through formal education. Consequently, those women who view themselves as "good Christians" must develop double selves in order to fit into two social environments, the church and the world outside the church. The Korean Christian culture in North America seems to perpetuate the image of women as an appendix to men.[33] Despite all these negative consequences for women, they still attend and are attached to the church.

Women's Identity and Marginalization

Korean North American women are caught between two cultural ideologies: Korean values and North American values. Korean values tend to ask women to be submissive and passive while North American values foster and demand, increasingly, individualism and assertiveness. For Korean immigrant women, the encounter with the North American feminist movement is a special source of identity disturbance. Korean culture demands conformity and obedience to family needs and societal norms, while the West admires individualism and personal success. In Korea, they were constantly told to obey men and then, when they immigrate to this new land, they are told to think for themselves and make decisions on their own without necessarily asking the advice of men. They also face the conflict of collective (familial) and individual interests. In their new setting they do not necessarily always place family first, but can indeed take care of themselves.[34] Korean North American women feel pressure to preserve their Asian cultural heritage, yet know that they must also assimilate themselves into Western sociocultural realities in order to survive.

32. Kim, *Women's Struggle for a New Life*, 91, 94.
33. Ibid., 160, 162.
34. Esther Ngan-Ling Chow, "The Feminist Movement: Where Are All the Asian American Women?" in *Making Waves: An Anthology of Writings by and about Asian American Women,* ed. Asian Women United of California (Boston: Beacon Press, 1989), 368.

Women who grew up in Korea (like women in many other places) have never had the opportunity to develop as authentic human beings with a true sense of self-worth. After immigration, their new environment prompts them to search for the self-realization and self-fulfillment they could not find in their childhood and youth. Their old-country self-image and self-identity do not fit in with contemporary North American society. A sharp contrast occurs between the traditional Korean women's role demanded of them at home and the contemporary Western image of womanhood portrayed in North American media and culture. Establishing a strong self-identity is crucial for Korean North American women who have experienced cultural and ideological transition and must survive as members of a doubly marginalized group (i.e., both female and Asian).[35] They do not belong to the dominant culture, nor to their homeland's culture, but are left in the margins. Korean North American women become separated from their native country and culture and, unable to melt into the dominant group, thus perceive themselves as "marginalized."

Marginalized people are "neither here nor there; they are betwixt and between the positions assigned and arranged by law, custom, convention and ceremony."[36] They stand on the borders of two cultural worlds but are not fully members of either. They straddle two societies, not completely accepted by the majority group in the society in which they live, because they belong to a visible minority. A part of these women longs for solidarity with their Korean heritage, and yet another demands a just place in the larger North American society, where many are still treated as strangers.[37] They identify with, or have internalized, the norms and ideals of the dominant group, but are often rejected by that group. In this sense, they are not only "in between" or "on the boundary" but also "outside or at the periphery of" the main group of a given society. The more they identify with the main group, the more they feel marginalized.[38]

---

35. Lee, "Korean American Women and Ethnic Identity," 190–93.

36. Kim, *Bridge-Makers and Cross-Bearers: Korean-American Women and the Church,* 16.

37. Fumitaka Matsuoka, *Out of Silence: Emerging Themes in Asian American Churches* (Cleveland: United Church Press, 1995), 1.

38. Sang Hyun Lee, "Called to Be Pilgrims: Toward an Asian-American Theology from the Korean Immigrant Perspective" in *Korean American Ministry: A Resource Book,* ed. Sang Hyun Lee (New York: Consulting Committee on Korean American Ministry, Presbyterian Church [U.S.A.], 1987), 92.

Many believe that Korean North American women (and immigrants in general) do not necessarily have to remain in the margins but can easily assimilate into the dominant culture. Yet this notion is false, because the theory of assimilation of different races does not stand up in North America. The total assimilation of racial groups in the United States has been depicted by the image of a melting pot. The idea of total assimilation, however, came to be realized only for those of homogenous national groups from the European continent, and not for those who came from other shores. As Frank Ichistita argues, "it seems to me that the melting-pot concept was valid only if one was white. Blacks were kept out entirely and other non-whites were invited in gingerly so as not to disturb the basic mix."[39] This melting pot model cannot work for "visible minorities" unless wholesale interracial marriages occur in North America, as was once suggested by the British historian Arnold Toynbee. As long as differences in outward appearance persist, people tend to be categorized and classified according to skin color and other physical characteristics,[40] which is why Korean immigrant women cannot fully assimilate into the main culture. Thus they continue to feel like outsiders and foreigners. Many people, especially those who have recently arrived, are unable to assimilate well with the dominant culture because of their lack of English language skills, as well as the lack of time to develop new friendships or relationships outside their Korean community.

Korean North American women feel a great deal of alienation and loneliness. In addition to being members of a marginalized Asian North American subculture that functions with rules the majority does not live by, women often experience the frustration of not having their experience recognized, validated, and supported by men within their own ethnic communities. Thus they are doubly alienated:[41] they experience alienation from within their ethnic community

---

39. Quoted in Young Jung Lee, *Marginality: The Key to Multicultural Theology* (Minneapolis: Fortress Press, 1995), 37.

40. Grace Sangok Kim, "Asian North American Youth: A Ministry of Self-Identity and Pastoral Care," in *People on the Way,* ed. David Ng (Valley Forge, Pa.: Judson Press), 205. Rather than promoting the melting-pot model, Canada has used the image of a mosaic. However, while in theory Canada sees itself as a mosaic, in practice many immigrants melt into the dominant group so that they can survive and be accepted into society.

41. Matsuoka, *Out of Silence: Emerging Themes in Asian American Churches,* 73, 74.

and from the broader North American culture.[42] These women's experiences are limited and constrained to a small, stifling, ethnocentric circle.

Furthermore, just as in Korea, a person's identity in this ethnic circle is not defined only by herself but by others around her, especially family members. Although transplanted to North American soil, Korean North American women's expressions of individuality lack the marks of individuality of the dominant North American culture. Rather, the Confucian identity of a woman is transferred to the new context. For example, all women are addressed in terms of their family relationships (or lack thereof). If married, her full name becomes obsolete and people call her "Mrs." or "so-and so's wife" or *seh-sek-shi* (a newlywed bride). If a woman has a child or children, she is referred to within the ethnic community as the mother of her firstborn. The only time a woman's full name is recognized and used is when she is relatively young and unmarried (approximately twenty-five years and younger). After a certain age, understood as marriageable age, a woman's name becomes obsolete and she is recognized as a *no-chea-nyeu* (old maid).[43] *No-chea-nyeu* is not by any means a favorable or honorable name but is a hurtful, pejorative term with negative connotations, because the Korean North American culture maintains that every woman should be married by a certain age. An unmarried woman is still looked down upon and despised, much as she was during the Confucian era. Thus the deep desire of these women to escape Confucianism is forsaken, as the burdens and limitations of Confucian philosophy are still visible within home, church, and work, and indeed are legitimized in different ways also by Christianity and its Bible. As an added burden, these women now have to deal with racism in their new culture.

As a whole, Korean North American women are powerless. They are powerless within their Confucian Korean culture and also in their new immigrant context. They are further left powerless in the churches as they are considered secondary to men. This powerlessness has become part of their identity. In their powerlessness, they have ac-

    42. Kim, *Bridge-Makers and Cross-Bearers: Korean-American Women and the Church*, 93, 97.
    43. Ibid., 112.

cumulated much *han*.[44] Korean North American women are not able to release their *han* through their immigrant life but still bear it and continue to accumulate more. Their theology needs to empower them to release their *han*.

HAN AND THE NEED FOR NEW THEOLOGY

As detailed above, Korean North American women experience burdens that come with adopting a new land. They must adjust to and accept double roles. They live in a land where they are marginalized and often experience racism; they also lose their own individual identity and are referred to by their marriage status in their own community. They become invisible and silenced just as they were in their homeland. Their thoughts do not seem to warrant any hearing, and their identity is lost in the tradition that brought them to the new land. They continue to live and experience *han*, which will always be with them unless they find new ways to release it. Just as for women living in Korea, not many channels exist for Korean North American women to eliminate their *han*.

In many ways, these women live a life of exile in this new land. They are like the biblical figure of Hagar, since many came here not by their own choice, but by someone else's and for someone else's sake. Many live in anguish worrying about their children, and many live with a sense of alienation and confusion. The ideal images of Korean women are of submissiveness and self-sacrifice, and these images leave defenseless victims helpless. These women's sense of wandering in the wilderness differs from that of men in the immigrant community, because women's exile is more a circumstantial, forced exile, rather than a voluntary flight. Their degree of uncertainty and lack of personal direction is greater than that of the men in their culture. Immigrant women are not able to pursue their own interests or professional ambition, but have to work for family members in low-paying and, often to their minds, degrading jobs such as cleaning and other manual work. This far-away-from-home wilderness often presents problems with their children, which are more than the women can handle. Overwhelmed by a sense of alienation and oppression, these women find

44. Chapter 7 presents a more detailed discussion on Korean North American women's powerlessness.

themselves needing a workable theology and spiritual guidance for survival and to release their accumulated *han*.[45]

Since many of these immigrant women are Christians, they turn to Christianity to find answers and a way out. Often, the church is viewed as a channel of release. The marginalized existence of these women determines the very character and function of their churches as "communitas,"[46] making the church very important to these women. Even though the church itself is patriarchal, the church is the place where women can gather together with others of similar interests, backgrounds, and problems. These women look forward to church and try to find some consolation there for all the burdens and problems that they are experiencing. The church, however, has not advanced greatly beyond the Yi dynasty in its social treatment and placement of women. In line with Confucian thought, Korean North American Christian women continue to exist for others and keep the rule of obeying men. They obey, follow, and provide for the various needs of their ministers "as to the Lord." They deny and sacrifice themselves by carrying others' crosses as their own. They believe that they have nothing to look forward to in this life, for their reward will be purely spiritual.[47] Women are taught to suffer and endure in this world, for a better life comes after death. Also, many women have internalized their assigned subordinate status, accepting it as normal and rationalizing it. Oppressed people often have an "oppressed mentality," buying into the dominant ideology and actively promoting it. Tragically, oppressed women often oppress other women and resent it when other women break free of their bonds. In a quest for a less oppressed life, they need to find a liberating theology that can assist in the process of the healing of their *han*.

Since Jesus Christ is central to Christianity, some theologians are searching with hope and anticipation for a new and liberative image and understanding of Jesus. One image proposed by Korean women is that of Jesus as a shaman priest. Jesus cried out for the pain of suffering humanity, and shamans do likewise for the suffering Korean

45. Lee, "An Exilic Journey: Toward Womanist Theology from Korean Immigrant Women's Perspectives," 24.

46. Kim, *Bridge-Makers and Cross-Bearers: Korean-American Women and the Church*, 16.

47. Ibid., 87.

people. Shamans comfort the *han*-ridden *minjung,* and similarly, Jesus comforts the *han*-ridden people. For Korean women, salvation or redemption means being exorcised from their accumulated *han* and untangling their many-layered *han,* which can be achieved through a shaman. Therefore, Korean women can easily link the Jesus of the New Testament, who also exorcised the possessed and healed the sick, with their shaman priest. The Korean shaman has been a healer, comforter, and counselor for Korean women just as Jesus Christ healed and comforted women in his earthly ministry.[48] Korean women are interpreting in fresh and creative ways the traditional images of Jesus. If Jesus Christ is to make any sense to Korean women, it is argued, then Jesus Christ must be an exorcist of their *han* and a "priest of *han.*" Since most shamans are women, many Korean women connect with a female image of Jesus more than the male. For some Korean women, Jesus can no longer be a white man in Jewish clothes, but a Korean woman shaman priest who releases their *han.*

This image of Jesus works well for many Korean women and is commendable as theologically creative and valuable. The image does not, however, resonate well with Korean North American women, most of whom have not directly inherited this shamanistic tradition. Many are unaware and ignorant of shamanic practices, and even see them as evil. Korean North American women do not want to embrace something that is not entirely authentic to their bisocial being and bicultural tradition. Neither can these women find liberation in the white male savior that Western society has been perpetuating for the last two thousand years, for they cannot identify with this white Jesus. Furthermore, the images of Jesus that some white feminist theologians are proposing also do not resonate very well with Korean North American women, whose experiences and context are very different from white women's.

As we have seen, Korean North American women are at times torn between two cultures as they try to embrace both and live by them both. One key to resolving such a tension between two cultures is to maintain a bicultural existence, through selecting appropriate elements of both cultural worlds to make the best adaptation according

---

48. Chung, *Struggle to Be the Sun Again,* 66.

to the demands of social circumstances.[49] At times, the decision to use one culture over the other is not a question of what is better than the other, but rather selecting what is good from both cultures. Similarly, their image of a Jesus who will release them of their pain, sorrow, and *han* should be retrieved from both worlds. This task will be an exciting and important endeavor as many Korean immigrant women continue to search for new ways of understanding Jesus. The next chapter examines the Asian figures of Wisdom and begins to propose a christological way forward for women who live in a "both/and" world.

---

49. Chow, "The Feminist Movement: Where Are All the Asian American Women?" 368.

~ Five ~

A Multifaith Interpretation
of Wisdom

SYNCRETISM HAS ALWAYS been integral to Korean culture and religion. Within the history of Christianity as well, syncretism was
present in the early church and throughout its history. "Pure Christianity does not exist, never has existed, never can exist."[1] Syncretism
is clearly evident in Old Testament texts[2] and a concrete example is
the development of Wisdom. Many scholars have demonstrated that
biblical and apocryphal *Hokmah*/Sophia was a syncretistic formation from a nearby Egyptian goddess Isis. This syncretic formation
of Sophia diminishes any argument for "pure orthodoxy" or a "pure
Christianity." An understanding of the syncretistic origin of Sophia
is also important for Korean North American women, who have
inherited syncretistic cultures, traditions, and religions — i.e., their
religio-cultural heritage is Shamanist, Buddhist, and Confucianist,
as well as Christian, and these coexist hidden within their minds
and souls.

To begin to understand Wisdom, examination of its etymology can
be helpful. The English word "wisdom" and related Germanic words
have their root in the Proto-Indo European term *weid,* which means
"knowledge" and "appearance." Thus the German word *wissen,* to
know, is closely related to the English term "wisdom," as well as to the
Latin-rooted English term "vision." The name of the ancient Sanskrit
Hindu Scriptures, the "Vedas" (knowledge), is also etymologically

---

1. "The Divine is always made present through human mediations which are always
dialectical.... Many...historians of Christian origins have shown that Catholicism is a
grandiose and infinitely complex syncretism." Leonardo Boff, *Church: Charism and Power*
(London: SCM Press, 1985), 92.
2. Many scholars discuss the existence of syncretism during biblical times, for example,
Wesley Ariarajah, *The Bible and the People of Other Faiths* (Geneva: World Council of
Churches, 1985).

closely related. The Greek word for wisdom, *Sophia,* fundamentally means a skill. In pre-Socratic Greece (before 470 B.C.E.), Sophia meant the mastery of a practical knowledge, and only during the classical period of Socrates, Plato, and Aristotle did the word come to signify theoretical, philosophical knowledge. Then, during the Hellenistic period (after 330 B.C.E.), Sophia came to mean both practical and theoretical knowledge.[3] The meaning of the term Wisdom has obviously gone through changes over a period of time.

This chapter will explore certain Asian concepts of Wisdom as a source for Korean North American women's Christology. I shall attempt to find in the riches of Asian religion and culture insights that complement biblical and other Christian sources, for the sake of a "multifaith hermeneutics" of Wisdom. We begin by exploring selected Wisdom figures in Asia to examine their similarities and differences with the Wisdom figure found in the Bible and Christianity. Then we explore the roots of biblical Sophia by examining the origins and deeds of Isis.

WISDOM FIGURES IN ASIA

The project undertaken in this thesis is precisely to inculturate the Gospel of Christ for Korean North American women. To do so, a syncretic approach is necessary, blending concepts from beyond Christianity in order to clarify and illuminate the gospel for this time and place, and for these people.

Wisdom can be found in almost every culture and religion. As we see in the next chapter, Wisdom appears in the Christian scriptures as *Hokmah* (Hebrew) and *Sophia* (Greek), both clearly feminine, and also in Buddhism as *prajna,* which is a grammatically feminine noun in Sanskrit. Wisdom (sagehood) is also found in the Confucian tradition and is very much a part of Asian religion, culture, and society. The concept of Wisdom deeply affects the lives of Asian women through their various religio-cultural traditions. This section examines Buddhism's *prajna* to understand her origins, deeds, and purposes, as well as Kuan-yin in the Buddhist tradition and sagehood in Confucianism.

---

3. Leonard Swidler, "A Christian Historical Perspective on Wisdom as a Basis for Dialogue with Judaism and Chinese Religions," *Journal of Ecumenical Studies* 33 (1996): 557–72.

I propose that Korean North American women may well relate to and accept the biblical notion of Sophia, finding within it resonances of their own Asian cultural heritages. As a Korean North American woman, I myself am heartened to know that biblical Wisdom is akin to the Wisdom of my forebears.

Prajna: Wisdom in Buddhism

Wisdom is an important concept in Buddhism, in that it manifests hope and liberation for Buddhists. Wisdom is generally believed to be the absolute knowledge through which enlightenment is attained. Absolute knowledge is the knowledge of nondiscrimination, namely, the knowledge of "suchness," which is free from all differentiating features. Since absolute knowledge is compassionate in its nature, the Enlightened One (Buddha) leads people to their emancipation. In short, Wisdom is regarded as the most essential concept within Buddhism, the essential virtue without which no being may claim to be an Enlightened One (Buddha).[4] Wisdom thus is a necessary incentive, and without it Buddhists have no serious goal to achieve. Wisdom is the very essence of Buddhism and Buddhism cannot exist without it.

The word *prajna* in Sanskrit comes from the word *pra,* which means "to know," and which can also mean "superior, excellent." Often, *prajna* is synonymous with *jnana,* a term preferred in the Bhagavad Gita. *Jnana* can be translated as "cognition" or "gnosis" because it is a special kind of knowledge, distinguished from cleverness and from scientific thinking.[5] The word *prajna* joined with *paramita* becomes supreme Wisdom, a perfect or transcendent form. The term *paramita* is a compound of *param* meaning "beyond" and *ita,* which may be translated as "she who has gone." Thus *paramita* means something that has "gone beyond" and *Param* has even been rendered "the other shore." This combination of meaning provides a very pleasant image of something that has crossed from our domain of ignorance to another shore where perfection dwells.[6]

4. Genryu Tsutsumi, "Karuna (Compassion) and Prajna (Wisdom): A Note of Seizan-Sect Doctrine," *Japanese Religions* 4 (1966): 45, 46.

5. Edward J. D. Conze, "Buddhist Prajna and Greek Sophia," *Religion* 5 (1975): 161.

6. Douglas A. Fox, *The Heart of Buddhist Wisdom* (Lewiston, N.Y.: Edwin Mellen Press, 1985), 74, 87.

The *Prajnaparamita* literature consists of thirty-eight different books composed in India between 100 B.C.E. and 600 C.E. Four distinct phases can be distinguished: the elaboration of a basic text (ca. 100 B.C.E. to 100 C.E.), the expansion of that text (ca. 100 to 300 C.E.), the restatement of the doctrine in short Sutras and versified summaries (ca. 300 to 500), and the period of Tantric influence and of the composition of Commentaries (ca. 500 to 1200). The oldest text to be composed is *Perfection of Wisdom in 8,000 Lines* in thirty-two chapters. About the time of the beginning of the Christian era the basic *Prajnaparamita* was expanded into a "Large *Prajnaparamita*," as represented today by three different texts — *Perfect Wisdom in 100,000 Lines* (S, Ch),[7] *Perfect Wisdom in 25,000 Lines* (Ch, T, em), and *Perfect Wisdom in 18,000 Lines* (s, Ch, T). These three texts are basically one and the same book and differ only in the extent to which the "repetitions" are excluded. The huge bulk of the large *Prajnaparamita* proved to be an obstacle to later generations. Even men like Asanga could no longer understand its meaning, due to the great number of the repetitions, and their inability to distinguish the different words and arguments. The challenge to overcome this difficulty was met in two ways: by new, shorter Sutras and by condensed Summaries of the large text.[8] Among these texts, the holiest of the holy is the *Diamond Sutra* (350 C.E.) and the *Heart Sutra* (350 C.E.). The first is known in Sanskrit as the *Vajracchedika Prajnaparamita,* the "Perfection of Wisdom which cuts like a thunderbolt." The second sets out to formulate the very "heart" or "essence" of perfect Wisdom.[9]

The two major classes of Buddhist scriptures, the *Abhidharma* and

7. Edward Conze uses initials to indicate the different languages in which the text appears. S is Sanskrit, Ch is Chinese, T is Tibetan. Small letters indicate where only a part is available in that language. Em indicates that the work forms part of Conze's typed translation of the *Prajnaparamita*. Edward Conze, *Selected Sayings from the Perfection of Wisdom,* 2d ed. (London: Buddhist Society, 1968), 11–13.

8. Ibid., 11–13.

9. Edward Conze, *Buddhist Wisdom Books* (London: George Allen & Unwin, 1958, 10.

The *Prajnaparamita Sutras* were revealed by the Buddha himself, but they were too difficult to be understood by his contemporaries. In consequence, they were stored in the Palace of the Serpents or Dragons called Nagas, in the Nether world. When the time was ripe, the great doctor Nagarjuna went down into the Nether world and brought them up. Edward Conze, *Buddhism: Its Essence and Development* (New York: Harper & Brothers, 1959), 29.

the *Prajnaparamita* group of texts, are largely devoted to the elucidation and advancement of knowledge and Wisdom. Practically every Buddhist treatise (sastra), written by an individual author in conformity with the Scriptures (sutras), is in some sense a document of the supremacy of knowledge and Wisdom over against traditional rituals and dogmatic beliefs. In the ultimate analysis, Wisdom is decisive, as it alone opens the door to liberation.[10]

In the Buddhist tradition, *prajna* has become personified as a woman but is not worshipped as a goddess. *Prajna* is a Wisdom supremely compassionate, rescuing humans from their ignorance and suffering. She is a nurturer, sustainer, and liberator. Faith in her will lead to the release of many fears and ensure that no division exists between matter and spirit, the world and nirvana. *Prajnaparamita,* commonly known as the Perfection of Wisdom, can be seen to be feminine, not only from the grammatical form of her name but also from the many statues and images of her feminine body.[11] The texts which present *prajnaparamita* do not present her as a divine being or an immortal essence. She is the ultimate saving Wisdom.[12] These characteristics are just some of the favorable traits that she possesses and displays.

In early Mahayana literature the feminine grammatical gender begins to take on more explicitly psychological overtones as *prajnaparamita* is presented as "the mother of all Buddhas."[13] This image of Wisdom becomes very powerful, conveying the conviction that all things originate from Wisdom. Wisdom is presented as the beginning of all things:

> The Buddhas in the world-systems in the ten directions bring to mind this perfection of wisdom as their mother. The Saviors of the world who were in the past, and also those that are [just

---

10. Lal Mani Joshi, "Faith and Wisdom in the Buddhist Tradition," in *Dialogue and Alliance* 1 (1987): 72.

11. Anne Bancroft, "Women in Buddhism" in *Women in the World's Religions, Past and Present,* ed. Ursula King (New York: Paragon House, 1987), 90.

12. Joanna Rogers Macy, "Perfection of Wisdom: Mother of All Buddhas," in *Beyond Androcentrism: New Essays on Women and Religion,* ed. Rita M. Gross (Missoula, Mont.: Scholars Press, 1977), 315.

13. Alan Sponberg, "Attitudes Toward Women and the Feminine in Early Buddhism," in *Buddhism, Sexuality and Gender,* ed. José Ignacio Cabezón (Albany: State University of New York Press, 1992), 26.

now] in the ten directions, have issued from her, and so will the
future ones be. She is the one who shows this world [for what
it is], she is the genetrix, the mother of the Jinas [=Buddhas].[14]

Thus her feminine characteristics are evident and clearly portrayed.
She is undoubtedly a feminine figure. *Prajnaparamita* is the highest or
perfect Wisdom, which means that she contains or suffers no shadow
of error. Wisdom is not something one acquires, but something one
discovers oneself to be. Wisdom is within oneself and thus one needs
to discover her. She is beyond all distinctions, even those of knower,
knowing, and known, for she is at once all three of these, making
them one. She is the insight that goes beyond any knowing about
anything and is therefore beyond words (which are always "about
something"). She is pure luminosity, the supreme attainment for mortals; she certainly leaves behind the ordinary working of reason,
perception, and analysis.[15]

The *Abhisamayalamkara,* one of the most important treatises
of the scholastic tradition of Mahayana Buddhism, begins with an
homage to the supreme perfection of Wisdom as the mother of the
various types of spiritually accomplished beings: "I bow down to the
Mother of the hosts of disciples (*sravakas*), Bodhisattvas and buddhas."[16] The mother has three aspects, her manifestation as Scripture
(here referring to the Prajnaparamita Sutras), as path (the series of
mental states that lead to illumination), and as result (enlightenment
itself). Sometimes a fourth aspect is added: "essence" (*rang bzhin*).
In this case, the "essential" *prajnaparamita* is emptiness, the essence
or final nature, of all phenomena. Wisdom is considered the mother
of the different spiritual types because she is their source. Just as the
mother is one of the two principle causes of a child, so too is Wisdom
one of the two chief causes of enlightenment. Wisdom is what nur-
tures the adept on the path; she is characterized as their "mother."
Just as a mother must bear the child in her womb for ten (lunar)

14. Prajnaparamita-Ratnagunasamcayagatha. XII, 1–2; trans. Edward Conze, *The Perfection of Wisdom in Eight Thousand Lines and Its Verse Summary* (Bolinas, Calif.: Four
Seasons Foundation, 1973), 31.
15. Douglas A. Fox, *The Heart of Buddhist Wisdom* (Lewiston, N.Y.: Edwin Mellen
Press, 1985), 74, 87.
16. Sravakabodhisatt-vaganino buddhasya matre namah/Abhisamayalamkara (I, 1d),
ed. R. Tripathi (Sarnath: Central Institute for Higher Tibetan Studies, 1988), 4 (of the
Sanskrit edition).

months, the natural gestation period, so too must Wisdom nurture the adept along the way through the ten *bhumis,* or stages of the Bodhisattva path. This gestation in mother Wisdom's womb brings about the birth of enlightened beings. The mother must continue to nurture the child in her womb until its birth, while the father's role in procreation occurs only at the beginning and by comparison is relatively short in duration.[17] Thus the mother is considered the more important partner in the whole birthing process. Just as a child is born of the Mother, so the full enlightenment of a Buddha comes forth from the Perfection of Wisdom. She shows them their way about in the world.[18]

Perfect Wisdom has many functions. She is the source of the all-knowledge of the Buddhas, the lords. Many people can also find protection in perfect Wisdom. In this Buddhist sutra, we recognize a remarkable parallel to the Hebrew and Greek *Hokmah*/Sophia.

The perfection of wisdom gives light, O Lord, I pay homage to the perfection of wisdom! She is worthy of homage. She is unstained and the entire world cannot stain her. She is a source of light, and from everyone in the triple world she removes darkness and leads them away from the blinding darkness caused by defilements and wrong views. In her we can find shelter. Most excellent are all her works. She makes us seek the safety of the wings of enlightenment. She brings light to the blind, so that all fear and distress may be forsaken. She has gained the five eyes and she shows the path to all beings. She herself is an organ of vision. She disperses the gloom and darkness of delusion. She does nothing about all dharmas. She guides to the path those who have strayed on to a bad road. She is identified with all-knowledge. She never produces any dharma, because she has forsaken the residues relating to both kinds of coverings, those produced by defilement and those produced by the cognizable. She does not stop any dharma. Herself unstopped and unproduced is the perfection of wisdom. She is the Mother of the Bodhisattvas on account of the emptiness of own-marks. As

17. José Ignacio Cabezón, "Mother Wisdom, Father Love: Gender-based Imagery in Mahayana Buddhist Thought," in *Buddhism, Sexuality and Gender,* ed. José Ignacio Cabezón (Albany: State University of New York Press, 1992), 185.
18. Conze, *Buddhism: Its Essence and Development,* 192.

the donor of the jewel of all the Buddha-dharmas she brings about the ten powers of a Tathagata. She cannot be crushed. She protects the unprotected, with the help of the four grounds of self-confidence. She has a clear knowledge of the own-being of all dharmas, for she does not stray away from it. The perfection of wisdom of the Buddhas, the lords, sets in motion the wheel of Dharma.[19]

Thus she is very attractive to those who are in fear and need a safe place to turn to, as she protects those who are weak. Not surprisingly she is very appealing to many people, especially those who are oppressed. In some particular doctrinal traditions, *prajna* is looked upon as productive energy. In Nepal, all those who desire to know the true doctrine worship Wisdom. In Japan, Java, and Indo-China she was well beloved, but in China she was unknown. *Prajna* is usually represented white in color, with one head and two arms. The right hand may hold a white lotus and the left the stem of a blue lotus, which supports the sutra on a level with her ear.[20]

Many people pay tribute to and adore Wisdom. "The Perfection of Wisdom gives light, O Lord. I pay homage to the Perfection of Wisdom!" cries Sariputra after listening to Subhuti. Wisdom is viewed as someone with supremely positive qualities who takes the darkness away. Overcoming darkness is important in a world that is full of hardships and difficulties. *Prajna* removes the darkness of ignorance and unfolds the true nature of reality. Having such a soothing light of Wisdom, she finally destroys the chains of attachment and helps people to achieve a state of desirelessness. *Prajna* inspires human beings to realize the threefold nature of reality for the total elimination of attachment. For Buddhist tradition she denotes proper or right understanding, insight, the highest knowledge, and by attaining it, one becomes able to visualize and to understand everything in its true

---

19. Conze, *Selected Sayings from the Perfection of Wisdom,* 61.

20. Alice Getty, *The Gods of Northern Buddhism,* translated from the French of J. Deniker (Rutland, Vt.: Charles E. Tuttle, 1962), 130, 131. *Prajnaparamita* emerges as the Third Noble Truth. Given the emptiness of dharmas, there is, if one can grasp this emptiness, nothing to desire, nothing to grasp; seeking this is liberation. From this come two corollaries: (1) one cannot think one's way into this *prajna;* it is a way of seeing; (2) wisdom is now raised from a means to an end. As transforming insight, it is both the ground of all the virtues and their goal. Joanna Rogers Macy, "Perfection of Wisdom: Mother of All Buddhas," in *Beyond Androcentrism: New Essays on Women and Religion,* ed. Rita M. Gross (Missoula, Mont.: Scholars Press, 1977), 318.

perspective. The human being is able, because of her, to give up all unnecessary craving. *Prajna* is not merely a theoretical knowledge but a practical way to detachment and escape from every sort of misery in life. The attainment of Wisdom is threefold: *sila* (virtue), *samadhi* (concentration), and *panna* (wisdom).[21]

Prajna does her utmost to assist people to forsake the blinding darkness caused by defilements and by false views. She makes us seek the safety of all the dharmas that act as wings to enlightenment. She brings light, so that all fear, terror, and distress may be forsaken. She shows the path so that all beings may acquire the five organs of vision. Perfect Wisdom is the source of all-knowledge of the Buddhas or lords. The perfection of Wisdom is the mother of the Bodhisattvas, the great beings, on account of her generation of the Buddhadharmas. She liberates from birth-and-death because she is not unmoved nor destroyed.[22]

Indeed, fundamental to Buddhism has been the cultivation, development, and perfection of Wisdom. Analysis, investigation, examination, argumentation, reasoning, and penetrating insight are all tools and techniques of acquiring knowledge and Wisdom.[23] All Buddhists, by definition, are in reality seekers of Wisdom. Hence Buddhist scriptures are replete with the depth, width, majesty, and luster of that Wisdom, which is variously known as *bodhi* (illumination), *vidya/vijja* (science), *jnana/nana* (knowledge), *vipasyana* (insight), *abhijna* (superknowledge), *aloka* (light), and *prajna* (wisdom).[24]

"Liberation" may be said to be an important aspect of any religion, an essential goal for everyone to obtain, and of course is conceived differently in different traditions. Buddhist scripture mentions a twofold liberation: liberation of mind (*ceto-vimutti*) and liberation through Wisdom (*panna-vimutti*). Wisdom has essentially a liberational or soteriological function in Buddhism. Mere speculative knowledge is considered not only meaningless but detrimental to the task of liberation. *Asrava* or impurities are identified with *duhkha* or suffering.

21. Baidyanath Labh, *Panna in Early Buddhism* (Delhi: Eastern Book Linkers, 1991), iii, v.

22. Edward Conze, trans., *The Large Sutra on Perfect Wisdom* (Berkeley: University of California Press, 1975), 283.

23. Lal Mani Joshi, "Faith and Wisdom in the Buddhist Tradition," in *Dialogue and Alliance* 1 (1987): 71.

24. Ibid., 71.

By destroying all *asravas* or flowing influxes, the saint destroys suffering and wins happiness (*sukha*). The task of Wisdom is to make
us *anasrava*, free from sufferings. The root evil or sin in the Buddhist doctrine is misconception, misknowledge, or ignorance. *Avidya*
does not merely mean ignorance or absence of knowledge; the term
means wrong knowledge, misconception based on misperception, or
illusion (*moha*). The *Dhammapada* teaches that *avidya* is the supreme
impurity and that illusion is the greatest snare. A wrong view (*mithya-
dristi*) leads to miserable conditions, and attainment of a right view
brings about happiness. Wisdom, like a lamp, removes the darkness
of false opinions, dispels doubts, and brings about tranquility and
joy. This liberative Wisdom is attained through methodical meditation on the subjects recommended in the scriptures. The connection
between Wisdom and meditation in the Buddhist scheme is basic and
essential.[25]

Prajna is pure liberation, empty of anything clinging or defiled. She
can thus be defense, shelter, and protection from the samsaric storms,
the suffering of worldly striving and desire. In this way, she helped
many to let go of their fears and jump into the enlightenment.[26]

There are many advantages that come to those who have *prajna*.
In the *Astasahasrika-prajna-paramita-sutra* (chapter 3), the sons or
daughters of a good family who seek *prajna* feel no physical or mental
fatigue. "At ease they lie down, at ease they walk about. At ease he
sleeps, at ease he awakes. His body, filled with energy, feels at ease and
light. While sleeping, he sees no evil dreams."[27] Thus goodness awaits
those who seek *prajna*. As a whole, only positive elements occur from
obtaining Wisdom. All Buddhists, then, are seekers of Wisdom and
Buddhism is chiefly a way of Wisdom.[28]

Kuan-yin

Another feminine figure of Buddhism is Kuan-yin. Kuan-yin originated as an Indo-Tibetan divinity and was introduced into China by

25. Ibid., 73.

26. Denise Lardner Carmody, *Women and World Religions* (Nashville: Abingdon,
1979), 55.

27. Yuichi-Kajiyama, "Mahayana Buddhism and the Philosophy of Prajna," in *Studies
in Pali and Buddhism,* ed. A. K. Narain (Delhi: B. R. Publishing Corporation, 1979), 200,
201.

28. Joshi, "Faith and Wisdom in the Buddhist Tradition," 71.

the Mahayana school[29] about the fifth century C.E. Kumerajiva,[30] who entered China in the fifth century, was the first to render the Hindu name Avalokitesvara (Sanskrit) by its Chinese equivalent "Kuan-shih-yin." The name Kuan-yin is a bad Chinese translation of the Bodhisattva "Avalokitesvara," emerging from a confusion between the Sanskrit words *isvara*, "lord," and *svara*, "sound."[31] Her name means "She who hears the sounds (prayers) of mortals; she who looks down upon the world and hears its cries." Kuan-yin signifies "looking at the sounds of the [living beings]" and "listening to the world's sounds."[32]

This female figure Kuan-yin was originally a male figure; the earliest Buddhist texts mentioned only male Buddhas and Bodhisattvas. Male Bodhisattvas were first introduced around the late fourth century.[33] In China numerous images in the caves at Yun-kang and Lung-men portray Kuan-yin as a male Bodhisattva; he even has a moustache in some presentations. These portrayals date as late as the tenth century. Then this male Bodhisattva from India went through a sexual transformation and became a beautiful white-robed Chinese woman, Kuan-yin. Kuan-yin eventually became viewed as female more often than male, from the Sung dynasty (960–1127) to the present. Referred to as the "Goddess of Mercy," Kuan-yin was transported through Asia even as far as Japan, where she was known as Kannon, who performed the same functions as she did in China.[34] The female symbolism of the Bodhisattva was expanded further by the addition of *yin* symbols (i.e., moon, water) from the yin-yang polarity of Chinese thought. She was also a popular subject for women

---

29. John H. Chamberlayne, "The Development of Kuan Yin: Chinese Goddess of Mercy," *Numen* 9 (1962): 47.

30. He translated in 406 a chapter of the *Lotus Sutra* entitled "The Universal Face," which became the most popular and definitive edition. Diana Y. Paul, *Women in Buddhism: Images of the Feminine in Mahayana Tradition* (Berkeley: Lancaster-Miller, 1979), 255.

31. J. Hackin, Clement Huart, Raymonde Linossier, H. De Wilman-Grabowska, Charles-Henre Marchal, Henri Maspero, and Serge Eliseev, *Asiatic Mythology: A Detailed Description and Explanation of the Mythologies of All the Great Nations of Asia* (New York: Thomas Y. Crowell, 1963), 352, 353.

32. Paul, *Women in Buddhism*, 249.

33. Barbara E. Reed, "The Gender Symbolism of Kuan-yin Bodhisattva," in *Buddhism, Sexuality and Gender* (Albany: State University of New York Press, 1992), 160.

34. Paul, *Women in Buddhism: Images of the Feminine in Mahayana Tradition*, 251.

artists from at least the time of the Ming dynasty (1368–1644).[35] Her popularity increased as artists created more and more images of her.

Beginning with the T'ang dynasty, in the seventh and early eighth centuries, a delicately slender, white-clad female figure becomes the dominant portrait of Kuan-yin. Kuan-yin Clad-in-White was introduced into China toward the middle of the eighth century with the translation of the Ta ji King. She is represented as a beautiful woman entirely covered by a white veil, which hides even her hair. Kuan-yin holds a white lotus flower, to symbolize the purity of the heart that, having uttered the vow to become Buddha, remains unalterably steadfast to its vow. To her right and left are her two attendants, the Young Man of excellent capacities, Shan-ts'ai tung-tsi, and the Daughter of the Dragon-king, Lung-want nu. She is often placed upon the rock of p'u-t'o. Sometimes her white garment is partly covered by an embroidered robe or even disappears to give place to a Chinese woman's dress.[36]

Kuan-yin has many attributes that are attractive to women. In a Chinese culture dominated by Confucian social values, Chinese women viewed this female symbol positively, as she was particularly understanding of their problems as women. Kuan-yin became an object of devotion for Chinese women, as she offered many solutions and support for women's hardships. In a group of indigenous Scriptures, she is primarily portrayed as a fertility goddess. She is the only Buddhist personage who is especially appealed to for the gift of children.[37] These scriptures emphasize Kuan-yin's power to grant sons. This attribute was appealing to women, since women felt pressure to bear sons, who were valued over daughters in a Confucian society. Women also called Kuan-yin for protection during their pregnancies and the assurance of safe childbirths.[38] In addition, Kuan-yin protected children and cured them when they were sick.

Playing a very important role as the great Bodhisattva who embod-

---

35. Reed, "The Gender Symbolism of Kuan-yin Bodhisattva," 159.

36. J. Hackin, Clement Huart, Raymonde Linossier, H. De Wilman-Grabowska, Charles-Henre Marchal, Henri Maspero, Serge Eliseev, *Asiatic Mythology: A Detailed Description and Explanation of the Mythologies of All the Great Nations of Asia,* 354, 357.

37. Ibid., 352, 353.

38. Chun-fang Yu, "A Sutra Promoting the White-Robed Guanyin as Giver of Sons," *Religions of China in Practice,* ed. Donald S. Lopez Jr. (Princeton, N.J.: Princeton University Press, 1996), 97.

ied the virtue of compassion, Kuan-yin was even considered superior to any single Buddha in bestowing great benefits and merits upon faithful followers.[39] Kuan-yin was said to be so concerned for humanity that, upon receiving enlightenment, she chose to retain human form rather than transcend it as pure energy. She wanted to stay until every living creature attained enlightenment. For centuries, as a result, she has been the chief symbol of human compassion.

According to the *Lotus Sutra*, seven powers are conjured with the invocation of Kuan-yin's name: extinguishing fires, stilling turbulent rivers and oceans, calming winds and storms, freeing the accused from executioners, blinding demons and spirits, freeing the imprisoned and enslaved, and disarming one's enemies.[40] She is a very powerful woman who can ward off demons and enemies. If one calls upon the name of Kuan-yin, one's fears disappear.

Kuan-yin is important to those who suffer and need help. According to Pure Land Buddhist scriptures, Kuan-yin liberates living beings from the six realms of suffering by leading them after death to the Pure Land of A-mi-t'o Buddha, where they are assured of eventual enlightenment. She also liberates them from specific sufferings within each of the realms. The sufferings from which she liberates in this world are listed in the *Lotus Sutra*. Kuan-yin offers liberation for all suffering beings, even if they do not deserve it.[41] Thus she is merciful and compassionate to those who are struggling and finding it hard to live. Kuan-yin immediately relieves the sorrows of all who call out her name. The text displays the magnificent powers of the celestial Bodhisattva in times of need for those who pay reverence and call out the name Kuan-yin. She is also a mother figure for those in need of a mother.[42] She is nurturing, faithful, steadfast, and gentle.

---

39. Diana Paul, "Kuan-yin: Savior and Savioress in Chinese Pure Land Buddhism," in *The Book of the Goddess Past and Present*, ed. Carl Olson (New York: Crossroad, 1988), 164.

40. Ibid., 164.

41. Reed, "The Gender Symbolism of Kuan-yin Bodhisattva," 164.

42. Paul, *Women in Buddhism: Images of the Feminine in Mahayana Tradition*, 252. Statues of Avalokitesvara were common throughout India by the fifth century. Avalokitesvara was the epitome of mercy and compassion who, as the chief assistant to the Buddha Amitabha, escorted the faithful to the Pure Land along with Amitabha's other chief assistant, the Bodhisattva Mahasthamaprapta. Simply hearing the name of Avalokitesvara would result in great happiness. Paul, *Women in Buddhism: Images of the Feminine in Mahayana Tradition*, 249.

The focal point in worshiping Kuan-yin was to be free from suffering in this present world and to increase the "good things in life." If the practitioner wanted to remove the negative elements in this decadent world and try to change her lifestyle for the better, then development of a cult to a savior, who would distribute benefits in response to devotion, was thought to be appropriate.[43] Kuan-yin promises to manifest herself in whatever form is effective to save all beings in distress — from fires, robbers, drowning, and more. She promises to grant the wishes of her worshipers.[44]

A popular folktale from Japan entitled "The Kannon [Kuan-yin in Chinese] Who Substituted" illustrates the saving power of Kuan-yin.

Looking up from a small village nestled at the foot of a certain mountain, one can see a little shrine of Kannon on the very top. A young couple used to live in that village. The wife, for all her youth, believed in Kannon with utmost sincerity. Every night, after she had finished her daily housework, she visited the shrine to worship the image. Her husband did not know the reason for her going and became suspicious of the wife who went out and returned to the house every night at the same time. One day he finally lost his patience with his wife and determined to kill her. So he hid in the dark woods by the roadside and waited for his wife to come back. At the usual time she returned. The husband watching her coming near and, carefully aiming at her shoulder, swung down his sword askance. At this moment the wife felt her blood run cold throughout her body.

The husband wiped the blood from his sword and put the sword back in its sheath. When he returned to his home, he was astonished to see his wife, whom he thought he had slashed to death. He marvelled, and went back to see the place he had struck his wife. Sure enough, there were the dots of blood on the ground. He retraced his steps homeward, and asked his wife: "Didn't you feel something strange at such and such a time in such and such a place?" Then the wife answered: "Just at that time something made my blood run cold." The husband could not but confess all that had happened.

43. Paul, "Kuan-yin: Savior and Savioress in Chinese Pure Land Buddhism," 170.
44. Reed, "The Gender Symbolism of Kuan-yin Bodhisattva," 160.

The next morning he awakened early and was surprised to see blood dotted all the way from the entrance of his house to the shrine on top of the mountain. When he looked at the statue of Kannon, he was again surprised to see a scar on the statue's shoulder, on the place where he had struck his wife the night before.[45]

This folktale shows that for those who seek her, Kuan-yin will not remain passive; she will restore wholeness and prevent suffering. She is powerful and will take pains away. Kuan-yin bore the pain of the wife in this folktale and made her live.[46]

Chung Hyun Kyung gives a powerful image of Kuan-yin, who seeks to save people. Kuan-yin is a Bodhisattva, an enlightened being.

She can go into nirvana any time she wants to, but refuses to go into nirvana by herself. Her compassion for all suffering beings makes her stay in this world, enabling other living beings to achieve enlightenment. Her compassionate wisdom heals all forms of life and empowers them to swim to the shore of nirvana. She waits and waits until the whole universe, people, trees, birds, mountains, air, water, become enlightened. They can then go to nirvana together, where they can live collectively in eternal wisdom and compassion.[47]

Wisdom as Kuan-yin is enabling, as she goes forth into the world to seek us and help us.

Kuan-yin is revered as a goddess by common folk and as a celestial Bodhisattva by scholars. She is a suffering Bodhisattva who has delayed entering Nirvana's final peace as long as other sentient beings are caught in the cycle of rebirth. Kuan-yin may provide Asian North American women with a female icon that incorporates some of our most deeply felt beliefs about relatedness, community and suffering. She is an embodiment of utter compassion. She also appears as a Wis-

---

45. As cited by C. S. Song, *Theology from the Womb of Asia* (Maryknoll, N.Y.: Orbis Books, 1986), 169.

46. This story of "Kannon" as "substitute" is very like the story of the cross, with Jesus as our "substitute."

47. Chung Hyun Kyung, "Come, Holy Spirit — Break Down the Walls with Wisdom and Compassion," in *Feminist Theology from the Third World,* ed. Ursula King (Maryknoll, N.Y.: Orbis Books, 1994), 394.

dom figure, and according to the Sanskrit version of the Heart Sutra, Kuan-yin was able to discern the teachings of the Buddha. In the mystical tradition of Kuan-yin, she often appears in a vision to persons in need. The subject of supplication and meditation, she is available to those who call upon her. She is the all-loving compassionate one who suffers for the benefit of others. She embodies values that are reflected both in Asian cultures and in Christian faith.[48]

Kuan-yin listens to all the cries of the world, not just those of human beings but of plants and animals, mountains and valleys, small creatures and large. Buddhists of many cultures have long addressed this feminine compassionate presence to relieve human sickness, grief, and poverty of spirit.[49] Due to her passionate and compassionate characteristics, she is deeply beloved among many people. The compassion and saving attributes of Kuan-yin have sustained the spirits of the women of Asia, who have suffered under conditions of extreme oppression, domination, sexism, and poverty.

Wisdom within Confucianism

Wisdom is also central to Confucianism, and links can be made here also to biblical Wisdom. Wisdom is closely related to the "Way" to live, a concept found in most religions, including the three Semitic religions — Judaism, Christianity, and Islam. For the major religions of the Far East, the Way is central: The very name of Chinese Taoism places the Way, *Tao,* at the center of its religion. The goal of Taoism is to discern the *Tao* of the universe and to live in harmony with it. This notion of the Way was also central to the doctrine of Confucius, who taught that "the Way of Humanity" (*Ren-Tao*) is to follow "the Way of Heaven" (*T'ien-Tao*). Confucianism has its own perspective and understanding of Wisdom, viewing Wisdom mainly through sageliness or sagehood.[50]

Sageliness is the traditional goal of moral life in Chinese culture. As

48. Naomi P. F. Southard, "Recovery and Rediscovered Images: Spiritual Resources for Asian American Women," *Asia Journal of Theology* 3 (1989): 629.

49. Stephanie Kaza, "Acting with Compassion" in *Ecofeminism and the Sacred,* ed. Carol J. Adams (New York: Continuum, 1993), 51.

50. Leonard Swidler, "A Christian Historical Perspective on Wisdom as a Basis for Dialogue with Judaism and Chinese Religion," *Journal of Ecumenical Studies* 33 (1996): 558, 559.

an individual, the ideal person is a sage (a wise person),[51] and ancient Confucianists aspired to be sages themselves.[52] Although Confucius believed that only a sage can envision and establish a harmonious social order, he did not regard the ideal of sagehood as practically attainable by ordinary moral agents, instead functioning more like a supreme but abstract ideal of a perfect moral personality. Sagehood is a standard of inspiration rather than a standard of aspiration.[53] One does not hope to realize the ideal completely.

Confucianists held that the learning of human ethical relations was the true "orthodox" learning. Acquiring moral purity is the way to become a sage. Knowledge is an operation of the mind, and the Confucian philosopher Chu Hsi (1130–1200) regarded knowledge as a function of Wisdom. Chu Hsi was the most influential Chinese philosopher since the time of Confucius (551–479 B.C.E.) and Mencius (372–289 B.C.E.). He was the only thinker in the Christian era to influence many phases of Asian life throughout East Asia. He wrote, commented on, compiled, and edited almost one hundred works. Aside from his commentaries on the Confucian classics, his works on social and religious rites shaped Chinese, Korean, and Japanese behavior for hundreds of years.[54] He considered Wisdom inseparable from knowledge, although he had to acknowledge some subtle difference between the two.[55] The Confucianist emphasis on Wisdom as essential to practical, moral life closely resembles the *Hokmah* of biblical Wisdom, especially as found in Proverbs. Asian people will naturally resonate to the wise practical advice of the biblical proverbs or wise sayings.

The idea of Wisdom as hidden and stored originated in the *Book of Changes* and has been handed down from generation to generation. Being a book of great Wisdom, with a grand and profound

51. Joseph S. Wu, "Western Philosophy and the Search for Chinese Wisdom," in *Invitation to Chinese Philosophy*, ed. Arne Naess and Alastair Hannay (Oslo: Universitetsforlaget, 1972), 11.

52. Tang Chun-I, "The Spirit and Development of Neo-Confucianism," in *Invitation to Chinese Philosophy*, 57.

53. Antonio S. Cua, "The Concept of Paradigmatic Individuals in the Ethics of Confucius," in *Invitation to Chinese Philosophy*, 41.

54. Wing-Tsit Chan, *Chu Hsi and Neo-Confucianism*, ed. Wing-Tsit Chan (Honolulu: University of Hawaii Press, 1986), 1, 3.

55. Okada Takehiko, "Chu Hsi and Wisdom as Hidden and Stored," in *Chu Hsi and Neo-Confucianism*, ed. Wing-Tsit Chan (Honolulu: University of Hawaii Press, 1986), 198, 199.

worldview, the *Book of Changes* has been valued highly in China
since ancient times, often said to constitute the nucleus of Chinese
thought. Chu Hsi's idea of Wisdom as hidden and stored is a com-
prehensive synthesis of ideas before the Ch'in period (221–206 B.C.E.)
and those handed down through the Han and T'ang periods as well
as the opinions of Northern Sung Confucian scholars in regard to
Wisdom. Chu Hsi examined all of these ideas in detail and clarified
the essence of Wisdom. His Wisdom is based on realization through
personal experience.[56]

"Humanity" is the virtue in which the will for life begins and
should be given great importance. Wisdom is the virtue in which the
will for life brings itself to perfection; without Wisdom humanity, propriety, and righteousness cannot bring their task to completion. Chu
Hsi took special note of the fact that Wisdom has a meaning of the
beginning and of the ending and tried to explain this by comparing it
to storage and preservation in winter, which in turn possess the meaning of the beginning and ending. Wisdom belongs to winter, a season
when the will for life is finally fulfilled. Because it contains the force
of activation, Wisdom therefore has the meaning of the beginning and
ending.[57]

Sagehood is seen as the goal of the learning process. The act of
orientation to this goal, not to be minimized, is the establishment of
a legitimate goal in the sense of a meaningful and proper end of the
learning process.[58] Sagehood was characterized as the state within
which full realization of the *hsing,* true nature, or the endowment
of the heavenly principle, *T'ien li,* occurred within oneself and all
things. The sage, as one whose true nature has been realized, is said
to live in rapport with the ordering of all things. Self-cultivation is
pursued through constant effort and diligent struggle to reach the
goal. Whether the activity is discussion with a friend, the reading of a
text, the aesthetic appreciation of nature, the admiration of someone
from the past, serving in office, or practicing quiet-sitting for Kao,
such endeavors are all self-cultivation. They each contribute toward
the eventual realization of the goal of sagehood itself. Sagehood is

56. Ibid., 200.
57. Ibid., 206.
58. Rodney Leon Taylor, *The Cultivation of Sagehood as a Religious Goal in Neo-Confucianism* (Missoula, Mont.: Scholars Press, 1978), 35.

the emergence of one's true nature and as such may be spoken of as a religious goal. Self-cultivation is the means through which to understand, develop, and express one's true nature. To pursue the goal of sagehood is to act in conformity with true nature. A life of self-cultivation may best be described as an "authentic life."[59] Sagehood offers a model of self-transcendence, and the way to achieve it is by self-cultivation. Contrasting sharply with the Christian concept of justification by grace through faith, Confucian sagehood believes that one is justified by oneself and is the realization of the immanent principle of innate human goodness.[60]

A sage has many attributes. Simplicity and tranquility are basic to the sage. The sage may serve as an example and act as a good influence on others. A sage is a person who realizes his or her[61] humanity in benevolence (*jen*) and extends this humanity to others. *Jen* (benevolence) may be seen as a Confucian's ultimate concern, as expressed by outward manifestations or social practices of propriety (*li*). *Jen* and *li* (propriety) are intimately related to each other in the Confucian model.[62] Thus Wisdom plays an important role within Confucian thought as a practical "way" that is essentially moral in character and has a transcendent dimension (heaven).

Although little of the feminine exists in Confucian wisdom, Asian Christians, including Korean women, may well find it especially meaningful to conceive of Jesus Christ as incarnate Wisdom, the human embodiment of Wisdom for a life of goodness and truth.

ISIS AND THE ORIGINS OF SOPHIA

Our reflections on syncretic sources for Wisdom lead us naturally into a discussion of the syncretic origins of biblical Sophia herself. This chapter ends with the origins of Sophia in Egyptian Isis and her culture. A study of the cult of Isis reveals her strong influence on

---

59. Ibid., 101, 103.
60. Julia Ching, *Confucianism and Christianity: A Comparative Study* (Tokyo: Kodansha International, 1977), 10.
61. A woman can be a sage, as may be seen in Eva Man Kit-Wah, "The Idea and Limitation of 'Sageliness Within and Kingliness Without,'" *Ching Feng* 38 (1995): 118.
62. Kit-Wah, "The Idea and Limitation of 'Sageliness Within and Kingliness Without,'" 116–18.

the character and actions of Sophia. Among the many goddesses of ancient times, Isis was one of the most popular. Her cult began about the third century B.C.E. and spread throughout the ancient world.[63] Isis began as one of the gods of Heliopolis. Her mother was Nut, the great sky goddess, who was portrayed in Egyptian iconography as arching over her lover Geb, the earth. Among Nut's children are Osiris, Nephtys, Set(h), and Isis. Osiris and Isis were both brother and sister, and husband and wife. The twin brother and sister were said to be already in love with each other from the time they were in the womb of their mother.[64] From this beginning, Isis's character became more developed over the years.

Isis had a special appeal to many people, and multitudes worshiped her. She had a primary place in the pantheon of deities and in the hearts of human beings. She and her cult became refashioned and exported to many places during Ptolemaic rule beginning in the third century B.C.E. A strong missionary effort out of the port city of Alexandria, aided by seafaring traders of whom Isis was the special protector, eventually spread her cult throughout the Hellenistic world. In this process, Isis assumed the attributes, roles, and names of other national goddesses, uniting their various aspects in herself so that she became praised as the "many-named" yet one power over the whole human race.[65] Her influential and attractive characteristics eventually reached the Israelites who were also drawn to her.

The character and the functions of Isis and Sophia share many similarities, which has led to the realization that the Jewish writers were borrowing from the cult of Isis to ascribe feminine aspects of Yahweh. Isis's popularity was experienced as a temptation to the Jews to turn away from the traditional faith of their ancestors. A personified Sophia, integrated into Jewish monotheism, was thus for orthodox Judaism the answer to this threat. Jewish authors transferred the character of the mighty Isis to the figure of personified

---

63. Harold Wells discusses the origin of the cult in "Trinitarian Feminism: Elizabeth Johnson's Wisdom Christology," *Theology Today* 52 (1995): 331.

64. Jonathan Cott, *Isis and Osiris: Exploring the Goddess Myth* (New York: Doubleday, 1994), 9.

65. Elizabeth A. Johnson, "Jesus the Wisdom of God: A Biblical Basis for Non-Androcentric Christology," *Ephemerides Theologicae Lovanienses* 61 (1985): 268. J. S. Kloppenborg also discusses the similarity between Isis and Sophia in his article, "Isis and Sophia in the Book of Wisdom," *Harvard Theological Review* 75 (1982): 57–84.

Sophia in a creative effort to counteract the religious and social influence of this most popular and enticing deity.[66]

Jewish writers adapted Isis and projected her characteristics onto Sophia for other reasons also. Isis possessed many qualities that were lacking in the masculine deity of the Jews. She was not remote but was a very approachable deity, in contrast to the law-giver Yahweh. Though Yahweh was thought of as a God of compassion and of loving-kindness, these characteristics were no doubt often forgotten. Yahweh was viewed as a wrathful judge who punished his people severely. Some Jewish people found a feminine motherly goddess appealing, as they needed a deity who was near and to whom they could pour out their troubles. Isis's feminine traits compensated for the lack of a feminine aspect to the divine in the Jewish tradition. She provided the image of a giver of life and fertility, which are features downplayed in the male Israelite God (especially in view of their rejection of the fertility deities of Canaan). Isis helped women in childbirth — obviously a valuable function for any deity. Isis provided the motherly image and was the protector, educator, and savior, particularly for the young. All these desirable motherly images were not emphasized in the worship of Yahweh. Given that feminine images of Yahweh are to be found elsewhere in Old Testament literature, the syncretic contextualization of a feminine deity was not totally alien to the Jews and did not fundamentally threaten their own faith tradition, for they already knew of a feminine dimension of Yahweh through the prophets.

That far more masculine than feminine images of God appear in the Bible reflects the patriarchal society. Despite the many efforts to eliminate the feminine dimension of the deity, however, this dimension was still present. For example, God is imaged as a seamstress, "And Yahweh God made tunics of skins for the man and his wife and clothed them" (Gen. 3:21). When the Israelites in the desert complained of their problems to Moses, he in turn complained to Yahweh: "Was it I who conceived all this people, was it I who gave them birth, that you should say to me, 'Carry them in your bosom, like a beloved little mother with a baby at the breast?'" (Num. 11:12). In the eighth century, Hosea makes use of the image of Yahweh as a parent teaching

---

66. Johnson, "Jesus the Wisdom of God," 269.

a child to walk, feeding and nurturing, tasks normally performed in that society by the mother (Hos. 11:1, 3, 4, 9). An image also appears of God crying out with labor pains, "Yahweh God goes forth. . . . But now, I will cry out as a woman in labor, gasping and panting" (Isa. 42:13–14).[67]

Another appealing aspect of Isis to the Jewish people was that she was a concrete and visible goddess for her followers to see. The representation of Yahweh in images was severely forbidden. But Isis's followers were able to paint her on the walls or carve her body into their temple walls, desiring a more tangible God with whom they could relate. The feminine character of Isis also illustrated the ability to express love, which was not so apparent in the patriarchal, male God. Or, to put it differently, the essentially loving, compassionate Yahweh, who loved his people passionately (as often depicted by the Hebrew prophets), found dramatic expression through the maternal figure of *Hokmah*/Sophia. The wisdom authors, whose writings are now part of our Scriptures, evidently appropriated the feminine characteristics of Isis and ascribed them to Yahweh. Yahweh's presence came to be identified in terms of Sophia — no longer far away in a distant place, but on the streets, in the marketplace, and in their homes. By personifying Sophia and linking her to Yahweh, the Israelites had a more concrete and approachable God to relate to and to worship. The personification of Sophia as a dimension of Yahweh thus made a positive impact upon the male concept of the Israelite God, allowing the Israelites to keep their faith in the one God of Israel rather than leaving him to follow this enticing cult goddess.

WISDOM AND MULTIFAITH HERMENEUTICS

As we have seen in chapter 2, the process of transmitting Christian faith from one culture to another is complex. To become the true faith of the people, Christianity needs to be inculturated and made comprehensible to those who receive it. In other words, it needs to be in some degree syncretistic. Inculturation and syncretism are not new phenomena, nor is multifaith hermeneutics. These strategies were practiced

---

67. For further discussion see Leonard Swidler, *Biblical Affirmations of Woman* (Philadelphia: Westminster Press, 1979), 29.

long ago. If Christ is to speak deeply to Korean North American women, Christology must draw upon their own Asian cultural and religious heritage, incorporating certain positive aspects of Asian religious traditions. In addition, since Korean North American women are bicultural, in-between women, they need to draw from their North American as well as their Korean culture if anything is to make sense to them.

Within the Asian cultures and religions, Wisdom is ever present in various forms. As an important concept within Buddhism and Confucianism, Wisdom has had a formative influence upon Korean women's lives, perhaps more than they consciously realize. Korean North American Christian women, as members of a permanently visible minority, need to be aware of their religio-cultural roots. Even though they are Christian, they can grow to be proud of a rich tradition, deepening their identity and dignity as Asian North Americans.

When comparing these various Wisdom figures, note the many similarities in deed and character. Both *Prajna* and Kuan-yin are feminine and have saving qualities. Both are much sought after by Asian women who cry out to them when they are in despair. Syncretizing these various figures into a Christian understanding of Wisdom is possible. Even Confucianism's central emphasis on Wisdom (though not feminine) is relevant to an inculturated Wisdom Christology. This chapter explored the ancient Hebrew (and syncretistic) roots of biblical *Hokmah*/Sophia by examining the character of Isis. To be meaningful for Korean North American women, Scripture must be read in the manner of a multifaith hermeneutics. In the next chapter, we use the lens of multifaith hermeneutics to study Wisdom as portrayed in the Bible.

~ Six ~

Biblical Sophia

WE COME NOW to the heart of our book, which proposes that Wisdom can usefully be retrieved for a Christology that is relevant to Korean North American women. A Christology must of course have scriptural foundations, and feminist biblical scholars and theologians have already found biblical Sophia to be fertile ground for feminist Christology. Since I wish to link biblical Sophia to Wisdom in Asian religious traditions, the issue of syncretism is a consideration of prime importance.

We have seen that the image of Sophia is similar to the other Asian female religious figures and images. We shall see that the character and roles of Sophia are similar to *prajna* and Kuan-yin. Because of these similarities, Korean North American women who are bicultural may well embrace Sophia as a way to understand the identity and works of Christ. As these women seek more appropriate ways to express how they have encountered the feminine aspect of the divine, Sophia provides an excellent way.

This chapter mainly examines Sophia as portrayed in the Hebrew Bible, the New Testament, and the Apocrypha, briefly exploring three books — Proverbs, Sirach (Ecclesiasticus), and Wisdom of Solomon — to see how they portray Sophia. These portrayals of Sophia are then linked with the New Testament understanding of Sophia. This chapter examines the books of Matthew and John and the writings of Paul to understand the association made between Jesus and Sophia, which association was very strong within New Testament times. Soon thereafter, Sophia Christology diminished and eventually almost disappeared. This chapter ends with a brief discussion of the similarities between Isis and Sophia, and *prajna* and Sophia.

SOPHIA IN THE HEBREW BIBLE
AND APOCRYPHAL WRITINGS

In Hebrew wisdom Scriptures and in Greek apocryphal wisdom writings, *Hokmah*/Sophia is evidently God and God's presence in the world. These ancient Jewish authors found in her "a way of speaking about YHWH in female imagery without falling into ditheism."[1] *Hokmah*/Sophia is found in Jewish Scripture and intertestamental literature. She is personified first in the late portion of the book of Proverbs (fifth century B.C.E.) and is more fully presented in the apocryphal books of Ecclesiasticus (second century B.C.E.) and the Wisdom of Solomon (first century B.C.E.).[2] Sophia is a complex female figure who personifies God's presence and creative action in the world. She comes forth from the mouth of the Most High, pervading and connecting all things. Sophia creates, redeems, sanctifies, establishes justice, and protects the poor. She searches the world for a dwelling place and pitches her tent in Jerusalem.[3]

Proverbs 1–9

Proverbs 1–9 portrays *Hokmah* (Wisdom) in a wide range of characters and roles. She emerges on the scene in the style of an Old Testament prophet, crying out in the streets, encouraging the "simple" and "scoffers" to gain deeper understanding (1:20–23; 8:1–6). She is an active character, participating closely in the lives of people. She does not wait for people to come to her, but rather takes the initiative herself. She confronts people in the market and at the city gates, crying a message of reproach, punishment, and promise. The people whom she confronts generally do not welcome or accept her, but rather reject her. People do not enthusiastically embrace her (1:24–27)[4] even though the author writes that "all the things you may desire cannot compare with her" (3:15), for "she is a tree of life" (3:18) and her

---

1. Harold Wells, "Trinitarian Feminism: Elizabeth Johnson's Wisdom Christology," *Theology Today* 52 (1995): 334.
2. Barbara Newman, "Some Medieval Theologians and the Sophia Tradition," *Downside Review* 108 (1990): 112.
3. Elizabeth A. Johnson, "Redeeming the Name of Christ," in *Freeing Theology,* ed. Catherine Mowry LaCugna (New York: HarperSanFrancisco, 1993), 120. Note that wisdom literature is also patriarchal and needs to be read with a hermeneutic of suspicion.
4. Elizabeth A. Johnson, "Jesus the Wisdom of God: A Biblical Basis for Non-Androcentric Christology," *Ephemerides Theologicae Lovanienses* 61 (1985): 264.

"fruit is better than gold" (8:19). Wisdom is beyond comparison with the jewels and riches of this world.

Hokmah is intimately associated with God and with creation, possessing a unique cosmic role: "I have been established from everlasting," she sings, "from the beginning, before there was ever an earth" (8:23). When God created the world, "I was beside him as a master craftsman; and I was daily his delight, rejoicing always before him ... " (8:30).[5] She is happy about her role in creation and six times emphasizes her existence before creation and her active engagement in the creative activity. "The Lord by wisdom founded the earth; by understanding he established the heavens"(3:19). Sophia describes herself as a "delight" and speaks of "playing" before God.[6]

Hokmah is portrayed as living wisdom in many passages in the book of Proverbs. For example, in Proverbs 4:1–2, 5–6, the author states, "Listen, my children, to a father's instruction; pay attention and learn what understanding is.... Do not forsake my teaching.... Acquire wisdom, acquire understanding, never forget her, never deviate from my words...love her, she will watch over you." She is also looked upon as the perfect teacher in Proverbs 8:1, 3–5, 8, 15–16, 18.[7] As teacher, she addresses the simple: "How long, O simple ones, will you love being simple?" (1:22) telling them that "those who listen to me will be secure and will live at ease, without dread of disaster" (1:33). Furthermore, she is spoken of as one by whom kings now and forever will reign, and by whom the social order is maintained. "I have good advice and sound wisdom; I have insight, I have strength ... " (8:14ff). She is to be found at the crossroads of life calling upon human beings to recognize her presence and receive her words which "are life to him who finds them" (1:20ff; 4:20ff; 8:1–36).[8] She is a beneficent, right-ordering power in whom God delights and by whom God creates; her constant effort is to lure human beings to life.[9] Proverbs 3:18 states that "She is a tree of life" and therefore those who come to know her will gain life. Her true value

5. Thomas Finger, "Holy Wisdom, Love So Bright: Sophia in Scripture and Worship," *Daughters of Sarah* 4 (1994): 29.

6. Roland E. Murphy, "Wisdom in the Old Testament," *The Anchor Bible Dictionary*, vol. 6, ed. David Noel Freedman (New York: Doubleday, 1992), 927.

7. Susan Cady and Hal Taussig, "Jesus and Sophia," *Daughters of Sarah* 14 (1988): 8.

8. Burton L. Mack, "Wisdom Myth and Mytho-logy," *Interpretation* 24 (1970): 47.

9. Elizabeth A. Johnson, *She Who Is* (New York: Crossroad, 1993), 88.

is her connection with life. She carries life in her right hand, "long life is in her right hand ... " (3:16) and is the bearer and sustainer of life to all who hold her in their decisive grasp; "she is a tree of life to those who lay hold of her; those who hold her fast are happy" (3:18).[10] She is bound by ties of love and affection to those who respond to her: "I love those who love me" (Prov. 8:17a). Proverbs 8:17b tells us how one loves wisdom and is loved by her: "those who seek me diligently find me." She is not only teacher, preacher, and principle of authority but also a lover.[11]

In *Hokmah*'s last appearance within the book of Proverbs, the street preacher, life giver, agent of just governance, and architect of creation becomes a compelling hostess (9:1–6). She builds a house, sets her table, and sends her maidservants out to the public cross-roads to be proclaimers of the invitation. To those who accept her invitation and seek her, she gives refreshment as she says, "Come, eat of my bread and drink of the wine I have mixed" (9:5). She is constantly trying to lure human beings to life, to leave foolish ways and walk in the ways of wisdom, which are ways of insight, justice, and peace. "Her ways are ways of pleasantness, and all her paths are peace" (3:17 and see also 8:20; 9:6).[12] To come to her table is to live in community and to share in the abundance of life. She delivers her invitation in four ways, as she shouts with joy, she lifts up her voice, she calls, and she speaks her words. She extends her invitation by her voice, by her spoken word, trying to catch the attention of everyone in the town. In Proverbs 1:22–33, she implores all within earshot, everyone who can hear her, to turn to her words, to accept her ad-vice, because it is all a matter of life and death.[13] Hence, the book of Proverbs portrays *Hokmah* as a prophet, creator, perfect teacher, and hostess.

Sirach

The book of Sirach, written in Greek, also contains some wisdom pas-sages as it builds upon the book of Proverbs. Sirach 24 has thirty-five

10. Kathleen M. O'Connor, *The Wisdom Literature* (Collegeville, Minn.: Liturgical Press, 1988), 74.
11. Celia Deutsch, "Wisdom in Matthew: Transformation of a Symbol," *Novum Testamentum* 32 (1990): 19.
12. Johnson, "Jesus the Wisdom of God," 265.
13. O'Connor, *The Wisdom Literature*, 70.

lines, and after a very brief introduction, personified Sophia delivers a twenty-two-line speech (24:3–22) in which she describes her origin from God, and also her heavenly and earthly activity.[14] The book of Sirach, like Proverbs, describes Sophia as having been created from the very beginning: "Wisdom was created before all other things" (1:4, and see also 24:9), as having been infused into all of God's works, "...he poured her out upon all his works" (1:9) and as a creator (1:7). However, Ben Sira adds a new dimension to the character of Sophia, for she now becomes identified with the Torah (24:23), "as a result of which both were conceived together as a heavenly element which descended from heaven to take up its abode among the children of Israel."[15] This identification with the Torah plays a significant role in the New Testament, since Jesus also becomes identified with the Torah. Ben Sira also shows that Sophia is to help and care for people. She is available to human beings and makes her dwelling among human beings (24:1–29) since her presence in the world is to be understood solely as a gift from God.[16] Thus, the familiar character of *Hokmah*, as found in the book of Proverbs, reemerges in the book of Sirach, but new characteristics are added to her identity.

In Sirach, Sophia holds sovereignty over all nations. Proclaiming her heavenly birth and queenship, she declares, "I came forth from the mouth of the Most High, and like a mist I covered the whole earth. I dwelt in the highest heavens, and my throne was in a pillar of cloud" (24:3, 4).[17] She declares how she alone made a grand proprietary tour of the heights and depths of the created world and its people. She searched the world for a resting place and was told by the creator to pitch her tent in Israel.[18] Sophia is also presented as a bride, characterized by images of fertility, such as fragrant spices, rivers, and the trees of life.[19] We see an increase, then, in Sophia's feminine characteristics and roles in the book of Sirach as compared to the book of Proverbs.

---

14. Alexander A. Di Lella, "Wisdom of Ben Sira," *Anchor Bible Dictionary,* vol. 6, ed. David Noel Freedman (New York: Doubleday, 1992), 937.

15. David Winston, "Wisdom of Solomon," *Anchor Bible Dictionary,* vol. 6, ed. David Noel Freedman (New York: Doubleday, 1992), 124.

16. Mack, "Wisdom Myth and Mytho-logy," 47.

17. Johnson, "Jesus the Wisdom of God," 265.

18. Johnson, *She Who Is,* 88.

19. Newman, "Some Medieval Theologians and the Sophia Tradition," 113.

In an imagery of love and feasting similar to Proverbs 8–9, Sophia invites everyone who desires her to come to her banquet (24:19–23). To those who eat at her table she promises a meal of sweet delicacies and the satisfaction of their deepest hungers (24:19–21). At the banquet, what is to be eaten and drunk is Sophia herself: "Those who eat of me will hunger for more, and those who drink of me will thirst for more" (24:21). She is food and drink; she is the source of nourishment, life, and refreshment. To partake of her, to eat her, to be joined with her, intensifies desire for communion with her. In language that anticipates the eucharistic language of Christians, the poem claims that the more one enjoys her, the more one seeks her, and less worthy desires fall away. Specifically, to eat at her table and to partake of communion with her mean to obey her and to labor with her. The obedience of which Sophia speaks, "whoever obeys me will not be put to shame ... " (v. 22) is obedience to the law (v. 23) and the labor that she enjoins (v. 22) is labor in the study of the Law, the book of the covenant of the Most High (v. 23). One participates in the festive banquet and lives in union with Sophia when one obeys the law of Israel.[20]

Specifically, in Sirach 51:13–20, we find a sage's invitation to come to him for instruction coupled with the exhortation to submit to Wisdom's yoke. The sage of Sirach 51 follows his invitation with an exhortation: "Submit your neck to her yoke, that your mind may accept her teaching" (v. 26). Yoke as an image for Wisdom and Torah also occurs in Sirach 6:18–37: "Put your feet into her fetters and your neck under her yoke. Stoop your shoulders and carry her and be not irked at her bonds" (vv. 25–26). The significance of "yoke" indicates labor in the quest for Wisdom and submission to her ways. In Sirach 51, the sage tells us that the way to procure the nourishment and refreshment of Sophia is to go to her: "Come aside to me. ... I open my mouth and speak of her: gain at no cost, Wisdom for yourselves" (vv. 23, 25).[21] Thus, in Sirach 51, Sophia summons people to draw close to her, to dwell in her house, and to put themselves under her yoke, so that they will discover that they have gained much rest.

---

20. Kathleen M. O'Connor, *The Wisdom Literature* (Wilmington, Del.: Michael Glazier, 1988), 143, 144.

21. Celia Deutsch, *Hidden Wisdom and the Easy Yoke: Wisdom, Torah and Discipleship in Matthew 11:25–30* (Sheffield: Sheffield Academic Press, 1987), 115.

Ben Sira stresses the paradoxical nature of the quest for Sophia. Her instruction occurs in a context of relationship between herself and her students, who are Sophia's "children" (4:11), and the one "who loves her loves life" (4:12). Her collar becomes a "glorious robe," her yoke a golden ornament (6:29–30).[22] Ben Sira begins his book by telling us that God created Wisdom and that she remains with God forever: "All wisdom is from the Lord, and with him it remains forever"(1:1). In this book, Sophia represents Torah, which is the book of the covenant of the Most High God (24:23). The universal and cosmic Sophia thus becomes particularly associated with the history of Israel and its precious covenant law.[23]

Wisdom of Solomon

The book of Wisdom, written in Greek, is probably the latest Jewish writing accepted as part of the Greek canon of the Jewish Scriptures. This writing is often entitled "Wisdom of Solomon," an attribution that may be explained by the fact that in the central section of the book, King Solomon speaks. Knowing who wrote the book of Wisdom is difficult.[24] Wisdom of Solomon was composed about the middle of the first century B.C.E., and it documents the convergence of Jewish Wisdom literature with apocalypticism and Hellenistic philosophy as well as with Israelite *Heilsgeschichte*.[25] In the first chapters of the book, we find only marginal reference to Sophia. Primarily the middle section (chs. 6–10) is devoted to the personified Sophia.[26]

Wisdom of Solomon can be divided into three parts. Part 1 (chs. 1–5) begins with an admonition in wisdom style to love justice and seek God (1:1–5) and to give no place to death in one's life. Part 2 (chs. 6–10) is a speech in praise of Wisdom. Part 3 (11:2–19:22) is a hymnic reminiscence of the exodus. The main theme is that

22. Celia M. Deutsch, *Lady Wisdom, Jesus and the Sages* (Valley Forge, Pa.: Trinity Press International, 1996), 11.

23. Johnson, *She Who Is*, 89.

24. Silvia Schroer, "The Book of Sophia," in *Searching the Scriptures: Volume Two: A Feminist Commentary*, ed. Elisabeth Schüssler Fiorenza (New York: Crossroad, 1994), 17, 21.

25. Robert L. Wilken, ed. *Aspects of Wisdom in Judaism and Early Christianity* (Notre Dame, Ind.: University of Notre Dame Press, 1975), 2.

26. Schroer, "The Book of Sophia," 23.

God's punishments of enemies correspond to God's favors to the just (11:5).[27]

In the Wisdom of Solomon, Sophia is presented as a figure of God as pure spirit, while retaining her role as creatrix and governor of the cosmos. Her identity, evoked in a fivefold metaphor, is linked to the mystery of God: Sophia "is a breath of the power of God, a pure emanation of the glory of the Almighty . . . a reflection of eternal light, a spotless mirror of the working of God and an image of his goodness" (7:25–26).[28] But Sophia is also immanent. Preexistent, she is "the fashioner of all things" (7:22; 8:6) and master architect shaping the world order according to Wisdom. She is the principle of order in the universe, " . . . and she orders all things well" (8:1). "She glorifies her noble birth by living with God" (8:3). Sophia is a divine consort who sits by God's throne; "give me the wisdom that sits by your throne" (9:4). She thus appears to be part of the ongoing creative process and is also the source of all good things (7:10–11) and present in all things (6:12–13; 7:27; 8:1). Because of her role in creation and because she lives with God, Sophia imparts to the one who receives her knowledge of the hidden things (7:17–22; 8:8), making them privy to the mysteries of the divine and created orders.[29] Sophia seems to gain more divine character and power over the earth than she had in the two previous wisdom books.

At the outset of Wisdom of Solomon, Sophia is presented as a people-loving spirit who will not, however, "enter a deceitful soul . . . " (1:4–6). Later she is described as being intelligent, holy, unique, subtle, loving the good, steadfast, clear . . . twenty attributes in all (7:22–23). Unlimited power is also ascribed to Sophia, as the author writes, "Though she is but one, she can do all things" (7:27) and " . . . while remaining in herself, she renews all things" (7:27). Sophia is presented as almighty and powerful. She is also the "mother" of all good things; "I rejoiced in them all, because wisdom leads them; but I did not know that she was their mother" (7:12), responsible for their existence and thus knowing their secrets.[30]

Among her many functions described throughout wisdom litera-

27. Ibid., 19–21.
28. Newman, "Some Medieval Theologians and the Sophia Tradition," 113.
29. Deutsch, "Wisdom in Matthew," 25.
30. Johnson, "Jesus the Wisdom of God," 267.

ture, Sophia has an intriguing role in the book of Wisdom of Solomon
as she plays a mediating character between God and human beings.
She is a consort of God on the one hand, and therefore knows all
mysteries, and a consort of the righteous man (King Solomon) on
the other, whereby the mysteries are then imparted to him (8:2–
9).[31] Furthermore, similar to the way Proverbs presents her, Sophia
is shown as a good teacher (9:9–12) and even directs Israel's history
(chapter 10).[32] The author associates Sophia with rest. He describes
Solomon as saying: "When I enter my house, I shall find rest with
her, for companionship with her has no bitterness and life with her
has no pain, but gladness and joy" (8:16).[33] Thus, Sophia provides
comfort and rest to those who seek her.

Redeeming agency belongs to her for she saves human beings;
"…and (they) were saved by wisdom" (9:18). Chapter 10 retells
Israel's salvation history from the first human being to the Exodus as
the story of Sophia's redeeming power, attributing to her the saving
deeds that are elsewhere recounted of Yahweh. She protected Adam
and delivered him from his sin (10:1). When Cain turned from her in
anger, he perished. When the earth was flooded, Sophia "again saved
it, steering the righteous man by a paltry piece of wood" (10:4).
She strengthened Abraham, saved Noah, rescued Lot, gave victory to
Jacob, and stayed in solidarity with Joseph when he went to the dun-
geon (10:3). She also worked through Moses to free the people from
bondage, leading them over the waters and guiding them through
the wilderness. Her saving power shows itself active in history as
she brings about the decisive revelatory and liberating events of her
people Israel.[34]

In the Wisdom of Solomon, she is spoken of as a guardian and
savior of God's people. She was the cloud by day and the fiery pillar
by night, the guardian who led the oppressed Israel out of Egypt and
punished the Egyptians. She also gave them water from a rocky cliff.[35]
Sophia is a mediator figure (8:2–9) who "rescued from troubles those

---

31. Mack, "Wisdom Myth and Mytho-logy," 48.
32. Cady and Taussig, "Jesus and Sophia," 8.
33. Celia Deutsch, "Wisdom and Torah Motifs in Matthew 11:25–30: A Critical and Comparative Study," Ph.D. thesis, Toronto School of Theology, 1984, 197.
34. Johnson, *She Who Is,* 89, 90.
35. Karen Jo Torjesen, "You Are the Christ: Five Portraits of Jesus from the Early Church," in *Jesus at 2000,* ed. Marcus J. Borg (Boulder: Westview Press, 1997), 76.

who served her" (10:9): "A holy people and blameless race wisdom delivered from a nation of oppressors" (10:15).[36]

The author of the Wisdom of Solomon identifies her as the spirit of prophecy: "in every generation she passes into holy souls and makes them friends of God and prophets" (7:27). She is the desirable bride — "...I desired to take her for my bride..."(8:2) — who is beyond all price (7:8–9) because she is herself the sum of all wealth. "All good things came to me along with her, and in her hands uncounted wealth"(7:11). She is the teacher who leads the student to discipline, understanding and a moral life (8:6–7; 9:11), and is acquired through prayer — "Therefore I prayed, and understanding was given me" (7:7) — and the search for instruction (6:17–20). The femaleness of this divine figure is also linked with knowledge, rule, teaching, counsel, the most exalted origins, the power to create, trustworthiness, salvation, guidance, virtue, and justice. Most of these characters are not ordinarily associated with the roles assigned to women in the patriarchal society.[37]

Wisdom of Solomon also links Sophia with the Spirit of God. She stands beside the throne of glory, "...and from the throne of your glory send her..." (9:10), and lives with God: "She glorifies her noble birth by living with God" (8:3). Thus, she is "an initiate in the knowledge of God." Wisdom's presence to God's counsels has a transcendent, hidden quality. She dwells with God, so human beings must seek her. Yet the author's final word is that Wisdom does indeed pervade all — "because of her pureness she pervades and penetrates all things" (7:24) — and thus she is easily found (6:12–14).[38] In Wisdom 9:17–18, God sends Wisdom from on High.

Wisdom is associated with the word through which God has made humankind (9:1–2). The author seems to identify the two in 9:1–2, and this identity becomes clear in 7:22, where Wisdom is said to possess an intelligent spirit, and again in 7:24, where the author tells us that Wisdom "pervades and penetrates all things."[39] She can also be spoken of in the same breath with God's *logos* in 9:1–2, as the

36. Lester L. Grabbe, *Wisdom of Solomon* (Sheffield: Sheffield Academic Press 1997), 79.
37. Schroer, "The Book of Sophia," 25.
38. Deutsch, *Hidden Wisdom and the Easy Yoke*, 59.
39. Ibid., 58.

means by which God fashioned humankind, a development that is employed in the *logos* hymn in John 1.[40]

The character of Sophia becomes fully developed over the centuries, as is evident in the three books of Wisdom. From the beginning of Sophia's appearance, she has a distinct personality and plays a definite role within society. As the three Wisdom books develop, Sophia becomes more feminine and even possesses maternal characteristics. Later Christians made a clear link between Sophia and Jesus, and Sophia served as a bridge between the Old and New Testaments. Soon, many of the characteristics and tasks of Sophia were transferred onto Jesus.

JESUS SOPHIA IN THE NEW TESTAMENT

At the time of Jesus, a community called Therapeutae worshiped Sophia. Therapeutae was comprised of celibate men and women living together in the same desert community. Therapeutae lived in the rural isolation in the vicinity of Alexandria and devoted themselves to prayer, Scripture, and an ascetic lifestyle. Out of a longing for eternal blessedness, they left earthly life behind them and fled into the countryside. Though they seemed to live and study separately during the week, women and men formed a single community in which women had the same status as men. The teaching of Sophia was a kind of heavenly food to them.[41] The faithful of the community, who probably relied on the Wisdom of Solomon as one of their key texts, practiced what was called the synousia, "spiritual marriage" with Sophia. This marriage hinged on the conviction that the soul can be united deeply and intimately, as in an actual sexual intercourse, with Sophia. Only through such an act of "knowledge" can the sage truly experience what or who God is.[42] Little evidence exists, however, of any other communities that venerated Sophia. When this community declined, so did the popularity of Sophia. Connections are possible between the Therapeutae and early Christianity.

---

40. Ben Witherington III, *Jesus the Sage: The Pilgrimage of Wisdom* (Minneapolis: Fortress Press, 1994), 108.

41. Schroer, "The Book of Sophia," 26.

42. Carl A. Raschke and Susan Doughty Raschke, *The Engendering God: Male and Female Faces of God* (Louisville, Ky.: Westminster John Knox Press, 1995), 44, 45.

The tradition of personified Sophia flourished anew when communities of Jewish Christians started to reflect on the saving significance and identity of Jesus of Nazareth. They tapped deeply into the tradition of personified Sophia to articulate the saving goodness they experienced in Jesus the Christ,[43] finding many similarities between the two. Belief in Jesus as Sophia's envoy or as Sophia's embodiment appeared very early in various areas — in Western Syria or Palestine (Q) and in Corinth (1 Cor. 1–4).[44] Since Jesus the Christ is depicted as divine Sophia, confessing Jesus as the incarnation of God imaged in female symbol is biblical. A Sophia Christology asserts that Jesus is Sophia in human form. Sophia as Jesus manifested the divine mystery in the creative and saving involvement in the world. Therefore, Sophia Christology reflects the depths of the mystery of God and points the way to an inclusive Christology in female symbols.[45]

Some of the earliest Christology understands the ministry and mission of Jesus as that of a prophet of Sophia who was sent to proclaim that the Sophia-God is the God of the poor, the outcasts, and all those suffering from injustice. New Testament studies show that two levels of reflection can be distinguished in early Christian theological discourses on Sophia. One, which may go back to the historical Jesus himself but barely traceable any longer, understands Jesus as messenger and prophet of Sophia. The other identifies Jesus with divine Wisdom. In early Christian discourses we find a middle stage where the attributes of Sophia were given to Jesus. Scholars debated whether the pre-Pauline hymns or the Fourth Gospel already identified Sophia and Christ or whether they see Jesus and his work only as a paradigm that interprets Jesus in analogy to divine Wisdom.[46] The God of Jesus is Israel's God in the gestalt and figure of divine Wisdom. Jesus proclaimed the *basileia* of God to everyone through his miracles and healing activities. One of the oldest sayings ascribed to Jesus stresses that "Sophia is justified or proven just by all her children" (Q Luke 7:35). This saying is likely set in the inclusive table-community of Jesus with sinners, tax collectors, and prostitutes. The Sophia God

43. Johnson, "Redeeming the Name of Christ," 121.

44. Johnson, "Jesus the Wisdom of God," 276.

45. Johnson, *She Who Is,* 99.

46. For further discussion see Elisabeth Schüssler Fiorenza, *Jesus: Miriam's Child, Sophia's Prophet* (New York: Continuum, 1994), 139.

of Jesus recognizes all Israel as her children. She is justified in and by all of them.[47] Sophia invites everyone into full human existence. She is the bridge between God and humans and between humans and the created world. She comes to the world to represent God.[48] The Gospels of Matthew and John, and the writings of Paul, all identify Jesus with Sophia.

Corinthians

Paul's first letter to the Corinthians declares the link between Sophia and Jesus. The first reference to Wisdom is 1:17, in the last sentence of the opening passage dealing with Corinthian factionalism; the last occurrence is 3:19, in the midst of a passage dealing with Paul's position as apostle in the Corinthian church. Paul goes so far as to suggest that true Wisdom is, in fact, nothing else but an understanding of the cross, the center of the Christian kerygma. Paul understands the crucifixion of Christ to be the center of a mystery belonging to God's redemptive plan (his Wisdom). None of the "rulers of this age" knew this plan, for if they had known this mysterious Wisdom then they would not have crucified Jesus.[49]

In Corinth, some scholars led by Wilckens[50] maintain that Sophia was a christological title used by an enthusiastic Christian group whom Paul opposed. Other scholars like Hengel[51] say that Paul independently associated Christ with Sophia through first characterizing him as the new Torah, already identified with Sophia since the time of Sirach (ch. 24). When Paul wrote that God has made Christ Jesus "our *Sophia,* our righteousness and sanctification and redemption"

---

47. This earliest tradition ascribes to Jesus and John the Baptist an eminence of meaning that heightens the significance of their work, emphasizing that the most prominent among the children of Sophia are John and Jesus, whose work continues in the Jesus communities. For further discussion see Elisabeth Schüssler Fiorenza, *Sharing Her Word* (Boston: Beacon Press, 1998), 166.

48. Kathleen M. O'Connor, *The Wisdom Literature* (Wilmington, Del.: Michael Glazier, 1998), 63.

49. Birger A. Pearson, "Hellenistic-Jewish Wisdom Speculation and Paul," in *Aspects of Wisdom in Judaism and Early Christianity,* ed. Robert L. Wilken (Notre Dame, Ind.: University of Notre Dame Press, 1975), 45, 57.

50. See Ulrich Wilckens, *Weisheir und Torheit: Eine Exegetisch-religionsgeschichtliche Untersuchung zu 1 Kor und 2* (Tübingen, 1959), as cited by Johnson, "Jesus, the Wisdom of God: A Biblical Basis for Non-Androcentric Christology," 277.

51. Martin Hengel, *Son of God,* as cited by Johnson, "Jesus, the Wisdom of God: A Biblical Basis for Non-Androcentric Christology," 277.

(1 Cor. 1:30), he was giving to Jesus the salvific function that pious Jews ascribed to Sophia-Torah. Divine Sophia is manifested in the cross and the preaching of the cross. This Wisdom of God is stronger than all human wisdom and is the source of our life.[52]

According to 1 Corinthians 1:18–31, the message of the cross is both folly to the wise, and at the same time the divine exposure of their alleged "wisdom" as folly. In 1 Corinthians 1:23–24, Paul writes, "we are preaching a crucified Christ...a Christ who is the power and the *Sophia* of God." "By God's action Jesus Christ has become our *Sophia*" (1 Cor. 1:30). Paul affirms that Christ is Wisdom as he describes Christ as "the power and Wisdom of God" (1 Cor. 1:24). The world did not know God through "wisdom," and so God chose to save it through folly instead, the folly of Christ crucified who is the Wisdom of God.[53] First Corinthians 1:30 states, "He is the source of your life in Christ Jesus, who became for us wisdom from God...." When the Greeks accept the foolishness of a crucified savior, he becomes the Wisdom of God for them. After their human philosophical categories are struck down, the crucified Christ turns out to be *Sophia* for them.[54] Thus Paul clearly identifies Jesus with divine Sophia.

The Sophialogical traces embedded in Paul's letter to the Corinthian community, in which women were leaders and active as prophets, recognize the Resurrected One as identical not only with the Spirit of God but also with Divine Sophia. This perspective was possible because in Hebrew and Aramaic both terms, "Spirit" and "Wisdom," are grammatically feminine. The meaning of Wisdom is probably expressed in the traditional christological formula of 1 Corinthians 1:24, "Christ the power of God and the wisdom of God," which confesses Christ as God's power and Sophia. The resurrected One is seen in 1 Corinthians as Divine Sophia who led Israel in the Exodus out of Egypt (1 Cor. 10:1–4). Christ is the Divine Sophia,

---

52. Johnson, "Jesus, the Wisdom of God: A Biblical Basis for Non-Androcentric Christology," 277.

53. Francis Watson, "Christ, Community, and the Critique of Ideology: A Theological Reading of 1 Corinthians 1:18–31," in *Nederlands Theologisch Tijdschrift* 46 (1992): 133.

54. Peter Lampe, "Theological Wisdom and the 'Word About the Cross': The Rhetorical Scheme in 1 Corinthians 1–4," *Interpretation* 44 (1990): 122.

secret and hidden: "But we speak God's wisdom, secret and hidden" (1 Cor. 2:7) but revealed to the initiates of Sophia.[55]

Paul applies to Jesus the unique creative role of Sophia and thus attributes to him a cosmic significance "extending far beyond the observable influence of the crucified prophet from Nazareth."[56] Paul described Wisdom as the knowledge of the divine realm that lay beyond the realm of chance, fate, and the daimonic powers that govern the created world. Paul's divine Wisdom is, in fact, hidden from the powers that rule the visible cosmos, those lower powers that control the material world. Like the writer of Matthew, Paul believes that Wisdom is the knowledge of God's secret purpose, of God's nature, of the depths that are beyond seeing, hearing, and imaging. Knowing Wisdom glorifies and dignifies the knower. In the Corinthian context the figure of divine Wisdom, who calls all and invites all to her banquet and becomes the teacher of all, was identified with Christ, who invites everyone — Jew and Greek, slave and free, male and female — to participate in divine Wisdom.[57]

Some notable parallels exist between Paul's letter and the book of Proverbs: "For us there is one God, the Father, from whom are all things and for whom we exist, and one Lord Jesus Christ, through whom are all things and through whom we exist" (1 Cor. 8:6). This passage is parallel to Proverbs 3:19, "The Lord by wisdom founded the earth," and with numerous other wisdom texts where Sophia is agent and mediator of creation, leading to the judgment that Paul here has implicitly identified Jesus Christ with the figure of personified Wisdom. By drawing similarities between Jesus Christ and Sophia, Paul was unmistakably attributing to Jesus a divine, cosmic significance.[58] He describes Jesus as "the Sophia of God" who by God's action has become "our Sophia" (1 Cor. 1:23–25; 2:6–8).[59] Human beings should thus cherish Jesus Sophia as a wonderful gift from God, who saves and liberates people.

---

55. Schüssler Fiorenza, *Jesus: Miriam's Child, Sophia's Prophet,* 149–50.

56. Karen Jo Torjesen, "You Are the Christ: Five Portraits of Jesus from the Early Church," in *Jesus at 2000,* ed. Marcus J. Borg (Boulder: Westview Press, 1997), 77.

57. Ibid., 77, 78.

58. Johnson, "Jesus, the Wisdom of God: A Biblical Basis for Non-Androcentric Christology," 278.

59. Letty M. Russell and J. Shannon Clarkson, *Dictionary of Feminist Theologies* (Louisville, Ky.: Westminster John Knox Press, 1996), 270.

Matthew

In Matthew too, the representation of Jesus as Sophia incarnate is developed nascently into a Sophia Christology. Just as Sophia came to earth in the Torah (Sirach 24), Matthew implies that she becomes present in the person of Jesus. Further, in Matthew, Jesus' rejection by his own bears resemblance to Sophia's rejection by the people. In the Sermon on the Mount, Matthew identifies Jesus as the true Torah just as Sophia is Torah personified in Sirach 24. Matthew understands that the disciples of Jesus are commissioned as envoys of Sophia to continue his work.[60] Much work remains to be done, and the workers left behind have a great task ahead of them.

The symbol of Wisdom provides an integrating element for the content of Matthew 11:1–14:13a. In the material of chapter 11, Jesus is presented as Sophia personified, assuming traits attributed to Sophia in the sapiential and intertestamental literature. Jesus is identified both as Messiah, Son of Man, and as Sophia (11:2, 19). He is rejected by the Galilean towns, who will not listen to him and will not repent (vv. 20–24). Jesus is presented as Son and Revealer, as intimate with the Father (vv. 25–27) and very clearly as Sophia, who invites all to come for rest and refreshment (vv. 28–30).[61] Chapter 13 depicts Jesus as a teacher of Wisdom, speaking at first to crowds, but then more and more to the disciples (vv. 10–23, 36–52), forming them to conserve and share the Good News (vv. 51–52). The Pharisees initiate opposition, each time in some way furthering the portrayal of Jesus as the Wise Man. Matthew also presents a scenario in which the person and mission of Jesus, already glimpsed as the Wisdom of God (11:2–30), is revealed ever more fully through continuing confrontation with the wise men of Judaism (12:6, 8, 28, 41, 42).[62]

Matthew puts Sophia's words in Jesus' mouth so that Jesus is presented as Sophia speaking. Matthew has Jesus say, "Therefore, I send you prophets and wise men and scribes, some of whom you will kill and crucify" (23:34). The saying is an oracle of Sophia: by transferring the words from Sophia, speaking in the future tense, to Jesus

---

60. O'Conner, *The Wisdom Literature,* 187, 188.

61. In these passages, it is understood that Jesus is associated with Wisdom. Sirach and Psalms both contain verses on Sophia inviting others (Ps. 9:1–6; Sir. 24:19–23).

62. B. Rod Doyle, "A Concern of the Evangelist: Pharisees in Matthew 12," *Australian Biblical Review* 34 (1986): 17, 30.

speaking in the present, Matthew ascribes her words to him and thus represents Jesus as Sophia speaking. Matthew attributes to Jesus one of Sophia's characteristic activities, that of sending envoys. In Matthew those envoys are now Jesus' disciples, including members of Matthew's own community who have known persecution.[63]

Matthew also edits Q to present Jesus' deeds as those of Sophia. "Wisdom is justified by her deeds" (Matt. 11:19). Jesus-Sophia, preacher of good news to the poor, healer of the suffering and friend of the marginalized tax collectors and sinners, becomes justified by those deeds, though in the end he is rejected. In the lament over Jerusalem, Jesus speaks a Wisdom oracle depicting himself as a caring mother bird before withdrawing like Sophia from the city that rejects him (Matt. 23:37–39).[64] In Matthew, Jesus is not just a lawgiver, but the embodiment of Torah-Sophia; he is not simply Sophia's child or envoy, but her embodiment. A clear association thus exists between Sophia and Jesus in the Gospel of Matthew. The writer believed that Jesus was a manifestation of Sophia and linked her words, deeds, and actions to Jesus.

Matthew 11:28–30 offers promise and hope to all who are burdened:

> "Come to me, all you that are weary and carrying heavy burdens, and I will give you rest. Take my yoke upon you, and learn from me; for I am gentle and humble in heart, and you will find rest for your souls. For my yoke is easy, and my burden is light." (Matt. 11:28–30, NRSV)

The passage contains concepts, familiar in wisdom literature, that are applied to the Torah and hence point to a trait of Matthew's Sophian Christology.[65] In this passage Jesus is described as Sophia, who is hidden, revealed, and transcendent. Matthew transforms the Wisdom myth as a vehicle through which the author legitimates Jesus' teaching and prophetic proclamation.[66]

---

63. Johnson, "Jesus, the Wisdom of God: A Biblical Basis for Non-Androcentric Christology," 281.

64. Ibid., 282.

65. James M. Robinson, "Jesus as Sophos and Sophia: Wisdom Tradition and the Gospels," in *Aspects of Wisdom in Judaism and Early Christianity,* ed. Robert L. Wilken (Notre Dame, Ind.: University of Notre Dame Press, 1975), 11.

66. Deutsch, "Wisdom in Matthew: Transformation of a Symbol," 47.

Every feature of Matthew 11:28–30 can be traced back to the Jewish Wisdom tradition. Most specifically, Sirach 51 has an invitation to "Submit your neck to her yoke..." (as discussed earlier in this chapter). In the New Testament, Matthew has Jesus speaking these words instead of Sophia,[67] which indicates that Jesus is Sophia, and like Sophia will offer us a place and give us rest. Matthew 11:28–30 shows Jesus to be not only Wisdom but sage, describing Wisdom as both hidden and revealed. Wisdom is Torah, and the yoke is that of Torah, or of God and God's reign. Wisdom is associated with rest and refreshment, but also with labor and discipline. Wisdom as Torah is the word of revelation that embodies the socio-religious order. So for Matthew, Jesus' yoke is sweet and he gives rest, because through him God is revealed. Just as Wisdom remains with Israel (Sirach 24; Wisdom of Solomon 10:13), Jesus, who is Wisdom, is also "God with us" (Matthew 1:23) who remains with his disciples until the consummation of the age (Matt. 28:20).[68]

Matthew 11:28–30 depicts Jesus as addressing all Israel and inviting them to leave their teachers and come to him. The rest promised by Jesus is not freedom from the law itself but rather his presence with his disciples, helping them to bear their yoke. The rest promised by Jesus is not simply a reward to be granted in the future but is a gift for the present life — a correlative of the response to the invitation to discipleship. In verse 28, one hears Jesus' call to those who have not yet become his disciples. In Matthew's Gospel, they are people who not only labor under the legal interpretation of the scribes and Pharisees, but more particularly, suffer from the lack of leadership. The yoke is an image for Wisdom or Torah, and it is easy and his burden light because the yoke brings one into fellowship with the gentle and lowly one.[69] In most Jewish literature, Wisdom or Torah gives rest or reward, providing refreshment and nourishment.

John

A connection also exists between Jesus and Sophia in the Gospel of John. Scholars even debate whether, according to the Fourth Gospel, Jesus is Sophia Incarnate or whether he replaces her altogether. The

---

67. Pheme Perkins, "Jesus: God's Wisdom," in *Word and World* 7 (1987): 275.
68. Deutsch, *Lady Wisdom, Jesus and the Sages,* 58, 59.
69. Deutsch, *Wisdom and Torah Motifs in Matthew 11:25–30,* 59, 62.

narrative characterization of Jesus seems to speak for the first. Like
Sophia-Isis, Jesus speaks in the revelatory "I am"–style, and with the
symbolism of bread, wine, and living water she invites people to eat
and drink. Jesus, like Sophia, proclaims a message aloud in public
places. Jesus, like Sophia, is the light and life of the world; to those
who seek and find her, Sophia-Jesus promises they will live and never
die. Similar to Sophia, Jesus calls people to make them her children
and friends.[70] Like Sophia, he is identified with the Torah. Those who
seek and find him (as with Sophia) are promised the gift of life.[71] Jesus
again gives this promise in John 3:16: "For God so loved the world
that he gave his only begotten son, that whoever believes in him will
not perish but have everlasting life."

The Gospel of John depicts Jesus as Sophia incarnate and the
outreaching love of God now enfleshed in a man. Jesus preexisted
creation as God's preexistent Wisdom. Jesus came down from above
in that he existed in the divine presence as Sophia.[72] John connects
Jesus to preexistent Wisdom in his *logos* prologue.[73] The author of
John uses the concept of *logos* (linguistic male gender) to identify
Jesus with God. Since the *logos* is not a strongly personified figure
in Jewish literature, the question arises of the origin of this term in
John. This prologue cannot have come into existence without the Jewish tradition of personified Wisdom. Word was made flesh and dwelt
among us (John 1:14) and can be the creative and saving presence of
Sophia in the world, coming to us in Christ.[74]

Scholars have shown the extensive parallels of the prologue to the
wisdom literature. The first fourteen verses appear to be a "patchwork
of phrases in praise of Wisdom." Harris argued that the hymn upon
which the prologue was based was actually a Jewish hymn in praise of
Sophia and not the original composition of the evangelist.[75] When the
evangelist's editorial additions have been removed, and Wisdom has
been substituted for *logos*, what remains is a Jewish hymn in praise

70. Schüssler Fiorenza, *Jesus: Miriam's Child, Sophia's Prophet,* 152.

71. Proverbs 9:6 has the Old Testament promise of "life" given by Wisdom.

72. Michael E. Willet, *Wisdom Christology in the Fourth Gospel* (San Francisco: Mellen
Research University Press, 1992), 126.

73. Letty Russell, "God with Us," in *Christian Century* 108 (1991): 1131.

74. Johnson, "Jesus, the Wisdom of God: A Biblical Basis for Non-Androcentric
Christology," 293.

75. J. R. Harris, *The Origin of the Prologue to St. John* (Cambridge: University Press,
1917), 4ff, 10–19, 43.

of Wisdom. The original hymn praised Wisdom as God's agent in creation, in whom was light and life, but who was rejected by the world. Sophia was received by the few, however, the "wise" and the "holy" among whom Sophia came to dwell, revealing her glory. Sophia was rejected not only by the world, but also by Israel.[76] When John reveals that Jesus is the *logos* by making life and light central attributes, John is clearly shaping Jesus in the image of Sophia. His portrait of Jesus shaped by the Sophia tradition is more than is found in any other Gospel.[77] This prologue is a powerful and eloquent affirmation that Jesus and Sophia are one.

The revelation of God in Sophia is also hidden. The inaccessibility of Wisdom is portrayed most prominently in the hymn of Job 28. Wisdom is hidden: "It (wisdom) is hidden from the eyes of all living" (Job 28:21) and the only one who knows the way to Wisdom is God (Job 28:23–27). Similarly, no one knows Jesus' way (John 7:35–36; 8:22; 14:5) except the Father. Jesus is at times hidden from unbelievers and even from the disciples, but out of the hiddenness, Jesus calls for persons to experience his revelation. Both Wisdom and Jesus are hidden revealers.[78]

Life is a central theme in the wisdom material. The revelation of Wisdom, like the revelation of Jesus, is the revelation of life. Like Jesus, Sophia bestows life upon her followers: "For whoever finds me finds life and obtains favor from the Lord" (Prov. 8:35–36). Just as Jesus is life (John 14:6), the Scriptures say of Sophia, "She is your life" (Prov. 4:13). The revelation of God brought by Sophia results in life for believers.[79]

Many similarities between Sophia and Jesus are apparent in John. Like Sophia, Jesus also calls out in a loud voice in public places and speaks in long discourses using the first-person pronoun. Like Sophia he invites people to come, eat and drink, making use of the symbols of bread and wine. He teaches divine truth and makes people friends of God, particularly instructing disciples and calling them children. Like Sophia he is identified with Torah, which is light and life for human

76. John Painter, "Christology and the History of the Johannine Community in the Prologue of the Fourth Gospel," in *New Testament Studies* 30 (1984): 465, 466.

77. Karen Jo Torjesen, "You Are the Christ: Five Portraits of Jesus from the Early Church," in *Jesus at 2000*, ed. Marcus J. Borg (Boulder: Westview Press, 1997), 77.

78. Willet, *Wisdom Christology in the Fourth Gospel*, 98.

79. Ibid., 124.

beings. Those who seek and find him (as with Sophia) are promised
the gift of life. Finally, he is rejected in ways that spell death and
destruction for the rejectors.[80]

BIBLICAL SOPHIA, ISIS, AND *PRAJNA*

We have discussed previously the character and identity of Sophia,
Isis, and *prajna*. At this point we take a closer look at similarities and
differences between these manifestations of Wisdom.

Sophia and Isis

Many likenesses between Isis and Sophia could indicate some borrowing and adapting. The similarities are important, for these indicate
that syncretism was present long ago during biblical times.

The Hebrew Wisdom literature speaks of *Hokmah* — Wisdom —
as God's own Wisdom. In the Greek (apocryphal) literature the term
Sophia is used, and both nouns are feminine, yet not only noun gender renders *Hokmah*/Sophia feminine. She is explicitly depicted and
personified as female. Isis, by identification as the Mother of the gods,
became without question the divine life force, and energizing and in-
dwelling nature, wherever she gained adherents. In her homeland, Isis
was depicted as mighty on the earth and great in the underworld. She
makes the Nile flood to swell, to embrace and fructify the field, creating all that exists.[81] Isis takes part in the creation and ordering of the
world, descending from her cosmic positions to establish and maintain the social order in relation to the cosmic. The wisdom hymn of
Proverbs 8:22ff also reflects this general cosmic, mythical pattern.[82]
Mythic material is thought to have been added in Proverbs 1:22ff
and 8:1ff to an older collection of Jewish wisdom sayings that had no
reference to a mythological figure of Sophia. Such additions were designed to deal with the problem of theodicy in the post-exilic Jewish
wisdom schools, or as a result of missionary and apologetic efforts to
offset the appeal of the Isis cult.[83]

---

80. Johnson, "Jesus, the Wisdom of God: A Biblical Basis for Non-Androcentric
Christology," 284.
81. R. E. Witt, *Isis in the Graeco-Roman World* (London: Camelot Press, 1971), 133.
82. Burton L. Mack, "Wisdom Myth and Mytho-logy," *Interpretation* 24 (1970): 54.
83. Robert L. Wilken, ed. *Aspects of Wisdom in Judaism and Early Christianity* (Notre
Dame, Ind.: University of Notre Dame Press, 1975), 29.

An analysis of the Wisdom hymn of Sirach 24:3ff reveals that the "mixing of motifs" is central to the Wisdom figure, and Isis and her myth are suggested as standing behind the hymn. A study of verses 3–7 reveals a hymn to Isis, taken up literally and retouched lightly at one or two points. In this passage, non-Jewish statements abound: "Wisdom goes forth from the mouth of God" (Sir. 24:3), for example, which comes from a statement from Egyptian theogony and cosmogony.[84] The words, "the mist rises to heaven," subsequently have Sophia/Isis reign on a pillar of cloud, which is heaven.[85] Isis also rules in the cosmos and over humankind as she is the "Mistress of every land" (Cyme 3a–Ios 2a). The words, "Alone I have made the circuit of the vault of heaven" (Sir. 24:5), are similar to those of Isis creating the cosmos and ruling it. Sirach 24:6 connects the goddess's rule in the cosmos with that over humankind. This corresponds to Isis as she claims to be the mistress of every land. These striking similarities reveal much borrowing from the cult of Isis.[86]

A study of the structure of the Wisdom of Solomon shows that the author was familiar with the goddess Isis. The book was most probably written in Alexandria in the late Ptolemaic or early Imperial period.[87] The author of the Wisdom of Solomon apparently patterned his book according to the structure of the Isis aretalogies as he used titles and concepts found in the Hellenized Isis cult. In this way he was able to deal with the craving of men and women in the Hellenistic age for unification with God and the salvation of the soul. The author wanted to portray an expression of his traditional faith that could

---

84. The Jewish concept would be that Wisdom was created (vv. 9ff, Prov. 8:22ff). In "Egypt: The Hymn of Creation," Gressmann, *Altorientalische Texte,* 1ff (Eng. trans. in Pritchard, *Ancient Near Eastern Texts,* 6f) the Almighty inseminates himself and spews out Shu (air) and Tefnut (mist); cf. the cosmogony of Heliopolis, in Siegfried Morenz, *Egyptian Religion,* trans. by Ann E. Keep (Ithaca, N.Y.: Cornell University Press, 1973), 163ff.; H. Kees, *Religionsgeschichtliche Lesebuch,* 10, p. 12. For more discussion see Hans Conzelmann, "The Mother of Wisdom," in *The Future of Our Religious Past: Essays in Honour of Rudolf Bultmann,* ed. James M. Robinson, trans. Charles E. Carlston and Robert P. Scharlemann (London: SCM Press, 1971), 235.

85. This pillar has nothing to do with the seven pillars of the House of Wisdom. It is Egyptian. Conzelmann, "The Mother of Wisdom," 236.

86. Other similarities, e.g., the passage about Wisdom finding her dwelling-place in Israel, can be traced back to Egypt. See Adolf Erman, *The Ancient Egyptians: A Source Book of Their Writings,* trans. Aylward M. Blackman (New York: Harper & Row Publishers, 1966), 140ff. (Hymn to Osiris, 18th Dynasty). For further discussion see Conzelmann, "The Mother of Wisdom," 240.

87. John S. Kloppenborg, "Isis and Sophia in the Book of Wisdom," *Harvard Theological Review* 75 (1982): 57.

match the depth of religious appeal of the Isis literature and cult. Thus the author incorporates concepts and materials from the Isis myth and cult into his own theological reflection.[88]

In Wisdom of Solomon, Sophia is presented as the divine agent by which the King first attains Kingship (6:20–21), by which he rules (8:10–16; 9:10–12), attains wisdom (8:2–21), influence and power (8:12–15), eternal Kingship (6:21), and immortality (8:13, 17). This depiction must have been borrowed from the Isis cult, since Isis was represented as counselor of the King. Isis determined who became King, fed the young King with the milk of life and good fortune, and supplied him with wealth, victory, and success. Isis promised wealth, success, prosperity, and long rule to people who were pious. Likewise, Sophia grants long life and eternal kingship to those people devoted to her. Clearly, Sophia as portrayed in Wisdom 8:2–9 displays remarkable similarities to the principal attributes of Isis.[89]

Isis's ability to act as savior derives from the fact that she was intimately associated with the powers of the cosmos. She was assigned major roles creating and sustaining, as well as controlling the stars, the crops, and the weather. Sophia too was given the ability to save the righteous in virtue of her intimate connection with cosmic forces. She was able to give instruction concerning ontology, cosmology, physics, astronomy, biology, and pharmacology, because she was responsible for the creation of all of these (Wisd. of Sol. 7:17–22). Like Isis, Sophia was responsible for the regulation and oversight of the cosmos. Furthermore, Sophia's guiding of boats is closely tied to one of Isis's major competencies, the protection and guidance of sailors. Sophia's act of making the righteous man wealthy (Wisd. of Sol. 10:11) is significant in view of the prevalent notion that Isis confers wealth upon the pious. Sophia's presence with the righteous person in prison also closely parallels Isis's promise to save prisoners when they pray to her.[90]

The general pattern of the three wisdom books and the figure of Sophia found within them show their similarities with her predecessor Isis. Eventually, Sophia's feminine attributes became accepted and welcomed by the Israelites. Sophia made her mark and took her place

88. Wilken, ed., *Aspects of Wisdom in Judaism and Early Christianity,* 30.
89. Kloppenborg, "Isis and Sophia in the Book of Wisdom," 61, 74, 75, 78.
90. Ibid., 68–71.

securely within the Jewish tradition. One of the foremost titles of Isis is "savior" (*pansoteria, soteira, soter*), and countless texts and inscriptions praise her as such. Like Isis, Sophia is pictured in the book of Wisdom as a Divine Savior figure who promises universal salvation. Yahweh, of course, was already "savior" in Israelite tradition, in Exodus, and in the prophets. This saving role of Yahweh is now ascribed to Sophia. "Sophia rescued from troubles those who served her" (10:9).[91]

Sophia and *Prajna*

The characteristics of *prajna* were discussed in the previous chapter, but many similarities between Sophia and *prajna* need to be highlighted. From ca. 200 B.C.E. onward, two distinct civilizations — one in the Mediterranean and the other in India — constructed from their own cultural antecedents a similar set of ideas about Wisdom, each one independently. In the eastern Mediterranean we have the Wisdom books of the Old Testament, nearly contemporaneous with the *Prajnaparamita* in its first form. Later, under the influence of Alexander, the Gnostics and Neo-Platonists developed a literature that assigned a central position to Wisdom (Sophia) which reveals a profusion of verbal coincidence with the *Prajnaparamita* texts.[92] Numerous similarities between *prajnaparamita* and Sophia exist. These similarities may provide a key as to how Korean North American women can easily and clearly identify with Sophia and use her as a way to understand Jesus that is nonoppressive and nonthreatening, and encouraging to them as Asian women.

Prajnaparamita (Supreme Wisdom), like Sophia, is supremely compassionate, rescuing humans from their ignorance and consequent suffering and *han*. *Prajna* is also a nurturer, sustainer, and liberator like Sophia. *Prajna* is empty of clinging and defilement. Faith in *prajnaparamita* will lead the disciple to release many fears and to recognize no division between matter and spirit, the world and nirvana.[93]

---

91. Elisabeth Schüssler Fiorenza, *Sharing Her Word* (Boston: Beacon Press, 1998), 161, 162.

92. Edward Conze, *Buddhism: Its Essence and Development* (New York: Harper & Brothers, 1959), 142.

93. Anne Bancroft, "Women in Buddhism," in *Women in the World's Religions, Past and Present,* ed. Ursula King (New York: Paragon House, 1987), 90.

Sophia and *prajna* are also similar in that Wisdom has essentially a liberation or soteriological function in Buddhism. Mere speculative knowledge is considered not only meaningless but also detrimental to the task of liberation. *Asrava* is identified with *duhkha* or suffering, and by destroying all *asravas,* the saint destroys suffering and wins happiness (*sukha*). The task of Wisdom is to make us *anasrava,* free from sufferings. The root evil or sin within the Buddhist doctrine is misconception, misknowledge, or ignorance. Wisdom, like a lamp, removes the darkness of false opinions, dispels doubts, and brings about tranquility and joy. Wisdom ultimately brings about purification (*Parisuddhi*) and liberation (*mukti*). This liberative Wisdom is attained through methodical meditation on the subjects recommended in the Scriptures.[94]

Jesus' association with Sophia in Matthew 11:28–30 illustrates that he is presented here speaking as personified Wisdom, indicating that Sophia Christology was vibrant during the time of the biblical writers. *Prajna* too offers hope for Korean North American women. *Prajna,* like Sophia, is a nurturer and takes care of those who are tired and weary, who need someone to nurture them since they are always the ones who are nurturing others. In addition *prajna* is a sustainer who will sustain those who are about to give up and uphold them throughout their life. Furthermore, like Sophia, *prajna* is a liberator, who offers freedom from the detrimental effects of a patriarchal and oppressive society.

The ultimate function of Wisdom within Buddhism is to open the door to liberation. A great deal of training in morals and meditation is required for its achievement.[95] Even the earliest Buddhists clearly held that one's sex, like one's caste or class (*varna*), presents no barrier to attaining the Buddhist's goal of liberation from suffering. Buddhism in its origins, above all else, was a pragmatic soteriology, a theory of liberation that sought to free humanity from suffering. Women were not excluded from this pursuit of liberation.[96] Similarly, Sophia

---

94. Lal Mani Joshi, "Faith and Wisdom in the Buddhist Tradition" in *Dialogue and Alliance* 1 (1987): 73.

95. Ibid., 74.

96. Alan Sponberg, "Attitudes Toward Women and the Feminine in Early Buddhism," in *Buddhism, Sexuality and Gender,* ed. José Ignacio Cabezón (Albany: State University of New York Press, 1992), 8.

also wants to liberate both men and women from all their struggles and pain.

The one difference between Sophia and *prajna* is that Sophia plays a definite role in the creation of the world, while *prajna* has no cosmic functions and remains unburdened by the genesis of the universe.[97] Putting Buddhism's *prajna* and Christianity's *Sophia* together is an example of an appropriate syncretism. The integration of these two religious concepts can be a helpful, constructive, and liberative venture for Korean North American women's theology and Christology.

Embracing the Feminine Wisdom Tradition

When one moves from Jewish Wisdom literature and the New Testament to the early Christian (postapostolic) writings, the figure of Divine Wisdom diminishes. Yet a critical reading of the texts shows that a submerged theology of Wisdom permeates the Christian Scriptures. Early Jewish discourses on divine Wisdom provided a theological "linguistic matrix" that was activated by early Christian communities. We have seen that in the Old Testament, Sophia was identified with the Torah, and in the New Testament, Jesus was sometimes identified with the Torah. As a result, some of the words, functions, and character of Sophia were now directly transferred to the human being Jesus. Jesus is seen as Sophia's envoy and even as Sophia herself. Jesus, like Sophia, was also rejected and exalted, and intimately related to God in the creating and saving activity in the world. The tradition of personified Sophia played a foundational role in the development of Christology, and some of the most profound christological assertions in the New Testament are made in its category.[98] Early Christian discourses after the New Testament period could have used the tradition of divine Wisdom together with other early Jewish tradition to elaborate the theological significance of Jesus.[99] However, this linkage did not occur to any significant degree.

The Israelites saw the importance of recognizing a feminine dimension to the divine. We, living in another time and place, should also recognize the importance of this approach, especially in our context

---

97. Conze, *Buddhism: Its Essence and Development,* 143.
98. Johnson, "Jesus, the Wisdom of God," 276.
99. Schüssler Fiorenza, *Jesus: Miriam's Child, Sophia's Prophet,* 139.

in which women have become so widely aware of their worth and essential equality with men. This feminine dimension is well exemplified through Sophia. Over the years, patriarchal forces have attempted to extricate Sophia from the Christian tradition. However, she offers many positive elements for women who seek to find liberative metaphors of the divine. She must remain with us. To follow Wisdom, to embrace her, and to live with her is to live with God — to recognize and to collaborate with the harmony and order of God in this world and to be transformed by it. Such a transformation means to leave behind the illusion of isolation, that we each live alone. To embrace Wisdom is to take up a communal holistic stance toward the world and its inhabitants, to live in community with all that is, to live in peace. Like women's culture, wisdom literature at its best insists on the centrality of relationship, on interconnection rather than independence, on reciprocity rather than competitive domination.[100] As we saw in the previous chapter, Korean women have an especially good reason to attend to Sophia Christology because of the feminine Wisdom tradition embedded in their ancient religio-cultural heritage.

Christianity has always been a mixing or adaptation of numerous religions. The similarities between Isis and Sophia and also between *prajna* and Sophia provide a strong argument for a new understanding of Sophia for Korean North American women, who are bicultural. Many themes found in the Wisdom literature are particularly important and beneficial for Korean North American women. The theme of new life in Sophia is clearly stated in many of the books. New life is what Korean North American women passionately desire as they try to find means to have new, fuller, less oppressive lives in a new time and place. They want their lives to be healed, restored, and revitalized. Sophia invites us to a banquet of life. If our lives are to be full, we must accept her invitation. Korean North American Christian women need to embrace Sophia as a way to understand who Jesus is for us. That embrace is the concern of the following chapter.

---

100. Kathleen M. O'Connor, "Wisdom Literature, Women's Culture and Peace: A Hermeneutical Reflection," in *Blessed Are the Peacemakers,* ed. Anthony J. Tambasco (New York: Paulist Press, 1989), 57.

~ Seven ~

The Grace of Sophia
and the Healing of *Han*

KOREAN NORTH AMERICAN WOMEN have been silenced and sub-ordinated for too long. They have endured hardships through their Confucian heritage and also from their immigrant lifestyles. Torn between two different cultures, they do not seem to fit in comfortably anywhere. To make matters worse, the church has rarely helped these women to become liberated. Instead, the church has reinforced their subordinate status by perpetuating notions of a masculine divinity. The imagery for God needs to expand to include more liberative metaphors from the Christian faith tradition. Female images of God are essential for maintaining the fullness of the image of God and for the promotion of equality between women and men. For a liberative understanding of God, Korean North American women need to break away from the present patriarchal framework and move to a more inclusive understanding of God and of Jesus Christ. Sophia Christology is already a major feature of white feminist theology. This chapter develops the proposition that Sophia Christology may also serve as a meaningful and liberative way forward for Korean North American women's Christology, particularly because of the wisdom tradition of Korean women's own religious and cultural roots. The insights of multifaith hermeneutics encourage us to seek a genuinely inculturated and syncretic Korean North American feminist Christology. Such a hermeneutic requires us to reinterpret the Scriptures from the perspective of different religious traditions.[1]

---

1. Kwok Pui-lan, *Discovering the Bible in a Non-Biblical World* (Maryknoll, N.Y.: Orbis Books, 1995), 93.

THE DISAPPEARANCE OF SOPHIA CHRISTOLOGY

The concept of an exclusively white male savior that has dominated Western Christology and therefore much of Christian thought is inadequate because women cannot identify with this image. Also, this image has marginalized women and people who are not white. In the first century C.E., the biblical community concentrated on what God had done for them in Jesus and who Jesus was in a functional way. The New Testament writers evidently had more than one Christology. In the second to seventh centuries, the Church used philosophical categories to talk about Jesus and raised questions about his nature and who he was that enabled him to be the Savior. Then during the eleventh to sixteenth centuries, a new process of reasoning and synthesizing occurred.[2] The historical development of Christology thus went through some changes. However, one approach that remained throughout history is the predominant identification of Christ with maleness.

Logos Christology reinforced the identification of Christ with maleness. The *logos* concept was a widespread and diffuse notion in the ancient world. The early Stoic philosophers believed that the *logos* was an impersonal "world soul," an ordering rational principle within the cosmos. In Greek thinking, the reason or mind is masculine because it derives from God. Women were considered deficient in reasoning and thus further in the chain of Being from the source of Reality. In the beginning of the Christian era, *logos* came to be understood in personal terms as a divine intermediary being who communicated knowledge of God to people. The Jewish philosopher Philo of Alexandria is considered a source for the Prologue to John's Gospel. The author of the Fourth Gospel drew on the Stoic-Platonic *logos* philosophy as well as Jewish biblical exegesis. Rosemary Radford Ruether argued that the founders of the Church need not have used the Greek philosophical concept of *logos* to explain their doctrine of the incarnation. They could have used the Jewish understanding of Wisdom.[3]

---

2. Elizabeth A. Johnson, *Consider Jesus: Waves of Renewal in Christology* (New York: Crossroad, 1990), 5–9.

3. Julie M. Hopkins, *Towards a Feminist Christology* (Grand Rapids: William B. Eerdmans, 1994), 83, 84.

Even though Sophia is present in many Old and New Testament passages, and a clear link exists between Jesus and Sophia, the interest in Sophia Christology seems to disappear by the end of the fourth century of the Christian tradition. As we have seen, John in his Prologue uses concepts that derive from earlier Sophia texts, but already replaces Sophia with *logos*. A reexamination of Church history reveals that *logos* Christology gradually gained prominence and attraction among the founders of the Church and theologians, which eventually contributed to the decline of Sophia. In the second century, Justin Martyr explained Jesus' deity, using the doctrine of the *logos*.[4] A little later, St. Irenaeus believed that the *logos* is associated with God. In the fourth century, Athanasius, the "winner" of the Council of Nicaea, reinforced the notion of *logos,* using it to talk about the Incarnation and the person of Christ to the detriment of Sophia Christology. This development emphasized the maleness of the second person of the Trinity and established an androcentric Christology, which still remains with us even today. Within the first four centuries of Church history, then, the association between Sophia and Jesus became lost and Jesus was soon identified only with *logos*. However, each generation must reexamine the past and the tradition that has been handed down. Theology must always be in dialogue with emerging cultures, societies, and other religions. Feminist theology offers a critique of this male notion of the incarnate one and suggests a return to Sophia Christology as a way of liberating both women and men from the apparent maleness of God.[5]

---

4. The interest in Sophia declined and remained in the background or in the footnotes of many thinkers and writers. A possible reason for the failure of Sophia Christology to flourish within the tradition may be due to the power of language. In a certain sense Christology is about naming our Christ figure and naming our God, and usually the one who holds power does the naming. The phenomenon of the power to name is illustrated in a book called *Black Sea*. This book examines the question of who the "barbarians" are and how they actually become labeled as barbarians. Researchers have discovered that nation-states often identified "barbarism" as the condition or ethic of their immediate eastward neighbor. Thus, for the French the Germans were barbarous, for Germans the Slavs, for the Poles the Russians, and for Russians the Mongol. Hence, barbarism depended on those who did the naming. Similarly within the Church, many of the issues surrounding Christology were resolved or adapted by groups or people who had the power to name. They preferred the term *logos* over Sophia. Neal Ascherson, *Black Sea: The Birthplace of Civilisation and Barbarism* (London: Vintage, 1996), 50.

5. Roman culture was eminently and innately patriarchal. The Germanic peoples of Northern Europe who fell heir to Caesar were equally so. In the meantime the Bible came to be read in Latin, and scholars in the West were not able to recover the original Greek and Hebrew texts until the sixteenth century. The name "Sophia" disappeared except in

Our North American society does not appreciate things that are resolved without "reason" and "knowledge." *Logos,* or reason, represents formal education. Sophia is thought to represent intuitive and informal edification. North American communities have thus suppressed the Sophia tradition. Anything different from reason, knowledge, or *logos* receives little honor, but people can move toward freedom through emphasizing Sophia. Sophia is another dimension of Jesus, who has been presented as *logos.* Sophia shows the other side of him, which is liberating, spontaneous, full of life, "feminine," and loving — elements that have been missing in Korean North American women's Christology.[6]

We have seen that feminist exegesis and theology have begun to retrieve the feminine aspect of the divine and are reexamining the Gospel story of Jesus as the story of Wisdom's child, Sophia incarnate. This association provides new possibilities for many feminist theologians who seek to find liberating aspects of Christ and to remain within the Christian faith. Feminist theology needs to reinterpret the symbol of Christ, to allow its ancient inclusivity to shine through[7] so that women will no longer be excluded or undermined, but rather, encouraged and strengthened in their womanhood.

With Jesus as Sophia, one encounters the mystery of God who is neither male nor female, but who, as Source of both and Creator of both in the divine image, can in turn be imaged as either.[8] E. Johnson, argues persuasively that Jesus came to be seen as God's "only begotten Son" only after he was identified with Sophia.[9] Thus he was first seen as an embodiment of Sophia, the female personification of the divine presence, and only later was he given the more popular title, Son of God. The *logos* Christology of John, masculinizing the

the Eastern church, where she became Hagia Sophia, "St. Sophia," after whom the great church in Constantinople was named. Carl A. Raschke and Susan Doughty Raschke, *The Engendering God: Male and Female Faces of God* (Louisville, Ky.: Westminster John Knox Press, 1995), 60.

6. This thought has been developed in conversation with Andrew Sung Park, Professor of Theology at United Theological Seminary, Dayton, Ohio.

7. Elizabeth A. Johnson, *She Who Is* (New York: Crossroad, 1993), 154.

8. Elizabeth A. Johnson, "Jesus the Wisdom of God," *Ephemerides Theologicae Lovanienses* 61 (1985): 280.

9. Elizabeth A. Johnson, "Redeeming the Name of Christ," in *Freeing Theology,* ed. Catherine Mowry LaCugna (New York: Paulist Press, 1970), 121. Elizabeth Johnson presents Sophia in a trinitarian manner. However, the focus here is on the second person, the one in whom Sophia is incarnate.

Sophia concept, came even later. Jesus' association with Sophia illustrates that Jesus' ability to be savior does not reside in his maleness but in his loving, liberating presence in the midst of evil and oppression. Theological speech about Jesus the Wisdom of God therefore shifts the focus of reflection away from maleness and onto the whole theological significance of what transpires in the Christ event.[10]

We have seen that *logos,* translated as "word," is a masculine concept and has been used to diminish or replace Sophia, which is clearly feminine. This Christology still remains dominant in many Christian Korean women's faith, but moving beyond this viewpoint to another Christology that is more welcoming of women is now necessary. Language is a truly powerful instrument that can mold or alter one's reality and perception of the world. Androcentric culture, classical theism, and *logos* Christology produced an exclusively masculine image and language about God and Jesus. Any feminine imagery or language about God was considered illegitimate or incorrect. Masculine language about God and Jesus has had negative effects on Christology. For example, if Jesus' maleness is interpreted as essential to his redeeming Christic function, then Christ serves as a religious tool for marginalizing and excluding women.[11] Some people take the gender of Jesus as the paradigm of what being human means, that maleness is closer to the human ideal than femaleness.[12] Furthermore, this paradigm perpetuates the idea that men (and not women) are created in the image of God and thus men are the only ones who can represent God on earth. The emphasis on the maleness of Jesus results in the understanding that men are better than women. Women thus come to be viewed as human beings in need of improving or bettering themselves by becoming more like men. The almost exclusive, historical use of *logos* Christology has diminished women and reinforced the patriarchal system that subordinates women to men in society and church.

KOREAN NORTH AMERICAN WOMEN'S STRUGGLE

Throughout my life, I have been trying to reconcile and re-image this male, white savior, whom I have found undesirable. I have struggled

---

10. Johnson, *She Who Is,* 167.
11. Ibid., 151.
12. Johnson, *Consider Jesus,* 104.

with the fact that a strictly male savior prevents women's search for the feminine aspect of the divine, with whom they can share and identify and by whom they can be empowered. The prayers said at church to the Father and to the Son have made me uneasy and caused me to question the legitimacy of using such language to address the holy one, who says, "I am who I am" (Exod. 3:14). The fact that Korean ministers and church members do not want women ministers because "it just does not seem right" has angered me and challenged me to find alternatives to the continuous use of male terms for Jesus. I have also had unpleasant experiences with male ministers who told me that I should not pursue ministry, for I am a woman and therefore cannot represent God. These male Korean ministers thought *they* could represent God, but *I* could not because of my gender. This has strengthened my continual search for an image of God and Jesus that would be more welcoming and embracing of all people, both women and men.

Furthermore, *logos* Christology has reinforced the thought that Western knowledge is better than Eastern thought or wisdom. Since *logos* in Greek philosophy connotes reason and rationality, the emphasis on *logos* in Christology seems to imply that "reason" and "rationality" are better than emotion and creativity. These dichotomies have not helped women's position historically — in society, family, and church — as women were usually identified with wisdom of a soft, inferior kind, and men with knowledge of a superior kind. Movement away from the dominant male mind-set, which has been part of our culture, society, politics, and religion, is necessary because this damaging mind-set hinders us from exercising the creativity that God has intended for us, preventing us from building a just society that can welcome and celebrate as whole beings women of all races, cultures, and religions. The search for a Christology that will be more inclusive and embracing of women and their gifts to the world is needed now.

Women are often powerless. Women are not powerless ontologically or by nature, but are made powerless by society, history, politics, and religion. These structures have radically removed power from women,[13] rendering them subordinate, subjugated, and oppressed.

---

13. I am graciously indebted to Dr. David Kwang sun Suh for his insights and conversation with me on power.

This section discusses these four ways in which women are left powerless so that we may understand what we need to do to obtain our original power and to regain full humanity.

First, Korean North American women experience powerlessness due to societal injustices. As we pointed out in chapter 3, the Confucian heritage and the patriarchal society of Korea have rendered women powerless. In many different ways, this socio-cultural milieu diminished women's voice, treating them as insignificant, unimportant, and unnecessary. Countless times I have been told by my parents and elders in the family to "be silent," for a woman is admired for her gentleness and silence. Silence is a virtue for Korean women. Elders in the family constantly remind me that no man, or in-laws, will appreciate a woman who voices her own opinions or makes criticisms of culture, society, or injustices in the world. A silent woman is much appreciated in Korean society. Hence, within this patriarchal society, people have attempted to render me powerless to do what is just and to make changes for a more equal society. My struggle has been to fight against the powers of a society that renders women powerless. In the process of fighting against this injustice, I have suffered socially by being labelled with undesirable names. This struggle has been difficult, but I feel the need to do so for the sake of the next generation of women.

Furthermore, Korean North American society generally prefers men to women. When a girl is born, there is less rejoicing than when a son is born. Sorrow accompanied the day that my cousin's wife gave birth to her second daughter. My aunt, the child's grandmother, even refused to visit her and the new baby at the hospital. For weeks, my aunt was angry, weary, and disturbed, and did not want to see her new granddaughter. She actually commented that a "death" has occurred in the family since her daughter-in-law did not bear a son. Korean society still values men so highly that women's powerlessness is present even at birth.

Second, history has repeatedly taught women to have little authority, be silent, and remain indoors. History reveals that patriarchy has been the dominant underlying ethos of most cultures. Patriarchy was prominent in Korean society, as revealed in its historical literature, religious practices, and cultural attitudes. Men's work, deeds, contributions, and thoughts are considered greater than those of any woman. Furthermore, remembering the male leaders, rulers, kings, teachers, and religious leaders is easy, but not so for the female ones. Women have not had many positions of power in history. Even in my own family history, the men were powerful and the authoritarian ones in the household. I still remember my grandfather ruling the house. Afraid to anger him or make him lose his temper, no one interfered with him. If he lost his temper, the whole house became chaotic, which no one wanted. Many of the women in our family lived in fear, and women obviously had less power than the men in the family.

Third, politics have favored men's rights over women's, which also has left women powerless. History reveals that the men in power developed and changed the laws, which favored those who already had power. For example, in many cases women are raped and the rapists evade prosecution. Throughout history, women have been raped often by father, brothers, or husbands, but the perpetrators are not charged. The following story of a rape victim illustrates how rapists are seldom charged in the courts.

> Bu-Nam Kim was born as the fifth daughter in a normal farmer's family. One day Bu-Nam (9 yrs.) was on the way to one of her friends' and bumped into Mr. Song (30 yrs.). She knew him well. He said, "Bu-Nam, can you run errands for me? Why don't you wait for me in my room?" She obeyed him and waited for him in his room. He came in and abruptly raped her. She felt a rupturing pain and was petrified by fear and terror. For ten days, she could not speak. From that time, she became quiet. Meeting any male made her heartbeat momentarily suspend. Unaware that this [was] happening, her mother used to say, "Like a cow, Bu-Nam is taciturn."
>
> At twenty-three, she married Mr. Choi, a farmer. But from the beginning, she had trouble in making love with him because of anxiety, guilt, and phobia created by the rape. One day, her husband asked the reason why she had been that way and she confessed the past incident. She was hospitalized and was divorced two months after the confession.
>
> Later, she married Mr. Lee, a truck driver, and had a son between them. When her husband was incarcerated due to an automobile accident and her life became miserable again, her

paranoia came back. Last June, while visiting her family at
Nam-Won-Kun, she met Mr. Song and demanded compensation
for her misery. Mr. Song avoided dealing with her directly but
only with her elder brother. Excluding her, they settled the issue
with the compensation of 400,000 Won ($570). When she re-
visited him to demand a suitable recompense, he reviled at her;
in return, she took the revenge into her own hands by killing
him.[14]

As women are made powerless within the political world, they are at
a loss as to where they can turn to seek justice.

Fourth, religion has played a large part in maintaining Korean
North American women in their powerless condition. Large components of Confucianism and Buddhism have honored men and
historically given power to them to allow only them to be teachers
and leaders. Christianity also has patriarchal roots. Women were only
ordained within the last fifty years in many of the dominant Protestant denominations, while Roman Catholic and Orthodox churches
refuse to ordain women even today. Korean North American women
are treated as second-class citizens and given menial tasks within the
church. They are prohibited from leadership positions, on the grounds
of "biblical teaching."

These four elements of powerlessness have grave effects on women's
day-to-day lives and have contributed to Korean North American
women's *han.* We have become immobilized to make changes in our
lives. We Korean North American women are thus the *minjung* of
society, who are doubly and triply oppressed. In this situation, what
will allow us to reclaim our full humanity? What will give us power
to make changes in our society? As a Christian theologian, I look to
Christ for liberative dimensions of his person and work that can help
in creating a just society.

A CHRISTOLOGY THAT SPEAKS TO TWO CULTURES

Some Korean theologians are reclaiming their indigenous religion of
Shamanism and are proposing that Jesus may be imaged as a shaman

---

14. As cited by Andrew Sung Park, *The Wounded Heart of God* (Nashville: Abingdon
Press, 1993), 32, from *The Korea Times* (Supplement), February 23, 1991.

priest. This approach, no doubt, has validity, especially in Korea. Korean North American women, however, are not likely to embrace something that is not authentic to their bisocial being and their bicultural experience. Western feminist theologians are also proposing new ways of understanding Jesus because his maleness is a problem for many white feminist women and for black womanist Christians. The male white Jesus is doubly alienating for Korean North American women, whose experiences, culture, and context are quite different from those of dominant white women.

Many feminist theologians have presented new understandings of Jesus that liberate us from narrowly male notions of Christ. Korean North American women cannot simply adopt many positive images of Christ in an unqualified way. Furthermore, as a Korean North American woman, I am dissatisfied with the Christologies that white feminist theologians present, in part because they do not speak to my cultural experiences, contexts, and religious heritages. Every group in society has its agenda, and white women's agenda is different from Korean North American women's. The white feminist theological agenda is essentially gender equality. Womanist theology also has its own agenda, which is to overcome racism and its influence on the church and on black people's consciousness, especially as this pertains to black women, who are doubly or triply victimized by sexism, racism, and poverty.[15] Although many Korean North American women are not economically poor, they have in common with African American women the need to deal with issues of sexism and of racism. Korean North American women too are a visible minority, suffering racial discrimination, together with the age-old sexism of both Korean and North American cultures. But Korean North American women need to go beyond these two issues and wrestle with yet another. These women have a distinct Asian history and culture, very different from that of either white or black women in North America. They still have vivid memories and often deep attachments to the religions and ways of life of another part of the world. Culture therefore plays a part in their agenda.

Asian culture, specifically Korean culture, plays an important role

---

15. Black women too have a distinct "culture," that is, the culture of African Americans, descended from slaves, and having a long history of severe oppression within the United States.

in the daily lives of Korean North American women. At the same time, these women find themselves within a North American culture that affects them daily at home, work, and church. This North American culture bears even upon their image of God. Korean North American women need to deal thoughtfully with cultural issues and to understand and critique their cultural situation systematically, which is why chapters 3 and 4 dealt at length with cultural heritage and related issues. Christology needs to arise authentically, not only from the Bible, but from the cultural roots of the people and also out of their experiences of *han* — oppression and domination. The premise of my argument is that culture is deeply important and that a Christology relevant to these particular women must include not only gender and race but also culture.

Every society has its own unique culture (or cultures), and women are generally said to be creators and sustainers of culture. Culture is always evolving and always needs criticism in light of changing circumstances. Both feminist consciousness (mainly learned from North American feminist thought) and postcolonial cultural consciousness have shown us that various elements of Asian culture, and of Christianity, have oppressed women. To break the cycle of oppression, women must engage in cultural criticism from the viewpoint of liberation and life. As we discussed earlier, Korean North American women are torn between two cultures as they try to embrace both cultures and attempt to live by them both. A very positive experience then, for Korean North Americans — both women and men — would be to maintain a bicultural existence, selecting appropriate elements of both cultural worlds to make the best adaptation according to the demands of social circumstances.[16] However, women often become pushed to the margins as they try to satisfy both cultures. On many occasions, they are caught also between generations, as they try to satisfy both older and younger family members. The older generation may prefer the traditional Asian values, while the younger generation may adapt to the more liberal, less rigid Western traditions. This dichotomy results in misunderstandings and conflict. Some resolution is required to help reconcile the generations.

---

16. Esther Ngan-Ling Chow, "The Feminist Movement: Where Are All the Asian American Women?" in *Making Waves: An Anthology of Writings by and about Asian American Women,* ed. Asian Women United of California (Boston: Beacon Press, 1989), 368.

As a Korean North American woman, I am bicultural and feel an intense need to reclaim the religious heritages of both Asia and the West. A (syncretic) contextualized Christian faith and theology could contribute to the emancipation of Korean North American women. Such a contextualized Christianity would have its basis in a new understanding of Jesus. We surely need a Jesus who will heal us of our pain, sorrow, and *han*. Many Korean North American women are abused and need healing from this situation. Our Christology must emerge from both worlds, resulting in a syncretic or hybridic understanding of Jesus. As discussed in the previous chapter, Wisdom is a concept or image that can come from both worlds.

In search of a Christology that addresses the issues discussed above, I am comforted to find feminine images of the divine in my Asian and Western cultures. Thus, to present a congruent and consistent Christology that satisfies the needs of Korean North American women, I present a syncretistic understanding of a Jesus who will heal, empower, and give courage to make changes in an unjust society. I propose, then, that Wisdom Christology, found in our Asian religions and culture as *prajna* and Kuan-yin, and also in our Christian tradition as Sophia, is a meaningful Christology for us. The Sophia Christology presented for Korean North American women is from their culture. What is needed is a multicultural and multifaith hermeneutic of Wisdom. As a Korean North American woman, I believe that the grace of Sophia can heal many deep wounds from *han* and can initiate the process of liberation.

Korean North American women live in the margins of society, which makes women experience themselves as shadows, semipersons who lack their own thoughts, feelings, and gifts. Life on the margin is spent trying to learn how to manipulate the people and groups with real power. The marginal life is a life of rage, expressed sometimes in child abuse, but more often unexpressed, except in depression or psychosis. Such a life is also one of invisibility, a life that sometimes even accepts as part of life battering and sexual abuse. Every woman in North America has experienced the life of powerlessness to some degree,[17] but visible minority women experience it in greater intensity.

---

17. Susan Cady, Marian Ronan, and Hal Taussig, *Sophia: The Future of Feminist Spirituality* (San Francisco: Harper & Row, 1986), 83.

Sophia can help transform this life. Korean North American women need to hold onto this promise and hope as they respond to the grace of divine Sophia, who will unconditionally accept and love them.

SOPHIA CHRISTOLOGY FOR KOREAN NORTH AMERICAN WOMEN

We have seen how *Hokmah*/Sophia, a personified hypostasis of God, grew in stature and importance for the Jews from the fourth to the first centuries B.C.E. until her power was equivalent or superior to that of any Hellenistic goddess. The goddess Isis was one of many deities, but *Hokmah*/Sophia was a dimension of the one God for the Jews. As a dimension of the one God of Israel, she allowed the Jews to remain monotheists, while providing a gracious feminine divine presence in their world. Then, by the beginning of the Christian era, Sophia was portrayed as acting in history and assuming the roles of judge and savior of the Jewish people. She became identified with Jesus and with his salvific powers. Matthew 11:28–30, which reflects Sirach 51, actually has Jesus speaking the words of Sophia. "Put your neck under her yoke, and let your souls receive instruction; it is to be found close by. See with your own eyes that I have labored but little and found for myself much serenity. Hear but a little of my instruction, and through me you will acquire silver and gold." This passage, which is discussed in greater depth in the next section, is meaningful for Korean North American women who are struggling and burdened.

The close identification between Jesus and Sophia became virtually lost as the strong influence of *logos* Christology made its way into the dominant theology. A similar situation exists in the Korean tradition, for many people are not familiar with the roles and powers of *prajna* and Kuan-yin. Even though these concepts are powerful and desirable, many Korean women have forgotten their existence.

In Korean culture, Sophia, "Wisdom," is generally identified with women, while *logos*, reasoning knowledge, is identified with men. In this respect, Eastern and Western perceptions coincide or overlap, perhaps because of the feminine aspect of wisdom in both cultures, which led to its decline in popularity. Sexism in the West and East seem to resemble one another, but, ironically, potentially feminist dimen-

sions of both Western and Eastern religions and cultures recognize the
strength and grace of the female. We have already seen in previous
chapters, in both biblical and Buddhist traditions, an acknowledge-
ment of the feminine dimension of the divine. Asian women have been
able to survive with dignity and grace through *prajna* and Kuan-yin.
In the Hebrew Bible, wisdom authors felt that life is worth living
even during the darkest moments, because of the gracious presence
of *Hokmah*/Sophia. Korean North American women often feel life to
be unbearable, but through Jesus/God they are able to persevere.

Sophia Christology emphasizes characteristics of Jesus that are traditionally associated with the feminine. As feminine, Sophia is caring
and nurturing, yet enduring and powerful. Sophia Christology makes
it clear that women have access to the divine and that the masculine
character of the divine does not stand between women and God. Another important aspect of Sophia Christology that may be attractive
for Korean North American women is that Sophia Christology does
not have the tendency of a *logos* Christology to turn Jesus Christ into
an abstraction.[18] Korean North American women's theology is formulated in part through an examination and analysis of their context and
experience. Presenting a concrete rather than abstract understanding
of Christ is important. These women need to encounter Christ in
direct relation to their own experience of oppression and marginalization. Culture can be their tool to grasp Jesus as Sophia. Sophia
Christology accomplishes this and also brings Sophia to the people
so that they can grasp her from the grassroots level. Korean North
American women can encounter Christ within the experiences of their
everyday lives.

Some of the earliest traditions of the Jesus movement understood
the mission of Jesus as that of a prophet of Sophia sent to proclaim
that the Sophia-God of Jesus is the God of the poor, the outcasts
and all people suffering from injustice.[19] Consonant with such a vision of God, Korean North American women may indeed be drawn
into movements of liberation and justice, not only for themselves,
but for all the poor, outcasts, and sufferers. Such women may indeed

---

18. John B. Cobb Jr., "Christ Beyond Creative Transformation," *Encountering Jesus: A
Debate on Christology,* ed. Stephen T. Davis (Atlanta: John Knox Press, 1988), 168.
19. Elisabeth Schüssler Fiorenza, *Jesus: Miriam's Child, Sophia's Prophet* (New York:
Continuum, 1994), 140.

be motivated to be at the forefront in movements that defend black people, especially black women, or Native or Hispanic people, or movements that defend the economic interests of third-world peoples. Sophia Christology should not lead Korean North American women only to a defense of their own interests.

Sophia is clearly given a place in creation and redemption, as she is both Creator and Savior. Wisdom was operative in salvation history, rescuing and protecting the early heroes of Israel's faith (Wisdom of Solomon 10). Wisdom of Solomon gives historical illustrations of how "people...were saved by Wisdom" (9:18). In six stanzas, salvation history is recounted from Adam to Moses. The leading actor is not "God" but Sophia. Sophia saved people in the Exodus, demonstrating that she stands for liberation and justice.[20] Sophia was a savior in Israel's past and she continues to be a savior in the present. She will continue to save, rescue, protect, and deliver people, including Korean North American women, in their struggle for an exodus from their restricted, marginalized existence.

Thus we see that Sophia is not only a cosmological principle but also a soteriological principle that God uses to bring people to God-self. Sophia does not remain passive but actively goes out in search of the faithful. Sophia calls people to come to her, as in Proverbs, but also goes in search of disciples so that she may reveal herself to them. In so doing, she reveals God, for she is "an initiate in the knowledge of God" (Wisdom of Solomon 8:4).[21] As Sophia goes out in search of Korean North American women, she will find those who have strayed away and have left the community of fellow believers. Sophia will seek and bring back those who have left the church because of the injustices and inequalities that they have experienced.

We should keep in mind, though, that some Korean North American women are very prosperous and comfortable. Some are quite unaware of their own oppressive situation and of their need for emancipation. They may not be conscious of their own subordinated condition. Sophia can also reach out to these women, to awaken and challenge them. She may well even disturb their lives so that they may contribute to the emancipation of all women and men.

20. Michael E. Willet, *Wisdom Christology in the Fourth Gospel* (San Francisco: Mellen Research University Press, 1992), 16. Also refer to chapter 4 of this book.
21. Ibid., 16.

Sophia, then, has many saving qualities. The gospel can be proclaimed as the story of the prophet and child of Sophia, sent to
announce that God is the God of all-inclusive love who wills the
wholeness and humanity of everyone, especially of the poor and the
heavy burdened, the outcast and those who suffer injustice, sent to
gather them all under the wings of their gracious Sophia.[22] Sophia
loves everyone and desires well-being and justice for all, both men
and women, without exception. Jesus-Sophia is preacher of the good
news to the poor, healer of the suffering, and friend of the marginalized tax collectors and sinners. She welcomes everyone that the world
has rejected. She is "justified by her good deeds," though in the end
she herself is rejected,[23] which is the graciousness of Sophia. Though
human beings do not deserve it, Sophia reaches out to humanity and
saves, liberates, and loves those who are burdened and oppressed.

Sophia, who is proud of herself, is also strong and assertive.
"Sophia speaks her own praises, in the midst of her people she glories
in herself" (Ecclus. 24:1).[24] Korean North American women should
emulate her and find within themselves aspects that are worthy of
praise. They should be proud and excited about what they find in
each other. In addition, Sophia is the warm and nurturing one. "A
tree of life for those who hold her fast" (Prov. 3:18), she provides
shelter and nourishment to those who seek her. The role of nurturer
is a familiar one for the majority of Korean North American women.
Sophia's divine status demands respect for the work that women can
do to enhance life and promote growth.[25]

The use of wisdom categories to interpret Jesus has profound consequences for the church and for Korean North American women.
This view enables the Korean North American Christian community
to attribute cosmic significance to the crucified Jesus, relating him to
the creation and governance of the world and deepening their understanding of Jesus' salvific power by placing them in continuity with
Sophia's saving work throughout history. Using the wisdom categories
in this way also becomes a vehicle for developing insight into Jesus'

---

22. Johnson, "Jesus, the Wisdom of God: A Biblical Basis for Non-Androcentric
Christology," 291.
23. Ibid., 282.
24. Cady, Ronan, and Taussig, *Sophia: The Future of Feminist Spirituality*, 84.
25. Ibid., 85.

ontological relationship with God.[26] In addition, Jesus identified in wisdom terms goes some way toward overcoming the detrimental effects of traditional Christology on women. Sophia provides an alternate image of God doing traditionally divine things, such as creating, saving, and guiding the world.[27] Furthermore, Korean North American women can gain power and courage to participate fully in the ministry of the Word that Sophia leads. Women can celebrate their womanhood and their differences rather than trying to become like men. Sophian Christology calls the church to conversion, away from sexism and toward a community of the discipleship of equals, for the sake of its mission in the world.[28] The knowledge of Jesus as Sophia opens the door for Korean North American women to seek and to claim their rich inheritance.

Sophia imagery does more than depict Jesus as prophet, sage, *logos,* and Son of God. Sophia changes the theological and spiritual landscape for all who recognize her presence. She provides images and characteristics that are lacking in the male notions of God, offering new ways of understanding the divine. A basic change is for women, especially Korean North American women, to be able to identify with her.[29] With this retrieved image of Jesus as Sophia, women who felt excluded and neglected as they were prevented from full participation in God's work will find comfort, hope, and strength in the knowledge that they resemble and are like her. The very identification of women with Sophia brings affirmation of women's own experience, bodies, and power,[30] which are different from men's. Therefore, through the association of Jesus as Sophia, women are finally able to freely name their experiences and rejoice in them. Sophian Christology paves the way for theologians to be creative when they talk about God and Jesus. The identity of Christ cannot be captured for all time but continues to be revealed even in the present time. No longer are Christians limited to the traditional notions of who God and Jesus are but are

---

26. Elizabeth A. Johnson, "Wisdom Was Made Flesh and Pitched Her Tent among Us," in *Reconstructing the Christ Symbol,* ed. Maryanne Stevens (New York: Paulist Press, 1993), 105.

27. Johnson, "Jesus the Wisdom of God," 293.

28. Johnson, "Redeeming the Name of Christ," 134.

29. Susan Cady and Hal Taussig, "Jesus and Sophia," *Daughters of Sarah* 14 (1988): 11.

30. Ibid., 11.

encouraged to delve into newer understandings of who Christ is and will become.

SOPHIA RELEASES KOREAN NORTH AMERICAN WOMEN'S *HAN*

As we have said, white women try to overcome the negative effects of the long centuries of a male Jesus and a male God. Black women try to overcome the destructive, racist effects of a white male Jesus. Korean North American women also need to overcome their cultural boundaries, their gender-related limitations, and their *han*. As we discussed in chapter 3, Korean North American women have a profound *han* accumulated throughout their lives. They are *minjung* who are triply oppressed in this Western culture. As Christian women, they seek to release their *han* through Christianity. Only a theology that releases their *han* can be truly salvific and health-giving. Different women have different needs and agendas when they engage in theology. Korean North American women as a group have suffered like the people of Israel in the past. They too asked the question, "Why must we suffer?" In the attempt to answer this question, Wisdom then becomes, as in Job, a way in which to come to terms with human suffering. In Baruch, suffering is explained as the result of the rejection of Wisdom, as known in the Law.[31]

Church history reveals that Sophia has been ignored for a long time, not only in the Jewish tradition but also in the Christian tradition. Perhaps this rejection may be related to Korean North American women's suffering, as they also have not embraced the liberating aspects of Wisdom. Openly accepting and embracing Sophia might be one way to rectify this situation. Korean North American women have not been able to articulate that through their own culture and religion they have already been embracing Sophia herself. In the past, through their religion and culture, they understood and welcomed *prajna* and Kuan-yin as part of their religious identity. Now that a clear connection can be made between feminine wisdom figures, embracing Sophia as a welcome addition to their Christian belief and faith is necessary. These women now need to understand and artic-

---

31. Willet, *Wisdom Christology in the Fourth Gospel,* 15.

ulate that they have already been embracing Sophia all along. They
need to connect their own Asian wisdom understandings with Sophia,
for ultimately divine Sophia incarnate in Jesus will release them of
their *han*.

Sophia offers many attributes that are favorable to Korean North
American women. The Matthew 11:28–30 passage contains two
helpful traits of Sophia. One trait is that Sophia can provide Korean
North American women with "rest." "Rest" in the biblical texts is
a profoundly spiritual term, having to do with inner peace, assurance, and hope. But at the most basic, mundane level, Korean North
American women need to give themselves permission for — and, if
necessary, demand — a reduction of their domestic labor. Korean
North American women often overwork with the burden of housework and work outside the home. Their actual work in the home
and for the family must be more fairly shared with men. Women deserve this basic issue of justice. Sophia can help them to know that
they deserve this rest and should demand it. In order for them to go
out and make a difference in their lives and the lives of their sisters,
they first need to rest. Through resting, these women may find peace
within themselves and release from all the demands of family. They
also need rest so that they can be refreshed and revived for a good,
healthy approach to life.

The second trait that is favorable for Korean North American
women is that Sophia offers refreshment and nourishment. Korean
North American women need to be fed and given the proper nourishment for them to be replenished and given the strength to carry on.
Even Proverbs 9 suggests that Sophia prepared her life-giving food for
people. Her whole house and granaries are full of fruits and harvest,
and she fills her guests with wine (Prov. 9:16).[32] Korean North American women are also the guests of divine Sophia and can be nourished
and revived as they try to live a new life with her. They have carried
and accumulated so much burden and *han* throughout their lives.
For many, their *han* just builds up until they eventually die with it. As
Sophia offers refreshment and nourishment, these women will be revived, renewed, and strengthened to carry on. Sophia offers women

---

32. Judith E. McKinlay, *Gendering Wisdom the Host: Biblical Invitations to Eat and
Drink* (Sheffield: Sheffield Academic Press, 1996), 148.

a place to bring their burdens and lay them at her feet. As Sophia feeds them, she offers them new interpretations of the Scriptures. She mediates the knowledge of God, which is good news for everyone. No longer do Korean North American women have to accept and be chained to traditional misinterpretations of the Bible, which have been used to keep women down as second-class citizens. Jesus Sophia is a powerful image that offers new hope, possibilities, and liberation to these women. The description of Sophia's yoke as "easy" and the "burden" light enhances the gracious quality of the invitation.[33]

The new vision that Sophia Christology provides for Korean North American women is also a life of harmony with creation. Sophia is related to ecofeminism in that Sophia wants harmony throughout all of creation, which includes humanity and nature. Sophia does not want humanity to dominate over nature but to live in harmony with it. To most men, and especially to men of the West, nature appears as something to be dominated, and unfortunately nature is frequently linked with women. "The domination of women's labor is essential to an understanding of the cultural metaphor of dominated nature as dominated woman."[34] The emancipation of women and the release of their *han* are closely related to the emancipation of nature and of nature's *han*. Creation itself is experiencing a vast and deep *han*, as humanity misuses it and tortures it for humanity's own convenience and benefit. Nature too must be saved before it is ultimately destroyed. In this way, Sophia helps to heal the *han* of the earth and of humanity.

Han is to a great extent the result of sin, usually someone else's sin of injustice, and can also result from natural calamities. Human beings cannot rectify sin alone; God needs to deal with sin. Changing the sinful ways of human beings is difficult, and we do not naively imagine that sin will disappear. *Han*, on the other hand, is different in that it is suffering — unjust suffering. We do not expect it to be completely eradicated. However, we do not have to resign ourselves to it without struggle. Human beings can try to reduce one's own

---

33. Russell Pregeant, "The Wisdom Passages in Matthew's Story" ed. David J. Lull, in *SBL Seminar Papers* (Atlanta: Scholars Press, 1990), 482.

34. Rosemary Radford Ruether, *Sexism and God-Talk: Toward a Feminist Theology* (Boston: Beacon Press, 1983), 74. Also Elizabeth A. Johnson, *Women, Earth and Creator Spirit* (New York: Paulist Press, 1993). The connection between the domination of nature and of women is explored by ecofeminist writers.

han or another's *han* by striving to eliminate the injustices of society. For this reason, Sophia is so important for Korean North American women, for Sophia not only releases their *han,* but also empowers them to release the *han* of others.

Han is not only a result of sin but is in some respects like sin. Sin has separated us from God, from one another, and from the natural world; someone/something was needed to break humanity away from the bonds of sin. *Han* also alienates in this way. Like sin, *han's* bondage over these women also needs to be broken. *Han* has been like a crucifixion for Korean North American women and has had many crippling effects. Now we need to crucify the way things were. We need to experience a resurrection from the past, which has been overbearing, overburdening, dominating, and suppressing. Now we need to envisage how we want things to be. Having *han* provided a framework in which Korean North American women operated. *Han* has been valuable (strangely enough), in that it realistically recognized and named the unjust suffering as part of life. The power and actions of Sophia can overcome *han.* We need to move away from *han* to deliverance and resurrection. We need to experience real deliverance — resurrection in this world and not just in the world to come. This deliverance can come through the grace of Sophia, for she will eliminate the overbearing stronghold that *han* has played in the lives of these women. The elimination of *han* from one's life is a liberating and empowering experience.

In Western society, *han* can be somewhat linked to "fate."[35] Fate in ancient Western tradition is like destiny, and it can become an excuse for something occurring and for not doing anything about it. We just resign ourselves and say, "Since it is fate, we cannot really change the situation." However, fate is self defeating, preventing change or willingness to change. Similarly, *han* becomes an excuse not to act or do anything to change a situation, as we fail to take responsibility for our actions. For any change to come about, we need to eradicate fate. Discrediting fate will allow us to make responsible, moral decisions, and for Korean North American women, removing fate is essential to removing *han. Han* thus needs to be unraveled, which can

---

35. This thought of the unconventional Sophia and "fate" has developed from conversation with Dr. Calvin Pater, professor of church history at Knox College, Toronto.

be done either negatively or positively. If resolved negatively, the *han*-ridden person may seek revenge, sometimes even killing oppressors or causing other serious damage. However, if unraveled positively, *han* can be transformed into the energy for social, religious, and political change for building up a new community.[36] This transformation can happen with the aid of Sophia, as Korean women have already been bringing their *han* to Kuan-yin.

Some people view Sophia as unconventional, for she exists in the realm of freedom. She insists that human beings are not puppets but have free will to choose. She challenges the ways things are, especially conventional things. Sophia is unpredictable and spontaneous, challenging the logic of systems. No one can contain her. Through her we rid ourselves of the confining elements of *han,* which is why Sophia is meaningful and powerful. But to be whole and authentic, women need to break the bonds of *han. Han* is not and should not be the essence of women. *Han* is a negative cultural conventional reality in which people find themselves and not a biological reality. We are to achieve freedom through the unconventional. Divine Sophia is indeed unconventional!

Sophia is important because she presents hope, new life, and liberation for Korean North American women who have lived under the bondage of *han.* The liberative elements of Kuan-yin and *prajna* have been diminished as unimportant and unnecessary in the Buddhist and other Korean religious traditions, and within Christianity as well. Sophia, who is also Kuan-yin and *prajna,* has been relegated to footnotes and has become a mere trace in someone else's memory. However, Sophia is relevant today and needs to be retrieved as liberator within the Christian faith.

THE GRACE OF SOPHIA BRINGS HEALING

The grace of Sophia will ultimately liberate Korean North American women from the devastating toll of racism, sexism, marginality, and patriarchy. As discussed, Sophia can help release these women's *han* but this release is not enough to allow them to reclaim their full

---

36. Andrew Sung Park, *The Wounded Heart of God* (Nashville: Abingdon Press, 1993), 137.

humanity. After their *han* is released, healing needs to take place. Without healing, Korean North American women will remain in the cycle of *han,* where one *han* is released but then another *han* begins. Unless the cycle is broken, this pattern will continue, so that these women perpetually remain and live in *han.* But this cycle must not continue. Sophia can help break the vicious cycle of oppression and *han.* Through the grace of Sophia the first step toward healing and wholeness occurs. The grace of wisdom appears in both the biblical literature and in the Korean culture.

The Grace of Wisdom in the Bible

Grace is an important and essential term within Christianity — the most basic and original Christian experience. Grace is an experience of God, whose love for humanity is so great that God gave Godself to and for humanity.[37] The Greek word for grace is *charis,* which means a free divine gift or favor. Grace is thus God's unmerited, unearned love. The first Christians used the term to express the understanding of the relationship between humanity and the divine made known in Jesus Christ.[38]

However, no word for grace exists in the Hebrew Bible. Other words describe God's loving relationship with Israel, and of these words, *hesed* is the most fundamental. *Hesed* is best translated as God's covenant faithfulness or loving-kindness. Yahweh's *hesed* not only creates people's communion with Yahweh but with one another. Yahweh shows *hesed* toward his people, and likewise, we are to show *hesed* to God and one another.[39]

Further, the term "grace" is never ascribed to Jesus in the New Testament. Although Jesus is not recorded as using the word "grace," his entire life and teaching were expressions of it. In fact, the word "grace" is rarely used in the Gospels. Matthew and Mark each use it only once and John uses it three times in the Prologue of his Gospel. Luke uses it eight times in his Gospel and then uses it seventeen times in Acts.[40]

---

37. Leonardo Boff, *Liberating Grace* (Maryknoll, N.Y.: Orbis Books, 1979), 3.

38. Jennifer King, "Forward in Grace," *Modern Believing* 36 (1995): 5.

39. Timothy A. Dearborn, "God, Grace and Salvation," in *Christ in Our Place,* ed. Trevor Hart and Daniel Thimell (Exeter: Paternoster Press, 1989), 273.

40. Boff, *Liberating Grace,* 48.

Through Paul the term "grace" gained its popularity and became
an expression of Christianity. The word "grace" occurs hundreds of
times in his writings to convey God's free and inexhaustible benevolence: "We want you to know, brothers and sisters, about the grace
of God that has been granted to the churches of Macedonia" (2 Cor.
8:1).[41] Grace is conveyed as the gift of God in Jesus Christ, the gra-
tuitous and merciful love of God and Christ that enters into human
beings, liberating them and turning them into new creatures. "So if
anyone is in Christ, there is a new creation; everything has become
new!" (2 Cor. 5:17); "For neither circumcision nor uncircumcision is
anything; but a new creation is everything!" (Gal. 6:15). According
to Paul, God gave Godself gratuitously to humanity in Christ, and
it was not due to any merit of human beings. This experience of an
unexpected gift is what Paul expresses through the word "grace."[42]

For Paul, grace always relates to the cross and the person of Jesus
Christ (Rom. 3:24–26, 5:1–21; 1 Cor. 1:14).[43] Grace cannot be
divorced from these, as grace is embodied in Jesus Christ and exemplified above all through his death on the cross. Paul uses "grace"
as a synonym for the gospel and its results. "When the meeting of
the synagogue broke up, many Jews and devout converts to Judaism
followed Paul and Barnabas, who spoke to them and urged them to
continue in the grace of God" (Acts 13:43). Grace was not only considered the content of the gospel, but was also viewed as the means
of bringing it to humanity. This viewpoint is illustrated in such passages as Acts 15:11, "On the contrary, we believe that we will be
saved through the grace of the Lord Jesus, just as they will," and
Acts 18:27, "On his arrival he greatly helped those who through
grace had become believers."[44] Furthermore, by grace people are redeemed, commissioned to serve, empowered, led, endowed with gifts,
and made skillful. The Christian life begins in grace and continues in
grace. "Stephen, full of grace and power, did great wonders and signs
among the people" (Acts 6:8). Grace denotes strength to fulfill one's
vocation: " ... through whom we have received grace and apostleship

41. "Grace" also appears in translations as charm (Col. 4:6), gift (Rom. 12:6; Eph. 4:7),
and thanksgiving (1 Cor. 10:30).
42. Boff, *Liberating Grace,* 49.
43. Dearborn, "God, Grace and Salvation," 274, 275.
44. Charles C. Ryrie, *The Grace of God* (Chicago: Moody Press, 1963), 59.

to bring about the obedience of faith among all the Gentiles for the sake of his name" (Rom. 1:5).[45]

Grace is also unconditional love and is sufficient for all. "My grace is sufficient for you, for my power is made perfect in weakness" (2 Cor. 12:9). Grace is a gift from God that helps us in all our daily struggles, and it is also abundant and given to all those who seek it. God offers grace with the purpose of accomplishing for humanity good things that human beings cannot achieve alone: "By grace you have been saved" (Eph. 2:5). The above passages all illuminate the meaning of grace and are helpful for Korean North American women, offering much that is beneficial for their healing and search for new life.

The Grace of Wisdom in Korean Culture

The grace of wisdom is also found in Korean culture, as expressed in three concepts: *hahn, jung,* and *mut.* These concepts are key to the comprehension of the fundamental spirit that informs the beliefs, customs, and practices of Koreans. The term *hahn* denotes divine supremacy and refers to the heaven or the sky. Koreans, whether Confucian, Taoist, Shamanist, or Christian, all call the Supreme Being *Hahn-u-nim. Hahn,* which is the character of the divine, describes the Supreme Being as great, bright, ultimate, infinite, majestic, and magnificent. The word *hahn* signifies Oneness, indicating a circle that has no beginning and no end. A circle symbolizes wholeness and totality. *Hahn* also symbolizes paradoxical inclusiveness, embracing one and many, whole and part simultaneously. *Hahn* emphasizes tolerance, acceptance, and creativity in spite of difference and lack of accord.[46] This characteristic is important and is similar to the biblical understanding of grace that Jesus portrayed and embodied through his life.

Jung is affectionate attachment, understood as a feeling of endearment, warmth of human-heartedness, compassionate attachment, and also as an intense longing for somebody or something. *Jung* is both

---

45. See also Romans 5:2; 12:6; 1 Corinthians 1:4; 3:10; 12:4–11. Samuel J. Mikolaski, *The Grace of God* (Grand Rapids: William B. Eerdmans, 1966), 54.
46. Andrew Sung Park, *Racial Conflict and Healing* (Maryknoll, N.Y.: Orbis Books, 1996), 107, 108.

the material cause of *han* and the power to transcend it.[47] *Mut* can be translated as "beauty of natural harmony" or "grace of gentleness." The incarnation of *hahn* in *jung* produces the gracefulness of *mut*. *Mut* can be defined as the rhythmic equilibrium of symmetric factors and asymmetric elements, the beauty of action and implying the beauty of inner creativity. *Mut* coincides with freedom and speaks of the creative struggle of life.[48] Of these three terms, *mut* speaks mostly to Koreans about grace. *Mut* is the strength of transforming the *han* of sexism and oppression into the higher ground of *hahn* and *jung*. This transformation is grace.

In certain ways, these three terms, *hahn, jung* and *mut,* can be seen as similar to the Trinity in Christianity. *Hahn* is the transcendent mind of the divine, and *jung* is the incarnation of *hahn;* when *hahn* enters human life, *jung* arises. When the congruity between *hahn* and *jung* is achieved, *mut* emerges from it.[49] So *hahn* can be likened to God the Father, *jung* as Jesus, and *mut* as the Holy Spirit. If these three resemble and represent the Trinity, then they can be understood as the grace of wisdom arising out of Korean religion and culture for the Korean people. As women strive with Jesus/Sophia's help for a life of *hahn, jung,* and *mut,* the *han* of alienation, marginality, sexism, and patriarchy will be overcome by grace, "the indispensable medium of experiencing and receiving the gift of life."[50]

Andrew Sung Park describes the ethos of Koreans as *han,* and *hahn, jung,* and *mut.* Of course, supposing that these concepts are strictly identical with the grace of the New Testament would be a mistake. They do, however, refer to a divine benevolence and strength reaching out to humanity. The biblical and Korean understandings of grace are important because they help us to formulate a Korean North American feminist discernment of grace. Korean North American women still function, with various degrees of consciousness, under the Korean ethos of *hahn, jung,* and *mut.* For these women to embrace the grace of Sophia, they must understand their own ethos, which also delivers grace. Without this ethos, Korean North American women are trapped within a narrowly Western notion of grace. For bicultural

47. Ibid., 111.
48. Ibid., 112, 113.
49. Ibid., 114.
50. Ibid., 117.

women, embracing both Western and Eastern understandings is essential, in order that the healing power of grace may be fully realized in our lives.

The Grace That Heals and Empowers

As we have seen, grace is a central reality for the New Testament thought and writings and for Christian existence. However, considering its importance to Christianity, that the word "grace" appears so seldom in the Gospels seems strange. Grace is mainly a Pauline concept, developed after the death and resurrection of Jesus and referring to God's overwhelming love disclosed in those events. In light of the cross and resurrection, Christians, looking back upon Jesus' life and ministry, found grace in his generous attitudes of acceptance and forgiveness, and his power to bring healing and new life into people's lives. Sometimes the same life-giving reality is referred to as the power of the Holy Spirit. Grace is an experiential reality.

The understanding and meaning of grace has gone through several shifts throughout church history. Since the sixteenth century, Luther's (Pauline) understanding of justification as God's free forgiveness of sins has greatly influenced Christian thought, especially among Protestants. Luther was deeply anxious that he could not earn God's approval through works; he came to realize that approval from God comes only through justification by grace through faith. This insight became the foundation for a new Christianity that witnessed to the power of God alone to declare the sinner righteous and worthy. This dimension of Christian faith is still valuable, because it signifies that our worth and worthiness as persons does not depend on our own moral achievements. We are loved and accepted unconditionally. Feminist theology, however, has questioned this prevailing emphasis on grace as forgiveness of sins. Feminist theologians and others often argue the need to move the focus away from forgiveness of the "sinner" to the well-being of the "sinned against" or victims.[51] Grace cannot be limited only to justification but needs to be recognized in the healing and strengthening of our ordinary lives. Feminist theologians believe that what most urgently needs repair is not the sins of

---

51. See Park, *The Wounded Heart of God*, 10.

individuals but the systemic evils of societies and communities.[52] We thus seek to find new ways of speaking about grace.

To begin repairing the systemic evils of society and community against Korean North American women, speaking of grace as healing may be advantageous. The grace of God[53] heals the wounds of *han* that have imprisoned Korean North American women. Sophia's grace can truly release the *han* and begin the process of rebuilding lives and just societies. Grace was not absent from Korean religious life but is exactly the tasks of *hahn, jung,* and *mut* found in Korean culture. Furthermore, shifting away from an exclusive focus on the cross is necessary to look for experiences of salvation in one's daily life — what is commonly called the movement of the Holy Spirit. Jesus is associated with the grace of God that brings forgiveness,[54] but the grace of Sophia/*prajna* also must be understood as empowerment. Women do not lack power because of their biological nature but because of culture, politics, history, and religion. God's grace, the grace of Sophia/*prajna,* can restore power to women, which has been unjustly removed from them. The grace of Sophia can embrace, heal, empower, and make people whole.

The concepts of healing and empowerment capture the essence of the grace of Sophia for Korean North American women. These women have experienced and endured many oppressions, domination, and *han.* For them to begin a life that God intended for all humanity, healing must begin. The mere release, or *han-pu-ri,* of their *han* is not enough in itself. They need healing from their pains of injustices, patriarchy, racism, and sexism. They also need to be healed from their brokenness — their broken bodies and spirits. Both body and spirit have endured many hardships. If these women are truly to live, healing must occur. Furthermore, they also need healing from their experiences of oppression and *han* in the church. When the church, which is called to be a nurturing, strengthening community, adds oppression and pain to these women's lives, confronting those forces of destruction is necessary. Grace must be understood, then, as

---

52. Susan Brooks Thistlethwaite and Mary Potter Engel, eds., *Lift Every Voice* (Maryknoll, N.Y.: Orbis, 1998), 173.

53. It is not the "image" or "concept" that heals. God's grace itself heals. But distorted ideas or images can hinder or undermine the power of grace to reach into our lives.

54. Thistlethwaite and Engel, eds., *Lift Every Voice,* 175.

more than the forgiveness of one's own sins. Grace is also the strength to confront the sins and injustices of others, within and outside the church for the sake of Sophia's reign of justice and peace. Healing needs to happen through the grace of Sophia, and her grace is at work in many different ways.

Grace as healing is the unconditional love that is poured into the wounded lives of hurting women. They experience this love in many deplorable circumstances, such as subjection to their elders, their husbands, their fathers, and other male figures. A young woman, Young Ran,[55] shares her tearful story of growing up in a household where everything was "conditional." Her mother and father were only loving to her if she "worked at the family business, cleaned up the house, looked after her nieces and nephews, got A's at school, and was obedient to her parents." If she didn't fulfill these enormous tasks, then she was beaten black and blue. Through the grace of Jesus-Sophia, she can know that the love of God is unconditional. Regardless of her heritage, societal beliefs, and upbringing, Sophia's love can embrace her. Grace is about acceptance, self-acceptance, and transformation. These women need — from their own culture and from the wider culture — acceptance for who they are, with all their unique traits and personality. They also need to accept themselves for who they are.

Grace gives self-worth, which these women need to experience as a step forward toward liberation and healing. They have been given worth only in connection to men, whether father, husband, or son. A middle-aged woman, Soo Young, shares her grief of losing her honorific title at church as soon as her husband passed away. To her sorrow, she realized that without a husband, she was made worth-less and unwelcome, even at the social gatherings of the church. A young woman, Ji-Heh, recounts her pain of overcoming racism. As a young girl, she grew up in a white neighborhood, suffering from racism. The children around the neighborhood teased her about her accent, her unfashionable clothes and the strange lunches that she occasionally brought to school. These racist remarks still bring much pain to her, even now as an adult, with a child of her own. Grace, however, is empowering, giving strength to resist and prevent oppression. These

---

55. I am relating the stories of Korean North American women whom I know personally. Their names have been changed to protect their privacy.

women thirst for empowerment, for they need Sophia's grace to fight against all forms of domination and oppression, both for themselves and for others. Grace offers new self-confidence. Grace empowers these women so that they can be agents for change and enables women to speak out to people who rape, oppress, and marginalize others.

The grace of Sophia as a healer provides restoration. Korean North American women need to be restored into wholeness. They have been stripped of their rights, privileges, and dignity. Grace can begin to renew and bring these women to reclaim their full humanity. The grace of Sophia is vast and overwhelming. She can embrace these women and strengthen them to carry on.

Healing through grace arises through courage. A middle-aged woman, Keum Joo, shares her pain of frequently being put down and made to feel worthless by her husband. This degrading process occurs in public and even among friends. This type of male behavior is common in Korea, and Korean immigrant men also feel that they are given the permission to do the same. Many women like Keum Joo struggle daily to overcome their humiliation. Grace is the courage to respond to such personal degradation, to refuse to put up with it. Women need courage to speak out against injustices against other women, which are often perpetrated in the name of "harmony within the family." They need courage to stand up for what is true, even if their reputation is destroyed in the process. The exercise of courage can be costly. The grace of Sophia, however, is the opposite of *han,* which immobilizes people and prevents them from making emancipatory changes in their lives. Grace enables and encourages women to live out their full humanity and to be in solidarity with others who also suffer.

For Korean North American women, a suffering Christ is not enough. It is important that their savior understands their suffering and is with them in their pain, but it is not enough. They need a powerful savior who can not only be with them in their suffering, but who can strive with them to eliminate the evil sources of their pain. They want a powerful savior who can save them and make changes in the world to eliminate sexism, racism, patriarchy, marginalization, subjugation, and powerlessness. This powerful savior is found in Jesus/Sophia. In Korea, women go to Kuan-yin because they are powerless. They take their *han* to her to receive healing. The grace of Jesus/*prajna* was already present. Kuan-yin is grace.

Sophia as *prajna* and Kuan-yin is more powerful than the prevalent male notion of *logos* in her ability to bring liberation and empowerment to others. Contrary to Western thought, wisdom is more powerful than knowledge, for wisdom transcends mere knowledge. *Logos* emphasizes reason, while Sophia emphasizes intuition. Intuition includes spontaneity, awareness, and enlightenment, and these three together are more powerful than reason. Furthermore, power is not found in the model of Western scientific knowledge, which dissects, analyzes, and destroys. Rather, power is found in wisdom, which is all-embracing, caring, and life-giving to human beings and nature. Wisdom is power indeed, and Korean North American women who have suffered immensely seek a power who will equip them to destroy the systemic evils of this world. The grace of Sophia is this power, powerful enough to sustain and make whole a person who has experienced the worst atrocities.

Thus, through the grace of Sophia, who gives power, committed and intelligent action can take place. Korean North American women who find healing through the grace of Sophia must in turn heal others. They must begin the process of healing the brokenness of humanity around them as they work toward justice and liberation. Korean North American women need to be committed to rejecting patriarchy as the accepted norm. They also need to eliminate the devastating power of *han* from themselves and from all people. They must also remember not to be the source of *han* to others. Korean North American women need to reconstruct a new, just society, to emancipate all creation, men and women, and all of nature, who are under the bondage and slavery of *han*. Korean North American women therefore need to embrace Wisdom as the grace of Sophia, who continues to search out and invite all people. The invitations have been sent, the table has been set. Now we need to accept Sophia's invitation and come joyfully to her banquet.

Bibliography

Inculturation

Azevedo, Marcello De Carvalho. *Inculturation and the Challenges of Modernity.* Rome: Centre "Cultures and Religions" — Pontifical Gregorian University, 1982.

Bosch, David J. *Transforming Mission: Paradigm Shifts in Theology of Mission.* Maryknoll, N.Y.: Orbis Books, 1991.

Crollius, Ary Roest, and Theoneste Nkeramihigo. *What Is So New about Inculturation?* Rome: Pontifical Gregorian University, 1984.

Geertz, Clifford. *The Interpretation of Cultures.* New York: Basic Books, 1973.

Lee, Peter K. H. "Contextualization and Inculturation of Christianity and Confucianism in the Contemporary World." *Asia Journal of Theology* 7 (1993): 84–91.

Nicholls, Bruce J. "Towards a Theology of Gospel and Culture." In *Gospel and Culture,* edited by John Stott and Robert T. Coote. Pasadena, Calif.: William Carey Library, 1979.

Rahner, Karl. *Concern for the Church: Theological Investigations XX.* Translated by Edward Quinn. New York: Crossroad, 1981.

Schineller, Peter. *A Handbook on Inculturation.* Mahwah, N.J.: Paulist Press, 1990.

———. "Inculturation: A Difficult and Delicate Task." *International Bulletin of Missionary Research* 20 (1996): 109–12.

Schreiter, Robert. "Inculturation of Faith or Identification with Culture?" In *Christianity and Cultures,* edited by Norbert Greinacher and Norbert Mette. Maryknoll, N.Y.: Orbis Books, 1994.

Shorter, Aylward. *Toward a Theology of Inculturation.* Maryknoll, N.Y.: Orbis Books, 1988.

Starkloff, Carl F. "Inculturation and Cultural Systems," *Theological Studies* 55 (1994): 274–94.

Syncretism

Anderson, J. N. D. *Christianity and Comparative Religion.* London: Tyndale Press, 1970.

Boff, Leonardo. *Church, Charism and Power.* London: SCM Press, 1985.

Carlson, Jeffrey. "Syncretistic Religiosity: The Significance of This Tautology." *Journal of Ecumenical Studies* 29 (1992): 24–34.

Gort, Jerald, Hendrik Vroom, Rein Fernhout, and Anton Wessels, eds. *Dialogue and Syncretism: An Interdisciplinary Approach*. Grand Rapids: William B. Eerdmans, 1989.

Hoornaert, Eduardo. *The Memory of the Christian People*. Translated by Robert R. Barr. Tunbridge Wells, England: Burns & Oates, 1989.

Mulder, D. C. "None Other Gods" — "No Other Name." *The Ecumenical Review* 38 (1986): 209–15.

Schreiter, Robert J. "Defining Syncretism: An Interim Report." *International Bulletin of Missionary Research* 17 (1993): 50–53.

Suh, Nam-dong. "Historical References for a Theology of Minjung." In *Minjung Theology,* edited by the Commission on Theological Concerns of the Christian Conference of Asia. Maryknoll, N.Y.: Orbis Books, 1983.

Thomas, M. M. "The Absoluteness of Jesus Christ and the Christ-Centered Syncretism." *Ecumenical Review* 37 (1985): 387–97.

Wells, Harold. "Korean Syncretism and Theologies of Interreligious Encounter: The Contribution of Kyoung Jae Kim." *Asia Journal of Theology* 12 (1998): 56–76.

Isis

Cott, Jonathan. *Isis and Osiris: Exploring the Goddess Myth*. New York: Doubleday, 1994.

Dimon, Karen Eileen, ed. "Re-Imagining: God...Community...the Church." Papers from Re-imagining Conference, Minneapolis, November 4–7, 1994. *Church and Society* 84 (1994): 5–135.

Engelsman, Joan Chamberlain. *The Feminine Dimension of the Divine*. Philadelphia: Westminster Press, 1979.

Farmer, A. Kathleen. *Who Knows What Is Good?* Grand Rapids: William B. Eerdmans, 1991.

Kloppenborg, J. S. "Isis and Sophia in the Book of Wisdom." *Harvard Theological Review* 75 (1982): 57–84.

Mack, Burton L. "Wisdom Myth and Mytho-logy." *Interpretation* 24 (1970): 46–60.

Witt, R. E. *Isis in the Graeco-Roman World*. London: Camelot Press, 1971.

Sophia

Blenkinsopp, Joseph. *Wisdom and Law in the Old Testament: The Ordering of Life in Israel and Early Judaism*. Oxford: Oxford University Press, 1995.

Brock, Rita Nakashima. "Dusting the Bible on the Floor: A Hermeneutics of Wisdom." In *Searching the Scriptures,* vol. 1: *A Feminist Introduction,* edited by Elisabeth Schüssler Fiorenza with the assistance of Shelly Matthews. New York: Crossroad, 1993.

Burnett, Fred W. *The Testament of Jesus-Sophia: A Redaction-Critical Study of the Eschatological Discourse in Matthew*. Lanham, Md.: University Press of America, 1981.

Cady, Susan, and Hal Taussig. "Jesus and Sophia." *Daughters of Sarah* 14 (1988): 7–11.

Cady, Susan, Marian Ronan, and Hal Taussig. *Sophia: The Future of Feminist Spirituality.* San Francisco: Harper & Row, 1986.

Camp, Claudia. *Wisdom and the Feminine in the Book of Proverbs.* Decatur, Ga.: Almond, 1985.

———. "The Female Sage in Ancient Israel and in the Biblical Wisdom Literature." In *The Sage in Israel and the Ancient Near East,* edited by Leo G. Perdue, Bernard Brandon Scott, and William J. Wisdman. Louisville, Ky.: Westminster/John Knox, 1993.

Cobb, John B., Jr. "Christ Beyond Creative Transformation." In *Encountering Jesus: A Debate on Christology,* edited by Stephen T. Davis. Atlanta: John Knox Press, 1988.

Conzelmann, Hans. "The Mother of Wisdom." In *The Future of Our Religious Past: Essays in Honour of Rudolf Bultmann.* Ed. James M. Robinson. Trans. Charles E. Carlston and Robert P. Scharlemann. London: SCM Press, 1971.

Deutsch, Celia. "Wisdom and Torah Motifs in Matthew 11:25–30: A Critical and Comparative Study." Ph.D. thesis, Toronto School of Theology, 1984.

———. *Hidden Wisdom and the Easy Yoke: Wisdom, Torah and Discipleship in Matthew 11:25–30.* Sheffield: Sheffield Academic Press, 1987.

———. "Wisdom in Matthew: Transformation of a Symbol." *Novum Testamentum* 32 (1990): 13–47.

———. *Lady Wisdom, Jesus and the Sages.* Valley Forge, Pa.: Trinity Press International, 1996.

Di Lella, Alexander A. "Wisdom of Ben Sira," *Anchor Bible Dictionary,* vol. 6, Si-Z, edited by David Noel Freedman. New York: Doubleday, 1992.

Doyle, B. Rod. "A Concern of the Evangelist: Pharisees in Matthew 12." *Australian Biblical Review* 34 (1986): 17–34.

Engelsman, Joan Chamberlain. *The Feminine Dimension of the Divine.* Philadelphia: Westminster Press, 1979.

Fang, Mark. "The Wisdom of Solomon in the Light of the Chinese Context." *Ching Feng* 36 (1993): 23A–37.

Finger, Thomas. "Wisdom Mythology and the Christological Hymns of the New Testament." In *Aspects of Wisdom in Judaism and Early Christianity,* edited by Robert L. Wilken. Notre Dame: University of Notre Dame Press, 1975.

———. *In Memory of Her: A Feminist Theological Reconstruction of Christian Origins.* New York: Crossroad, 1983.

———. "Holy Wisdom, Love So Bright: Sophia in Scripture and Worship." *Daughters of Sarah* 4 (1994): 29, 54–55.

———. *Jesus: Miriam's Child, Sophia's Prophet: Critical Issues in Feminist Christology.* New York: Continuum, 1994.

Gese, Hartmut. "Wisdom, Son of Man, and the Origins of Christology: the Consistent Development of Biblical Theology," translated by U. Mauser. *Horizons in Biblical Theology* 3 (1981): 23–57.

Grabbe, Lester L. *Wisdom of Solomon.* Sheffield: Sheffield Academic Press, 1997.

Gray, William. "Wisdom Christology in the New Testament." *Theology* 89 (1986): 448–59.

Harris, J. R. *The Origin of the Prologue to St. John.* Cambridge: University Press, 1917.

Hefling, Charles C., Jr. "On the Possible Relevance of Lonergan's Thought to Some Feminist Questions in Christology." In *Lonergan and Feminism,* edited by Cynthia S. W. Crysdale. Toronto: University of Toronto Press, 1994.

Hopkins, Julie M. *Towards a Feminist Christology.* Grand Rapids: William B. Eerdmans, 1994.

Horsley, Richard A. "Spiritual Marriage with Sophia." *Vigiliae Christianae* 33 (1979): 30–54.

———. "Wisdom of Word and Words of Wisdom in Corinth." *Catholic Biblical Quarterly* 39 (1977): 224–39.

Humphrey, Hugh M. "Jesus as Wisdom in Mark." *Biblical Theology Bulletin* 19 (1989): 48–53.

Johnson, Elizabeth A. "Wisdom Was Made Flesh and Pitched Her Tent among Us." In *Reconstructing the Christ Symbol,* edited by Maryanne Stevens. New York: Paulist Press, 1970.

———. "The Incomprehensibility of God and the Image of God Male and Female." *Theological Studies* 45 (1984): 441–65.

———. "Jesus the Wisdom of God: A Biblical Basis for Non-Androcentric Christology." *Ephemerides Theologicae Lovanienses* 61 (1985): 261–94.

———. *Consider Jesus: Waves of Renewal in Christology.* New York: Crossroad, 1990.

———. "Redeeming the Name of Christ." In *Freeing Theology: The Essentials of Theology in Feminist Perspective,* edited by Catherine Mowry LaCugna. New York: HarperSanFrancisco, 1993.

———. *She Who Is: The Mystery of God in Feminist Theological Discourse.* New York: Crossroad, 1993.

———. *Women, Earth and Creator Spirit.* New York: Paulist Press, 1993.

Johnson, Marshall D. "Reflections on a Wisdom Approach to Matthew's Christology." *Catholic Biblical Quarterly* 36 (1974): 44–64.

King, Jennifer, "Forward in Grace." *Modern Believing* 36 (1995): 4–10.

LaCugna, Catherine Mowry, ed. *Freeing Theology: The Essentials of Theology in Feminist Perspective.* New York: HarperSanFrancisco, 1993.

Lamp, Peter. "Theological Wisdom and the 'Word about the Cross': The Rhetorical Scheme in 1 Corinthians 1–4." *Interpretation* 44 (1990): 117–31.

Lang, Bernhard. *Wisdom and the Book of Proverbs: An Israelite Goddess Redefined.* New York: Pilgrim Press, 1986.

McKenzie, J. J. *I Will Love Unloved: A Linguistic Analysis of Woman's Biblical Importance.* Lanham, Md.: University Press of America, 1986.

McKinlay, Judith E. *Gendering Wisdom the Host: Biblical Invitations to Eat and Drink.* Sheffield: Sheffield Academic Press, 1996.

McKinney, Richard W. A., ed. *Creation, Christ and Culture.* Edinburgh: T. & T. Clark, 1976.

Murphy, Roland E. "Wisdom in the Old Testament." In *The Anchor Bible Dictionary*, vol. 6, Si-Z, edited by David Noel Freedman. New York: Doubleday, 1992.

Newman, Barbara. "Some Medieval Theologians and the Sophia Tradition." *Downside Review* 108 (1990): 111–30.

———. "The Pilgrimage of Christ-Sophia." *Vox Benedictina* 9 (1992): 9–37.

O'Connor, Kathleen M. *The Wisdom Literature*. Collegeville, Minn.: Liturgical Press, 1988.

———. "Wisdom Literature, Women's Culture and Peace: A Hermeneutical Reflection." In *Blessed Are the Peacemakers,* edited by Anthony J. Tambasco. New York: Paulist Press, 1989.

Painter, John. "Christology and the History of the Johannine Community in the Prologue of the Fourth Gospel." *New Testament Studies* 30 (1984): 460–74.

Pearson, Birger A. "Hellenistic-Jewish Wisdom Speculation and Paul." In *Aspects of Wisdom in Judaism and Early Christianity.,* edited by Robert L. Wilken. Notre Dame, Ind.: University of Notre Dame Press, 1975.

Pentz, Rebecca D. "Jesus as Sophia." *Reformed Journal* 38 (1988): 17–22.

Perkins, Pheme. "Jesus: God's Wisdom." *Word and World* 7 (1987): 272–80.

Piper, Ronald A. *Wisdom in the Q-tradition: The Aphoristic Teaching of Jesus.* Cambridge: Cambridge University Press, 1989.

Pregeant, Russell. "The Wisdom Passages in Matthew's Story." In *SBL Seminar Papers 1990,* edited by David J. Lull. Atlanta: Scholars Press, 1990.

Raschke, Carl A., and Susan Doughty Raschke. *The Engendering God: Male and Female Faces of God.* Louisville, Ky.: Westminster John Knox Press, 1995.

Reese, James M. "Christ as Wisdom Incarnate: Wiser than Solomon, Loftier than Lady Wisdom." *Biblical Theology Bulletin* 11 (1981): 44–47.

Robinson, James M. "Jesus as Sophos and Sophia: Wisdom Tradition and the Gospels." In *Aspects of Wisdom in Judaism and Early Christianity,* edited by Robert L. Wilken. Notre Dame, Ind.: University of Notre Dame Press, 1975.

Ruether, Rosemary Radford. *Sexism and God-Talk: Toward a Feminist Theology.* Boston: Beacon Press, 1983.

Russell, Letty M. "God with Us." *Christian Century* 108 (1991): 1131.

Russell, Letty M., and Shannon J. Clarkson, ed. *Dictionary of Feminist Theologies.* Louisville, Ky.: Westminster John Knox Press, 1996.

Schreiter, Robert J. "Anonymous Christian and Christology." *Occasional Bulletin of Missionary Research* 2 (1978): 2–11.

Schüssler Fiorenza, Elisabeth. *Sharing Her Word.* Boston: Beacon Press, 1998.

Schroer, Silvia. "The Book of Sophia." In *Searching the Scriptures,* Vol. 2: A *Feminist Commentary,* edited by Elisabeth Schüssler Fiorenza. New York: Crossroad, 1994.

———. "Wise and Counselling Women in Ancient Israel: Literary and Historical Ideals of the Personified Hokma." In *A Feminist Companion to Wisdom Literature,* edited by Athalya Brenner. Sheffield: Sheffield Academic Press, 1995.

Scott, Martin. *Sophia and the Johannine Jesus.* Sheffield: Sheffield Academic Press, 1992.

Stevens, Maryanne, ed. *Reconstructing the Christ Symbol: Essays in Feminist Christology.* New York: Paulist Press, 1993.

Suggs, M. Jack. *Wisdom, Christology, and Law in Matthew's Gospel.* Cambridge Mass.: Harvard University Press, 1970.

Sugirtharajah, R. S. "Wisdom, Q, and a Proposal for a Christology [Jesus as Sage]." *Expository Times* 102 (1990): 42–46.

Tolpingrud, Amy C. "Light Shines in the Darkness and The Darkness Has Not Overcome Her." *Word and World* 7 (1987): 294–97.

Torjesen, Karen Jo. "You Are the Christ: Five Portraits of Jesus from the Early Church." In *Jesus at 2000,* edited by Marcus J. Borg. Boulder, Colo.: Westview Press, 1997.

Watson, Francis. "Christ, Community, and the Critique of Ideology: A Theological Reading of 1 Corinthians 1:18–31." *Nederlands Theologisch Tijdschrift* 46 (1992): 132–49.

Wells, Harold. "Trinitarian Feminism: Elizabeth Johnson's Wisdom Christology." *Theology Today* 52 (1995): 330–43.

Wilken, Robert L., ed. *Aspects of Wisdom in Judaism and Early Christianity.* Notre Dame, Ind.: University of Notre Dame Press, 1975.

Willet, Michael E. *Wisdom Christology in the Fourth Gospel.* San Francisco: Mellen Research University Press, 1992.

Winston, David. "Wisdom of Solomon." In *The Anchor Bible Dictionary,* vol. 6, Si-Z, edited by David Noel Freedman. New York: Doubleday, 1992.

Witherington, Ben, III. *Jesus the Sage: The Pilgrimage of Wisdom.* Minneapolis: Fortress Press, 1994.

Asian Theology and Culture

Abraham, K. C. *Third World Theologies: Commonalities and Divergences.* Maryknoll, N.Y.: Orbis Books, 1990.

Carmody, Denise Lardner. *Women and World Religions.* 2d ed. Englewood Cliffs, N.J.: Prentice-Hall, 1989.

Ching, Julia. *Confucianism and Christianity: A Comparative Study.* Tokyo: Kodansha International, 1977.

———. *Chinese Religions.* Maryknoll, N.Y.: Orbis Books, 1993.

Cho, Haejong. "Republic of Korea: Those Left Behind." In *Women in the Villages, Men in the Towns.* Paris: UNESCO, 1984.

Cho, Wha Soon. *Let the Weak Be Strong: A Woman's Struggle for Justice.* Bloomington, Ind.: Meyer-Stone Books, 1988.

Choi, Han Ja. "Feminine Images of God in Korean Traditional Religion." In *Frontiers in Asian Christian Theology: Emerging Trends,* edited by R. S. Sugirtharajah. Maryknoll, N.Y.: Orbis Books, 1994.

Choy, Bong-Youn. *Koreans in America.* Chicago: Nelson-Hall, 1979.

Chung, Hyun Kyung. *Struggle to Be the Sun Again: Introducing Asian Women's Theology.* Maryknoll, N.Y.: Orbis Books, 1990.

Chung, Lee Oo. "The Traditional Religion of Korea." In *Faith Renewed: A Report on the First Asian Women's Consultation on Interfaith Dialogue*. Hong Kong: Asian Women's Resource Centre for Culture and Theology, 1989.

Chung, Lee Oo, et al., eds. *Women of Courage: Asian Women Reading the Bible*. Seoul: Asian Women's Resource Centre for Culture and Theology, 1992.

Deuchler, Martina. *The Confucian Transformation of Korea: A Study of Society and Ideology*. Cambridge, Mass.: Council on East Asian Studies, Harvard University, 1992.

Erickson, Victoria Lee. *Where Silence Speaks: Feminism, Social Theory and Religion*. Minneapolis: Fortress Press, 1993.

Fabella, Virginia. "Overview of Ecumenical Association of Third World Theologians (EATWOT) in Asia." *Voices from the Third World* 7 (1984): 7–13.

Fabella, Virginia, ed. *Asia's Struggle for Full Humanity*. Maryknoll, N.Y.: Orbis Books, 1980.

Fabella, Virginia, and Sergio Torres, eds. *Irruption of the Third World: Challenge to Theology*. Maryknoll, N.Y.: Orbis Books, 1983.

———. *Doing Theology in a Divided World*. Maryknoll, N.Y.: Orbis Books, 1985.

Fabella, Virginia, and Mercy Amba Oduyoye, eds. *With Passion and Compassion: Third World Women Doing Theology*. Maryknoll, N.Y.: Orbis Books, 1988.

Fabella, Virginia, and Sun-Ai Lee, eds. *We Dare to Dream*. Maryknoll, N.Y.: Orbis Books, 1990.

Fabella, Virginia, Peter K. H. Lee, and David Kwang-sun Suh, eds. *Asian Christian Spirituality: Reclaiming Traditions*. Maryknoll, N.Y.: Orbis Books, 1992.

Falk, Nancy A., and Rita M. Gross, eds. *Unspoken Worlds: Women's Religious Lives in Non-Western Cultures*. San Francisco: Harper & Row, 1980.

Ferm, Deane William. *Third World Liberation Theologies: An Introductory Survey*. Maryknoll, N.Y.: Orbis Books, 1986.

———. Ferm, Deane William. *Third World Liberation Theologies: A Reader*. Maryknoll, N.Y.: Orbis Books, 1986.

Gelb, Joyce, and Marian Lief Palley, eds. *Women of Japan and Korea: Continuity and Change*. Philadelphia: Temple University Press, 1994.

Grayson, James Huntley. *Korea: A Religious History*. Oxford: Clarendon Press, 1989.

Grosjean, Yasuko Morihara. "Japan: The 'Silent Victims' Speak." *Journal of Feminist Studies in Religion* 3 (1987): 107–14.

Jin, Yan. "The Quest of Chinese Women: Toward a Chinese Feminist Liberation Theology." M.A. thesis, St. Michael's College, Toronto, 1992.

Katoppo, Marianne. *Compassionate and Free: An Asian Women's Theology*. Maryknoll, N.Y.: Orbis Books, 1980.

Kendall, Laurel, and Mark Peterson, ed. *Korean Women: View from the Inner Room*. Cushing, Maine: East Rock Press, 1983.

Kim, Elli. "Confucianism and Women in Korea." In *Faith Renewed II: A Report on the Second Asian Women's Consultation on Interfaith Dialogue.* Seoul: Asian Women's Resource Centre for Culture and Theology, 1991.

Kim, Hyon-Ja. "The Changing Role of Women in Korea." *Korea Journal* 11 (1971): 21–24.

Kim, Yung-Chung. ed. and trans. *Women of Korea: A History from Ancient Times to 1945.* Seoul: Ewha Womans University Press, 1976.

King, Ursula. *Feminist Theology from the Third World: A Reader.* Maryknoll, N.Y.: Orbis Books, 1994.

Kingston, Maxine Hong. *The Woman Warrior: Memoirs of a Girlhood Among Ghosts.* New York: Alfred A. Knopf, 1975.

Kwok Pui-lan. "Claiming a Boundary Existence: A Parable from Hong Kong." *Journal of Feminist Studies in Religion* 3 (1987): 121–24.

———. "Roundtable: A Vision of Feminist Religious Scholarship." *Journal of Feminist Studies in Religion* 3 (1987): 98–103.

———. *Chinese Women and Christianity 1860–1927.* Atlanta: Scholars Press, 1992.

———. "Special Section on Appropriation and Reciprocity in Womanist/ Mujerista/Feminist Work: Speaking from the Margins." *Journal of Feminist Studies in Religion* 8 (1992): 102–5.

———. *Discovering the Bible in the Non-Biblical World.* Maryknoll, N.Y.: Orbis Books, 1995.

Lee, Helie. *Still Life with Rice.* New York: Scribner, 1996.

Lee, Jung Young, "The Yin-Yang Way of Thinking." In *Asian Christian Theology: Emerging Themes,* edited by Douglas J. Elwood. Philadelphia: Westminster Press, 1980.

Lee, Sung-Hee. "Women's Liberation Theology as the Foundation for Asian Theology." *East Asia Journal of Theology* 4 (1986): 2–13.

Lewis, Nantawan Boonprasat. "An Overview of the Role of Women in Asia — A Perspective and Challenge to Higher Education." *East Asia Journal of Theology* 3 (1985): 139–46.

Mace, David, and Vera Mace. *Marriage: East and West.* Garden City, N.Y.: Doubleday, 1959.

Madrigal, Moon Jee Yoo. *The Role of Women in Korean Society with Emphasis on the Economic System.* Palo Alto, Calif.: R&E Research Association, 1979.

Members of Women Church. "Women Church of Korea." *In God's Image* 6 (1990): 56–57.

Okihiro, Gary Y. *Margins and Mainstreams: Asians in American History and Culture.* Seattle: University of Washington Press, 1994.

Ortega, Ofelia. *Women's Visions: Theological Reflection, Celebration, Action.* Geneva: World Council of Churches, 1995.

Paper, Jordan. "The Persistence of Female Deities in Patriarchal China." *Journal of Feminist Studies in Religion* 6 (1990): 25–40.

Park, Kyung Ae. *Women and Social Change in South and North Korea: Marxist and Liberal Perspectives.* East Lansing: Women and International Development Program: Michigan State University, 1992.

Pieris, Aloysius, S.J. *An Asian Theology of Liberation.* Maryknoll, N.Y.: Orbis Books, 1988.

Pobee, John S., and Barbel Von Wartenberg-Potter, eds. *New Eyes for Reading: Biblical and Theological Reflections by Women from the Third World.* Geneva: World Council of Churches, 1986.

Rhim, Soon Man. *Women of Asia: Yesterday and Today.* New York: Friendship Press, 1983.

Russell, Letty M., Kwok Pui-lan, Ada María Isasi-Díaz, and Katie Geneva Cannon, eds. *Inheriting Our Mother's Gardens: Feminist Theology in Third World Perspective.* Louisville, Ky.: Westminster Press, 1988.

Sharma, Arvind. *Women in World Religions.* Albany: State University of New York, 1987.

Song, C. S. *Third-Eye Theology.* Maryknoll, N.Y.: Orbis Books, 1979.

———. *Theology from the Womb of Asia.* Maryknoll, N.Y.: Orbis Books, 1986.

Southard, Naomi, and Rita Nakashima Brock, eds. "The Other Half of the Basket: Asian American Women and the Search for a Theological Home." *Journal of Feminist Studies in Religion* 3 (1987): 135–50.

Suh, Kwang-sun David. "A Biographical Sketch of an Asian Theological Consultation." In *Minjung Theology: People as the Subjects of History,* edited by the Commission on Theological Concerns of the Christian Conference of Asia (CTC-CCA). Maryknoll, N.Y.: Orbis Books, 1983.

Suh, Nam-Dong. "Towards a Theology of Han." In *Minjung Theology: People as the Subjects of History,* edited by the Commission on Theological Concerns of the Christian Conference of Asia (CTC-CCA). Maryknoll, N.Y.: Orbis Books, 1983.

Sun, Soon-Hwa. "Women, Work and Theology in Korea." *Journal of Feminist Studies in Religion* 3 (1987): 125–34.

Sunoo, Harold Hakwon, and Kim Dong Soo, eds. *Korean Women in a Struggle for Humanization.* Memphis: Association of Korean Christian Scholars in North America, 1978.

Yoo, Choon-ja. "Fire at the Suffering Place: The Reverend Cho Wha-Soon Does Theology with Her Whole Being." *In God's Image* 11 (1992): 37–43.

Asian North American Feminist/Immigration Theology and Resources

Brock, Rita Nakashima. "Special Section: Asian Women Theologians Respond to American Feminism." *Journal of Feminist Studies in Religion* 3 (1987): 103–5.

———. *Journeys by Heart: A Christology of Erotic Power.* New York: Crossroad, 1988.

Chang, Won H. "Communication and Acculturation." In *The Korean Diaspora: Historical and Sociological Studies of Korean Immigration and Assimila-*

tion in North America, edited by Hyung-chan Kim. Santa Barbara, Calif.: American Bibliographical Center, 1977.

Chow, Esther Ngan-Ling. "The Feminist Movement: Where are all the Asian American Women?" In *Making Waves: An Anthology of Writings by and about Asian American Women,* edited by Asian Women United of California. Boston: Beacon Press, 1989.

Choy, Bong-Youn. *Koreans in America.* Chicago: Nelson-Hall, 1979.

Ghymn, Esther Mikyung. *Images of Asian American Women by Asian American Women.* New York: Peter Lang, 1995.

Gordon, Milton M. *Assimilation in American Life: The Role of Race, Religion and National Origins.* New York: University Press, 1964.

Grosjean, Yasuko Morihara. "Japan: The 'Silent Victims' Speak." *Journal of Feminist Studies in Religion* 3 (1987): 107–14.

Hurh, Won Moo, and Kwang Chung Kim. *Korean Immigration in America: A Structural Analysis of Ethnic Confinement and Adhesive Adaptation.* Cranbury, N.J.: Association University Presses, 1984.

Kang, K. Connie. *Home Was the Land of Morning Calm: A Saga of a Korean American Family.* Reading, Mass.: Addison-Wesley, 1995.

Kim, Ai Ra. *Women's Struggle for a New Life.* Albany: State University of New York Press, 1996.

Kim, Elaine H. "Defining Asian American Realities Through Literature." *Cultural Critique* 6 (1987): 87–112.

———. "Poised on the Inbetween: A Korean American's Reflections on Theresa Hak Kyung Cha's Dictee." In *Writing Self, Writing Nation,* edited by Elaine H. Kim and Norma Alarcon. Berkeley: Third Woman Press, 1994.

Kim, Grace Ji-Sun. "Crafting an Asian Immigrant Feminist Theology." *In God's Image* 16 (1997): 57–58.

Kim, Jung Ha. *Bridge-Makers and Cross-Bearers: Korean-American Women and the Church.* Atlanta: Scholars Press, 1997.

Kim, Kwang Chung, and Won Moo Hurh. "The Burden of Double Roles: Korean Wives in the U.S.A." *Ethnic and Racial Studies* 11 (1988): 151–67.

Kitano, Harry H. L., and Roger Daniels. *Asian Americans: Emerging Minorities.* 2d ed. Englewood Cliffs, N.J.: Prentice-Hall, 1988.

Kwak, Tae-Hwan, and Seong Hyong Lee, eds. *The Korean-American Community: Present and Future.* Seoul: Kyungnam University Press, 1991.

Kwok Pui-lan. "The Emergence of Asian Feminist Consciousness of Culture and Theology." In *Sisters Struggling in the Spirit: A Women of Color Theological Anthology,* edited by Nantawan Boonprasat Lewis, Lydia Hernandez, Helen Locklear, and Robina Marie Winbush. Louisville, Ky.: Women's Ministries Program Area, 1994.

Lee, Hwain Chang. *Confucius, Christ and Co-Partnership.* Lanham, Md.: University Press of America, 1994.

Lee, Inn Sook. "An Exilic Journey: Toward Womanist Theology from Korean Immigrant Women's Perspectives." In *Sisters Struggling in the Spirit: A Women of Color Theological Anthology,* edited by Nantawan Boonprasat Lewis,

Lydia Hernandez, Helen Locklear, and Robina Marie Winbush. Louisville, Ky.: Women's Ministries Program Area, 1994.

Lee, Jung Young. *Marginality: The Key to Multicultural Theology.* Minneapolis: Fortress Press, 1995.

Lee, Jung Young. ed. *An Emerging Theology in World Perspectives.* Mystic, Conn.: Twenty-Third Publications, 1988.

Lee, Mary Paik. *Quiet Odyssey: A Pioneer Korean Woman in America.* Edited and with an introduction by Sucheng Chan. Seattle: University of Washington Press, 1990.

Lee, Sang Hyun. "Called to Be Pilgrims: Toward an Asian-American Theology From the Korean Immigrant Perspective." In *Korean American Ministry.* Edited by Sang Hyun Lee. New York: Consulting Committee on Korean American Ministry, Presbyterian Church (U.S.A.), 1987.

———. "How Shall We Sing the Lord's Song in a Strange Land?" *Journal of Asian and Asian American Theology* 1 (1996): 77–81.

Lee, Sang Hyun, and John V. Moore, eds. *Korean American Ministry: A Resource Book.* Expanded English ed. Louisville, Ky.: General Assembly Council-Presbyterian Church (U.S.A.), 1993.

Matsuoka, Fumitaka. *Out of Silence: Emerging Themes in Asian American Churches.* Cleveland: United Church Press, 1995.

Min, Anselm Kyongsuk. "The Political Economy of Marginality: Comments on Jung Young Lee, *Marginality: The Key to Multicultural Theology.*" *Journal of Asian and Asian American Theology* 1 (1996): 82–94.

Min, Kyung Bae. "The Presbyterian Church in Korean History." In *Korean American Ministry.* Edited by Sang Hyun Lee. New York: Consulting Committee on Korean American Ministry, Presbyterian Church (U.S.A.), 1987.

Ng, David, ed. *People on the Way: Asian North Americans Discovering Christ, Culture, and Community.* Valley Forge, Pa.: Judson Press, 1996.

Ortega, Ofelia. *Women's Visions: Theological Reflection, Celebration, Action.* Geneva: World Council of Churches, 1995.

Park, Andrew Sung. *The Wounded Heart of God: The Asian Concept of Han and the Christian Doctrine of Sin.* Nashville: Abingdon Press, 1993.

———. *Racial Conflict and Healing: An Asian-American Theological Perspective.* Maryknoll, N.Y.: Orbis Books, 1996.

Park, Hee-Min. "The Relevant Ministry to Korean Immigrants in Metro Toronto Area." D.Min. thesis, Knox College, University of Toronto, 1982.

Sunoo, Sonia Shinn, ed., *Korea Kaleidoscope.* Davis, Calif.: Korean Oral History Project, Sierra Mission Area, United Presbyterian Church, U.S.A., 1982.

Takaki, Ronald. *Strangers from a Different Shore: A History of Asian Americans.* New York: Penguin Books, 1989.

Yim, Sun Bin. "Korean Immigrant Women in Early Twentieth Century America." In *Making Waves: An Anthology of Writings by and about Asian American Women,* edited by Asian Women United of California. Boston: Beacon Press, 1989.

Yu, Eui-Young, and Earl H. Phillips. *Korean Women in Transition: At Home and Abroad.* Los Angeles: Center for Korean-American and Korean Studies, California State University, 1987.

Methodology

Ariarajah, Wesley. *The Bible and the People of Other Faiths.* Geneva: World Council of Churches, 1985.

Bevans, Stephen B., S.V.D. *Models of Contextual Theology.* Maryknoll, N.Y.: Orbis Books, 1992.

Cone, James H. *God of the Oppressed.* New York: Seabury, 1975.

———. *Bread Not Stone.* Boston: Beacon Press, 1984.

Grant, Jacquelyn. *White Women's Christ and Black Women's Jesus: Feminist Christology and Womanist Response.* Atlanta: Scholars Press, 1989.

Gutiérrez, Gustavo. *A Theology of Liberation: History, Politics, and Salvation.* Rev. ed. with a new introduction. Translated and edited by Sister Caridad Inda and John Eagleson. Maryknoll, N.Y.: Orbis Books, 1988.

Hall, Douglas. "On Contextuality in Christian Theology." *Toronto Journal of Theology* 1 (1985): 3–16.

———. *Thinking the Faith: Christian Theology in a North American Context.* Minneapolis: Augsburg, 1989.

Isasi-Díaz, Ada María, and Yolanda Tarango. *Hispanic Women: Prophetic Voice in the Church.* San Francisco: Harper & Row, 1988.

Johnson, Elizabeth A. *She Who Is: The Mystery of God in Feminist Theological Discourse.* New York: Crossroad, 1993.

Knitter, Paul. *No Other Name? A Critical Survey of Christian Attitudes Towards the World Religions.* Maryknoll, N.Y.: Orbis Books, 1985.

Legge, Marilyn J. "Multidialogical Spiralling for Healing and Justice." In *Gender, Genre and Religion,* edited by Morny Joy and Eva K. Neumaier-Dargyay. Waterloo: Wilfred Laurier University Press, 1995.

Lind, Christopher J. L. "An Invitation to Canadian Theology." *Toronto Journal of Theology* 1 (1985): 17–26.

Nolan, Albert. "Contextual Theology: One Faith, Many Theologies." Chancellor's Address VIII delivered at Regis College, Toronto, November 12, 1990.

Ruether, Rosemary Radford. *To Change the World.* New York: Crossroad, 1990.

Russell, Letty M. *Household of Freedom: Authority in Feminist Theology.* Philadelphia: Westminster Press, 1987.

Russell, Letty M., ed. *Changing Contexts of Our Faith.* Philadelphia: Fortress Press, 1985.

Schreiter, Robert J. *Constructing Local Theologies.* Maryknoll, N.Y.: Orbis Books, 1986.

Schüssler Fiorenza, Elisabeth. *In Memory of Her: A Feminist Theological Reconstruction of Christian Origins.* New York: Crossroad, 1983.

Segundo, Juan Luis. *The Liberation of Theology.* Translated by John Drury. Maryknoll, N.Y.: Orbis Books, 1976.

Wells, Harold. "Social Analysis and Theological Method: Third World Challenge to Canadian Theology." In *A Long and Faithful March,* edited by Harold Wells and Roger Hutchinson. Toronto: United Church Publishing House, 1989.

———. "Ideology and Contextuality in Liberation Theology." In *Liberation Theology and Sociopolitical Transformation in Latin America,* edited by Jorge Farcia Antezana. Burnaby, B.C.: Institute for the Humanities, 1992.

———. "The Making of the United Church Mind — No. II." *Touchstone* 8 (1990): 17–29.

———. "Review Article; *She Who Is: The Mystery of God in Feminist Theological Discourse.*" *Touchstone* 13 (1995): 37–44.

Young, Pamela Dickey. *Feminist Theology/Christian Theology: In Search of Method.* Minneapolis: Fortress Press, 1990.

Buddhism

Cabezón, José Ignacio, ed. *Buddhism, Sexuality and Gender.* Albany: State University of New York Press, 1992.

Carmody, Denise Lardner. *Women and World Religions.* Nashville: Abingdon, 1979.

Chamberlayne, John H. "The Development of Kuan-Yin: Chinese Goddess of Mercy." *Numen* 9 (1962): 45–52.

Conze, Edward. *Buddhist Wisdom Books.* London: George Allen & Unwin, 1958.

———. *Buddhism: Its Essence and Development.* New York: Harper & Brothers, 1959.

———. *The Prajnaparamita Literature.* Netherlands: Mouton, 1960.

———. "Buddhist Prajna and Greek Sophia." *Religion* 5 (1975): 160–67.

Conze, Edward, ed. and trans. *Selected Sayings from the Perfection of Wisdom.* 2d ed. London: R. H. Johns Limited, 1968.

Conze, Edward, trans. *The Perfection of Wisdom in Eight Thousand Slokas.* Calcutta: Asiatic Society, 1958.

Fox, Douglas A. *The Heart of Buddhist Wisdom.* Lewiston, N.Y.: Edwin Mellen Press, 1985.

Getty, Alice. *The Gods of Northern Buddhism,* translated from the French of J. Deniker. Rutland, Vt.: Charles E. Tuttle, 1962.

Hackin, J. Clement Huart, Raymonde Linossier, H. De Wilman-Grabowska, Charles-Henri Marchal, Henri Maspero, and Serge Eliseev, eds. *Asiatic Mythology: A Detailed Description and Explanation of the Mythologies of All the Great Nations of Asia.* New York: Thomas Y. Crowell, 1963.

Joshi, Lal Mani. "Faith and Wisdom in the Buddhist Tradition." *Dialogue and Alliance* 1 (1987): 66–77.

Kaza, Stephanie. "Acting with Compassion." In *Ecofeminism and the Sacred,* edited by Carol J. Adams. New York: Continuum, 1993.

King, Ursula. *Women in the World's Religions, Past and Present.* New York: Paragon House, 1987.

Labh, Saidyanath. *Panna in Early Buddhism.* Delhi: Eastern Book Linkers, 1991.

Macy, Joanna Rogers. "Perfection of Wisdom: Mother of all Buddhas." In *Beyond Androcentrism: New Essays on Women and Religion,* edited by Rita M. Gross. Missoula, Mont.: Scholars Press, 1977.

Paul, Diana Y. "Kuan-Yin: Savior and Savioress in Chinese Pure Land Buddhism." In *The Book of the Goddess Past and Present,* edited by Carl Olson. New York: Crossroad, 1988.

———. *Women in Buddhism: Images of the Feminine in Mahayana Tradition.* Berkeley: Lancaster-Miller, 1979.

Reed, Barbara E. "The Gender Symbolism of Kuan-yin Bodhisattva." In *Buddhism, Sexuality and Gender,* edited by José Ignacio Cabezón. Albany: State University of New York Press, 1992.

Southard, Naomi P. F. "Recovery and Rediscovered Images: Spiritual Resources for Asian American Women." *Asia Journal of Theology* 3 (1989): 624–38.

Tsutsumi, Genryu. "Karuna (compassion) and Prajna (wisdom): A Note of Seizan-Sect Doctrine." *Japanese Religions* 4 (1966): 45–49.

Yu Chun-fang. "A Sutra Promoting the White-Robed Guanyin as Giver of Sons." In *Religions of China in Practice,* edited by Donald S. Lopez Jr. Princeton, N.J.: Princeton University Press, 1996.

Yuichi, Kajiyama. "Mahayana Buddhism and the Philosophy of Prajna." In *Studies in Pali and Buddhism,* edited by A. K. Narain. Delhi: B. R. Publishing Corporation 1979.

Confucianism

Ching, Julia. *Confucianism and Christianity: A Comparative Study.* Tokyo: Kodansha International, 1977.

Kit-Wah, Eva Man. "The Idea and Limitation of 'Sageliness Within and Kingliness Without.'" *Ching Feng* 38 (1995): 116–27.

Naess, Arne, and Alastair Hannay, eds. *Invitation to Chinese Philosophy.* Oslo: Universitetsforlaget, 1972.

Swidler, Leonard. "A Christian Historical Perspective on Wisdom as a Basis for Dialogue with Judaism and Chinese Religion." *Journal of Ecumenical Studies* 33 (1996): 557–72.

Takehiko, Okada. "Chu Hsi and Wisdom as Hidden and Stored." In *Chu Hsi and Neo Confucianism,* edited by Wing-tsit Chan. Honolulu: University of Hawaii Press, 1986.

Taylor, Rodney Leon. *The Cultivation of Sagehood as a Religious Goal in Neo-Confucianism.* Missoula, Mont.: Scholars Press, 1978.

Other Sources

Boff, Leonardo. *Liberating Grace.* Maryknoll, N.Y.: Orbis Books, 1979.

Carr, Anne. *Transforming Grace.* New York: Continuum, 1996.

Dearborn, Timothy A. "God, Grace and Salvation." In *Christ in Our Place,* edited by Trevor Hart and Daniel Thimell. Exeter: Paternoster Press, 1989.

Driver, Tom. *Christ in a Changing World: Toward an Ethical Christology.* New York: Crossroad, 1981.

Edwards, Denis. *Jesus the Wisdom of God*. New York: Maryknoll, 1995.

Fabella, Virginia, M.M., "Contextualization and Asian Women's Christology." In *Workshop on Asian Women's Theology, "Asian Women's Christology."* Seoul: Asian Women Resource Center Institute for Women's Theological Studies, Ewha Womans University, 1994.

Kierkegaard, Søren. *Training in Christianity, and the Edifying Discourse Which "Accompanied" It*. Translated by Walter Lowrie. Princeton, N.J.: Princeton University Press, 1941.

Mikolaski, Samuel J. *The Grace of God*. Grand Rapids: William B. Eerdmans, 1966.

Ruether, Rosemary Radford. "The Liberation of Christology From Patriarchy." In *Feminist Theology: A Reader,* edited by Ann Loades. Louisville, Ky.: John Knox Press, 1990.

Ryrie, Charles C. *The Grace of God*. Chicago: Moody Press, 1963.

Sohn, Seung-Hee. "Christology of Laughter." In *Workshop on Asian Women's Theology, "Asian Women's Christology."* Seoul: Asian Women Resource Center Institute for Women's Theological Studies, Ewha Womans University, 1994.

Thistlethwaite, Susan Brooks, and Mary Potter Engel, eds. *Lift Every Voice*. Maryknoll, N.Y.: Orbis Books, 1998.

Index